The Best of

DENVER
and THE ROCKIES

An impertinent insiders' guide

By Don and Betty Martin

DISCOVERGUIDES ● *Las Vegas, Nevada*
A Division of Pine Cone Press, Inc.

BOOKS BY DON AND BETTY MARTIN

Adventure Cruising • 1996
Arizona Discovery Guide • 1990, 1993, 1994, 1996, 1998
Arizona in Your Future • 1991, 1993, 1998
The Best of the Gold Country • 1987, 1990, 1992
The Best of Denver & the Rockies • 2001
The Best of San Francisco • 1986, 1990, 1994, 1997
The Best of the Wine Country • 1991, 1994, 1995, 2001
California-Nevada Roads Less Traveled • 1999
Inside San Francisco • 1991
Las Vegas: The Best of Glitter City • 1998, 2000
Nevada Discovery Guide • 1992, 1997
Nevada In Your Future • 2000
New Mexico Discovery Guide • 1998
Northern California Discovery Guide • 1993
Oregon Discovery Guide • 1993, 1995, 1996, 1999
San Diego: The Best of Sunshine City • 1999
San Francisco's Ultimate Dining Guide • 1988
Seattle: The Best of Emerald City • 2000
The Toll-free Traveler • 1997
The Ultimate Wine Book • 1993, 2000
Utah Discovery Guide • 1995
Washington Discovery Guide • 1994, 1997, 2000

Copyright © 2001 by Don W. Martin and Betty Woo Martin
Printed in the United States of America. All rights reserved. No written material, maps or illustrations from this book may be reproduced in any form, including electronic media, other than brief passages in book reviews, without written permission from the publisher.

Library of Congress Cataloging-in-Publication Data
Martin, Don and Betty —
The Best of Denver and the Rockies
Includes index.
1. Denver, Colorado—description and travel
2. Denver, Colorado—history
3. Colorado Rockies—description and travel

ISBN: 0-942053-35-4
Library of Congress catalog card number: 2001-126375

COVER DESIGN • **Vicky Biernacki**, Columbine Type and Design, Sonora, Calif.

JUST THE BEST; NOT ALL THE REST

This is a different kind of guidebook. Instead of saturating readers with details on everything there is to see and do in Denver and the Colorado Rockies, the authors have sifted through the region's hundreds of lures and selected only the Ten Best in various categories. This is more than a mere book of lists, however. Each listing is a detailed description, with specifics on location, hours and price ranges.

There is plenty from which to choose. *The Best of Denver and the Rockies* offers Ten Best lists covering nearly fifty different subjects, from playing to dining to reclining. It's a great resource for visitors with limited time, visitors with lots of time and Colorado residents who'd like to make new discoveries in Denver and its majestic sheltering mountains.

A guidebook that selects only on the best must, by its very nature, be rather opinionated. Some would even suggest that it's impertinent. Further, many readers may not agree with the authors' selections, which is part of the fun of reading it.

This is another in a series of "Ten Best" city guides by Don and Betty Martin, winners of a gold medal in the prestigious Lowell Thomas Travel Writing Competition. Check your local book store for these titles:

The Best of San Francisco.
The Best of Phoenix & Tucson
Las Vegas: The Best of Glitter City
San Diego: The Best of Sunshine City
Seattle: The Best of Emerald City

These and other remarkably useful *DISCOVERGUIDES* also can be ordered on line at *www.amazon.com, bn.com* and *borders.com. See the list in the back of this book.*

Keeping up with the changes

One of the fastest growing cities in the American West, Denver is a place of constant transition. The towns, resorts and attractions of the neighboring Rockies often change as well. If you discover something afresh on your Colorado visit, or if you catch an error in this book, let us know. Drop us a note if you find that a cowboy bar has become a laundromat or the other way around.

Address your comments to:

DISCOVERGUIDES
P.O. Box 231954
Las Vegas, NV 89123

CONTENTS
PART I: THE MILE HIGH CITY

A few words of thanks

We could not have written such a detailed and opinionated guide to Denver and the Rockies without the assistance of many other people. We are particularly grateful to "Mr. Denver," **Rich Grant**, the longtime director of communications for the Denver Metro Convention & Visitors Bureau, and his able assistant, public relations manager **Jill Strunk**, for helping us discover the best of the Mile High City.

Key contributors to the book's Rocky Mountain section were **Holly Johnson** and her staff of Johnson Communications, Lafayette, Colorado, who helped us discover the lures of Boulder and the resort areas of the Vail Valley; and **Melissa Schiff** of the Boulder Convention and Visitors Bureau, who also assisted us in that fine city. Also of great help were **Emily K. Jacob**, former communications manager of the Vail Valley Tourism & Convention Bureau and now public relations director for Beaver Creek Resort; and **Ian S. Anderson**, information services manager for the Vail Valley Tourism & Convention Bureau.

Doing Denver and the Rockies

Unless one lives here—not really a bad idea—it would be difficult to experience all that Denver and the nearby Rockies have to offer. A typical vacation or business trip allows one to barely scrape the surface of this fascinating region.

That of course is why we created this book. Since you probably won't have time to discover the very best that Denver and its mountains have the offer, we've done it for you. We spent many weeks prowling Denver's streets, sampling its restaurants, hiking and biking its streamside trails, visiting its attractions and museums. We ate more buffalo burgers and quaffed more microbrews than we care to admit, and consumed enough Mexican food to cater a *Cinco de Mayo* celebration. As lobby lizards, we explored the city's most elegant hotels, and we window-shopped from Larimer Square to Cherry Creek. We looked for the best views and photo stops, the best pubs and nightclubs. For those on a budget, we sought out the best free attractions and the cheapest places to eat and sleep.

After we'd done it all in Denver, we headed out in three directions, headed for the adjacent Rocky Mountains to explore further. We checked out the liberal lures of Boulder, Colorado's penultimate university town, and we enjoyed the grandeur of Rocky Mountain National Park. We sampled the summertime appeal of Colorado's famous Vail Valley ski resorts of Keystone, Breckenridge, Vail and Beaver Creek; and we walked the streets of historic Rocky Mountain mining towns. We then headed south to Colorado Springs and Manitou Springs to have a look at their many tourist attractions.

So we've been there and done that. We've seen it all, explored it all and sampled it all. And we saved the very best just for you.

Welcome to Denver and the Rockies!

Don W. Martin
Hanging out on Sixteenth Street Mall

PART I

DENVER

Colorado's largest city isn't fascinating because it's a mile high. It's fascinating because it's a thriving, culturally-rich metropolis with an abundance of attractions. The "Mile High" moniker comes from a geographic novelty that its founders didn't realize—it's 5,280 feet above sea level, give or take a foot here and there.

The Mile High City likes to identify with America's loftiest mountain range, the Rockies. The symbol for the City and County of Denver is two peaks cradling the sun. Its baseball team is the Colorado Rockies and one of its daily newspapers is the Denver Rocky Mountain News. However, first-time visitors may be surprised to discover that Denver is flatter than a travel writer's bank account, for it sits on the edge of the Great Plains. The Rockies, while forming a dramatic backdrop to the west, are several miles away.

Yet, those mountains are an integral part of this very level city. They're the favorite playground of its citizens, and the city-county recreation department even has several parks among the peaks. Of Denver's several million annual visitors, as many as eighty percent include the Rockies in their vacation plans. This book does the same, and that's why we call it *The Best of Denver and the Rockies*. Part I explores the very best that the Mile High City has to offer, and then Part II takes you where it's really high.

We are bound to have a territory if not a state, and the capitol will be Denver City, with the state house near my claims.
— Comment in 1858 by Denver's founder William Larimer

Chapter one

READY TO GET HIGH?

A SPLENDID ISOLATION

It's one of the most curiously located big cities in America—a mile high and hundreds of miles from nowhere. With a metropolitan population exceeding two million, Denver is the most isolated major city in America—maybe in the world.

If you galloped off in all directions, you won't encounter another sizable city for 600 miles. If Denver were in the middle of Europe and you traveled 600 miles east, you'd be in Russia; go 600 miles west, young man, and you'd reach England's shores. Go that distance north and you'd freeze your fanny off, for you'd be near the Arctic Circle.

Yet Denver is one of America's most livable, most vibrant and most popular cities, drawing ten million tourists and conventioneers a year. It's also one of America's fastest growing cities, having gained a third of a million people in the past five years.

Don't take our word for Denver's appeal. In 1996 and 1997, *Fortune Magazine* called it America's second best city in which to live and work. *Money Magazine* said it was the second most livable city in the West in 1998. *Sporting News* called it America's Best Sports City in

1997 and *American Health Magazine* rates it among the top ten cities for women's health.

However, we aren't urging you to move there. Some locals fuss that the greater Denver area already is growing too fast. We're simply recommending that you pay it a visit. And after you've done so, we urge you to explore the nearby mountains, as most visitors do. However, travelers who fly into Denver International Airport, then rent a car and head straight for the hills are making a large mistake. With its many lures, this town is too interesting to be bypassed. Any vacation to this region should include both Denver and its Rocky Mountain neighbors.

Denver's isolation offers advantages both to residents and visitors. As a metropolitan center serving an area nearly as large as Europe, it has more services and facilities, cultural lures, visitor attractions, restaurants and lodgings that most cities of its size. For sports fans, it's America's smallest city to support all four major league teams—football, baseball, basketball and ice hockey.

You need specific reasons for visiting this flat city beside the Rockies? How about 310 days of sunshine a year, more than a dozen fine museums, one of America's greatest aquariums, a downtown amusement park, sports action from those major league franchises, 2,500 restaurants of many ethnic persuasions, fine shopping, a handsomely restored historic area, a landscaped downtown pedestrian mall, America's largest performing arts center under one roof and—oh, yes—a dozen brewpubs.

And that's just Denver.

In the nearby Rockies, you've got hundreds of miles of hiking and mountain biking trails, great whitewater streams, some of America's top summer and winter resorts, Colorado Springs with its many tourist lures plus the U.S. Air Force Academy, fascinating old mining towns, the suburban yet urbane city of Boulder and—oh, yes—America's largest brewery.

While Denver is a mile high, give or take a few dips and hillocks, it's rather low when compared to its next door mountains. Although California's Mount Whitney is America's highest peak outside of Alaska at 14,496 feet, the Rockies overall are the country's highest mountain range. Fifty-four peaks are more than 14,000 feet high, compared with twelve in California's Sierra Nevada and only one in the rest of the lower U.S.—Washington's Mount Rainier.

GETTING THERE

Now that we've convinced you that Denver is worth visiting, we'll tell you how to get there and find your way about. Despite its isolation, the Mile High City is an easy reach. Build a city that is large enough and attractive enough and it becomes not an isolated way station, but a hub.

By highway ● Freeways gallop into town from five different directions. Interstate 70 comes from the east and west. I-25 offers north-south access from Wyoming and New Mexico, and I-76 angles southwesterly from Omaha.

I-70 also provides quick access to Denver's mountains, climbing high into the Rockies and then slipping through the mile-long Eisenhower Memorial Tunnel which—at more than 11,000 feet—is one of the world's highest highway tubes.

If you're approaching from north or south, note that Interstate 25 passes just west of the heart of the city. Take exit 210-A (Highway 40) onto Colfax Avenue, head east toward the Civic Center and you'll be in the middle of Denver. Coming from the west on I-70, fork to the right onto U.S. Highway 6 just east of Golden, since it's a more direct route to downtown. Then go north briefly on I-25 and take the Colfax Avenue exit.

From this point, you'll want a detailed city map to find your way to your hotel or motel and assorted downtown visitor lures. Several green signs on Colfax and other major streets point the way to some of the attractions. Many of the city's motels are along Colfax, since that was the U.S. Highway 40 before the days of freeways. Others are clustered about freeway interchanges.

By air ● We don't know why—in one of America's flattest cities—the new Denver International Airport was located halfway to Kansas. Although it's twenty-three miles northeast of town, DIA is served by a fast four-lane highway, and it's a fine flying field. It should be, since it cost $4.3 billion. The Department of Transportation says it's second best in America for on-time arrivals, with the lowest percentage of air traffic control delays, and it was rated third best in North America by readers of *Business Traveler International Magazine.* So forget those scary snowbound scenes from *Airport,* the film based on Arthur Hailey's book. Besides, that was old Stapleton Airport. Further, you'll be glad to know that DIA's state-of-the-art luggage routing system no longer eats Samsonites.

Denver International is home base for Frontier Airlines and United Airlines' second largest hub. Served by more than twenty other carriers, it's the sixth busiest airport in America, handling more than 35 million passengers a year. If you're among those numbers, signs will direct you to a variety of ground transportation choices, including shuttles, taxis, limos, rental car counters and—if you're on a budget—Regional Transit District buses. (See below.)

By train ● Amtrak's *California Zephyr* offers daily east and west service via Denver's grand old Union Station at Wynkoop and Seventeenth streets. Call (800) USA-RAIL or locally (303) 534-2812.

By bus ● Greyhounds gallop in and out of town several times a day. The station is at 1055 Nineteenth St.; (800) 231-2222 or (303) 293-6555. It's a few blocks from there to the Regional Transit District's

Market Street Station, where you can transfer to the Denver area's very comprehensive local bus service or a fixed rail system called The Ride. Call (800) 366-RIDE or (303) 299-6000 for transit information. (*www.rtd-denver.com*)

GETTING ABOUT

Newcomers may find Denver difficult to navigate, since the original city was platted southwest to northeast along the banks of Cherry Creek. As it grew, streets were aligned to the compass points. Thus, Denver sits at a 45-degree angle to itself, much to the consternation of traffic engineers and visitors. If you get lost, look for snowcapped peaks and you'll know that's west.

Many of Denver's attractions and most of its better restaurants and hotels are in the downtown area. That's the section sitting at an angle to the rest of the city. One of the first things you should do upon arrival, shortly after you've found lodging and unpacked your suitcases, is take our favorite Denver walk, outlined in Chapter Ten, page 147. This easy three-mile stroll will deliver you through the heart of the commercial area and into historic Larimer Square and LoDo District. You don't have to walk the entire route, since most of it is served by a free shuttle along Sixteenth Street Mall. Walking or riding, you'll become oriented with the downtown area.

The lowdown on LoDo

Feeling the need to mimic London's SOHO theater district and San Francisco's SOMA (south of Market), Denverites call their old town section LoDo, meaning **Lo**wer **Do**wntown. It refers to the area's northwest corner, yet one normally regards north as *up*. However, "UpDo" would sound really dumb. Blame it on the Colorado State Capitol. It stands on a slight rise on the southeastern edge of downtown, and heart of the city is downhill from there, northwest toward the South Platte River.

Originally, the capitol was nearly a mile from downtown, standing alone on that knoll. Then newer development spread southeasterly toward it, leaving the original business district in a state of urban blight. The new highrise section is regarded as upper downtown (but not UpDo). LoDo's redevelopment and gentrification started in the 1970s and continues to this day. It is a handsome area of restored century-old brick and masonry buildings, including some really imposing warehouses that are being converted into lofts. A two-block section of LoDo has been designated Larimer Square, busy with boutiques, galleries and restaurants.

After doing downtown, you'll find that the rest of Denver is easier to navigate, since streets are aligned to the compass points. Colfax Avenue is the main east-west artery; it skirts just below downtown, passing the state capitol and Civic Center, site of several major attractions. If you continue east on Colfax, you can turn north onto Colorado Boulevard and follow it to the large Denver City Park with its zoo and museum of natural history; or go south to the upscale Cherry Creek shopping area. If you go west on Colfax, then take Speer Boulevard northwest along Cherry Creek, you'll reach Six Flags Elitch Gardens amusement park and the South Platte River. Across the river is Colorado's Ocean Journey, one of America's finest aquariums.

If you're staying downtown and headed for a restaurant or attraction that's a fair distance south, it's often faster to take one-way Broadway and merge onto southbound I-25 at interchange 207-A, instead of going west on Colfax to pick up the freeway. On your return, exit onto northbound one-way Lincoln Street.

WEATHER OR NOT

Denver is one of the most outdoor-oriented cities in America, with walking and biking trails along the Platte River and Cherry Creek, 200 parks and many sidewalk restaurants and of course the allure of outdoor recreation in the next-door Rockies. Surveys have shown that its citizens are among the most fit of any city in America.

And why not? Denver receives more than 310 days of sunshine a year and annual precipitation is only fifteen inches, about the same as Los Angeles. Summer and fall days usually are gorgeous; hot days are tempered by the city's high altitude and the relatively dry air. Denver is a rather breezy city, as winds sweep down onto the plains from the Rockies. All the better to cool down summer days and blow the smog away.

"But it's a dry cold..."

What about winter? Doesn't it get colder than a well-digger's fanny in the Klondike? Not really, according to the Denver Metro Convention and Visitors Bureau. Average daytime temperature in January and February is around 44 to 46 degrees, which isn't exactly toasty. However, the air is high and dry, so it's less penetrating than damp cold. Unless the wind is blowing, crisp winter days aren't that uncomfortable. Snowfall is relatively light and it doesn't generally stay on the ground. Besides, aren't you supposed to be up on the ski slopes this time of year? Of course it does get cold at night, dropping into the teens from November through February.

Actually, Denver's worst weather is in the spring. That's when it gets most of its wind, rain and occasional blowing snow. The wettest months—which aren't really that wet—are May with 2.64 inches of precipitation, followed by April and June. The driest months? Would you believe December, January and February?

Because Denver's elevation, if you're coming from a place near sea level, you might want to pace yourself the first couple of days to get used to the altitude. Full acclimation to high altitudes actually takes several weeks, as any mountain climber will attest. However, this isn't the Himalayas; it's *only* a mile high, so the change isn't extreme.

IS LIKKER QUICKER?

Although Colorado generally is regarded as a rather free spirited state without a lot of confining regulations, it has some archaic liquor laws left over from Prohibition. As a matter of fact, Coloradans voted to outlaw booze four years before the feds, in 1916—much to the consternation of Adolph Coors. Beer sold in supermarkets can be only 3.2 percent alcohol and that's *all* they can sell. Only licensed liquor stores can sell full strength beer, along with liquor and wine. Package sales of any alcohol is forbidden on Sunday, although you can get a drink in a bar or restaurant that day.

Liquor stores aren't state operated as they are in places like Utah, Oregon and Washington. They're relatively plentiful and offer a good assortment—unless you get suddenly thirsty on the Sabbath. Since liquor stores have a corner on the market, we found booze to be rather expensive in Colorado.

VISITOR INFORMATION

For a copy of the *Denver & Colorado Official Visitors Guide,* contact the Denver Metro Convention & Visitors Bureau, 1555 California St., Suite 300, Denver, CO 80202; (800) 645-3446 or (303) 892-1505. (www.denver.org; e-mail: info@denver.org) Once you arrive, you'll find information centers at Denver International Airport, in Tabor Center on the Sixteenth Street Mall at Larimer Street, in Larimer Square downtown at Larimer and Fifteenth Street, and in the Cherry Creek Shopping Center at First Avenue near University Boulevard.

Other "best" sources

Denverites apparently love to make lists of what they like—and in some cases dislike—about their city. Three local publications feature annual lists of Denver's best offerings, with editors' and/or readers choices. Like crocuses, they all come out in the springtime.

Westword, a deliberately politically incorrect, alternative lifestyle newspaper, publishes a thick "Best of Denver" edition in late June. This tabloid-size publication is available free at news racks around town. If you aren't here when the "Best of Denver" edition hits the streets, you can buy a back copy at the office at 969 Broadway, near the corner of Tenth. "Best of Denver" selections are made by staff members, with alternate choices by readers in some categories. The list is lengthy, many selections are silly and most of them won't interest visitors. Who wants to know about "the best hairdo on a female TV personality" or "the best bug mural?" However, the Food and Drink section will provide many leads to interesting restaurants and pubs in the greater Denver area. (www.westword.com)

The **Denver Post** prints its annual "Colorado Peaks" selections the first Sunday in June. It, too, has some rather strange categories, such as the "most scenic free-standing restroom" and "best Colorado guidebook written by grade school students." (Maybe we should hire those kids.) However, it has many useful categories as well, covering restaurants, cultural lures, family attractions and nightlife. One particularly useful feature—it has locator maps of many of its selections.

Denver's slick and upscale city magazine, **5280**, published six times a year, announces its "Top of the Town" awards in the June/July issue, which hits newsstands and book stores in late May. Focusing on restaurants, cocktail lounges, food specialties and shopping, it's the most interesting of the three. There are no silly "ugliest billboard" or "best weed maintenance crew" categories. The only gimmickry is the magazine's "mile high" preoccupation, claiming that its selections are made by a team of 5,280 editors and writers.

As a matter of fact, we'd like to submit a new category to all three publications: "The most overused Denver cliché." And the winner, of course, is "Mile High City." If America were on the metric system like virtually all of the rest of the world, Denver would have to find a new gimmick. (On the other hand, it's probably better than being named after an omelet.)

AN UNAUTHORIZED HISTORY

How did it happen? How did a dusty prairie town—started by a claimjumper, bypassed by the transcontinental railroad and fed by a river too thick to drink and too thin to plow—become the largest city in the Intermountain West? In fact, the largest city between Los Angeles and Chicago.

During the 1850s, thousands of fortune hunters were streaming through—not to—Colorado, headed for the promise of California gold. The discovery of glitter in the tailrace of a sawmill in the Sierra Nevada foothills in 1848 had spurred history's greatest gold rush, and the greatest human migration since the Crusades. At the time, America essentially ended at the Missouri border, except for a few settlements in the Northwest. Areas that were to become Kansas, Nebraska, Colorado, Utah and Nevada were uncharted territory, informally called "Kansas Country." The Southwest was still owned by Mexico and future northwestern states were lumped together as "Oregon Country," whose boundaries were being disputed by England and the United States.

The vast spread of prairie, desert and mountains between Missouri and California was considered a hindrance to folks headed for the gold fields. Toward the end of the 1850s, as California gold fever began to subside, prospectors began poking about the foothills of the Rocky Mountains. If the streams of the Sierra Nevada had yielded gold, they reasoned, why not the rivers of the Rockies? In 1858, a group from Georgia found gold in a little stream called Cherry Creek, near the mouth of the South Platte River. It amounted to only a few hundred dollars. However, "it was magnified with each retelling of the story," according to one historian.

Although the strike fizzled, several people saw the potential of a trading center at the confluence of Cherry Creek and the South Platte, to serve gold and silver mining camps higher in the Rockies. The weather was milder down here and the land was flat, with plenty of room to stake out and sell lots. Two communities were started in 1858. The Georgia prospectors platted Auraria (for *aura*, the Latin word for gold) on the east side of Cherry Creek, and a group from eastern Kansas led by Charlie Nichols laid out the perimeters of St. Charles on the west side. Then the Nichols group started back to file a claim at the territorial capital of Lecompton. By this time, the Kansas Territory had been established, which included most of Colorado.

However, Nichols got word that another party was headed for the area. He retreated to make a "good faith improvement" on the townsite as required by law, starting the framework of a log cabin. Nichols either wintered at the site or resumed his trek to Lecompton and returned in the spring, depending on your historian. The other party— headed by "General" William Larimer—arrived at Cherry Creek in late 1858, liked the looks of Nichols claim and promptly jumped it. (He had acquired the title of general while serving with the Missouri militia.) He formed the Denver City Town Company, naming it in honor of Kansas territorial governor James W. Denver in an effort to win political favor. He had no way of knowing that Denver had resigned over the slavery issue, which had become so violent that the territory earned the title of "Bleeding Kansas."

Still, Larimer held onto his land and set about establishing Denver City. When Nichols objected to the land grab, Larimer's group said that if he didn't stop making trouble, "a rope and noose would be used on him." They eventually gave Nichols a few lots, which he sold and then left the area, preferring a small profit to a noose.

In 1859, a group of citizens met at Uncle Dick Wootton's Saloon on the banks of Cherry Creek and, fortified with a few drinks, drew up a petition to create the territory of Jefferson, although the federal government ignored their request. Later that same year, the fledgling settlement shriveled and nearly died in 1859 when gold strikes in the Black Hawk and Central City areas siphoned off most of its population. It managed to survive as a provisioning center. When Horace Greeley passed through that year, he made note of a "log city of 150 dwellings, not three-fourths completed nor two-thirds inhabited, nor one-third fit to be."

Askew towns

Three towns had been platted along Cherry Creek and the South Platte—Denver, Auraria and Highland. Street patterns of each sat slightly askew of the others, a condition that persists to this day. After months of squabbling, the three merged into the City of Denver in April, 1860. Legend says that Larimer bribed other officials with a barrel of whiskey. In reality, he held the most votes, since his group had established both Denver and Highland. The merged community of log and whipsaw board cabins grew slowly, then most of it burned back to the dirt in 1863. Taking a cue from similar disasters in California mining towns, officials decreed that future businesses had to be built of brick or masonry.

As more gold strikes were made in the nearby foothills, Denver gradually secured its position as a provisioning center for the mines. The federal government, now eager for the area's mineral wealth and needing resources to fight the Civil War, agreed to carve a chunk of land free from Kansas in 1861 to create a new territory. Ignoring the earlier petition, officials decided to name it Colorado instead of Jefferson. It's Spanish for "color of red," referring to the silt-laden lower reaches of the great river of the Southwest. *Rio Colorado* flows fresh and clear from the Rockies. However, it's rather ruddy by the time it reaches Arizona, several hundred miles downstream. There, early Spanish missionaries named it for its reddish hue.

A number of communities wanted to be Colorado's territorial capitol and for several years, the legislators "moved around to wherever they could find free drinks," wrote Thomas J. Noel in *Colorado: A Liquid History & Tavern Guide to the Highest State*; © 1999. They first met in Golden, then in Colorado City before settling permanently in Denver in 1866. In 1876, Colorado became America's 38th state.

Denver had its problems

Meanwhile, back in Denver, the new town's troubles weren't finished, even though nearby mines continued yielding their treasures. Cherry Creek and the South Platte River flooded in 1864, washing away most of Auraria and drowning twenty people. Then an Indian war erupted in Colorado and Denver was cut off from supplies for several weeks. And finally, builders of the transcontinental railroad decided to bypass Denver in favor of Cheyenne, not wanting to build rails through one of the steepest escarpments of the Rockies.

"Cheyenne will rapidly emerge as the queen city of the mountain and plain and Denver will be too dead to bury," said Union Pacific officials.

Some local investors panicked. Would this prairie town born of a fizzled gold strike, sitting beside a river too shallow for navigation finally die? By this time, mining had ebbed in the adjacent Rockies and the future looked bleak.

Officials realized that the key to survival was to build a connecting rail line to Cheyenne. Although it was completed in 1870, it was rather a boondoggle. Two-thirds of the $6.5 million raised for the Denver Pacific Railroad was siphoned off by fund-raisers and thieves. And a group of miners from Georgetown who had crafted a silver spike for the final link got drunk the night before the completion ceremony and gambled it away. Two months after the first train chugged into Denver, the Union Pacific completed its own line to the Mile High City, angling southwest through Kansas.

The rail links brought prosperity to Denver and assured its future. And, according to Phil Goldstein, author of *The Seamy Side of Denver,* the rails also brought "gamblers, con men and prostitutes who had been servicing the railroad construction crews." Typically, red light districts grew up near railroad tracks and—according to legend—the name comes from the red lanterns carried by train signalmen. Like most other Western cities, Denver indeed had its seamy side, and its main avenue of sin was Holladay Street in present-day LoDo. It gained national prominence as one of the bawdiest red light districts in the American West. The street had been named in honor of Ben Holladay, the legendary stage coach driver and founder of the Central Overland, California and Pikes Peak Express Company. Family members became so upset over the street's reputation that they petitioned officials to have its name changed. In 1887, it was renamed Market Street.

An assortment of colorful characters helped shape early Denver, and we aren't referring to prostitutes. Henry Cordes Brown and his wife paused here in 1860, headed for the California gold fields. Weary of the trail, they decided to go no further. A builder by profession, Brown eventually became one of the town's wealthiest and most influential men. He built the legendary Brown Palace Hotel and donated the land for the state capitol building.

Another Brown, James Joseph, arrived in 1894 after starting his fortune as a mining engineer in Leadville. He was accompanied by his pretty red-headed wife, Margaret Tobin Brown, who is now known to the world—incorrectly—as Molly Brown. These Browns also became community leaders and Margaret was one of Denver's most prominent activists, working for the rights of women and children. She became a world traveler and her survival of the *Titanic* sinking and her successful efforts to create safety at sea laws brought her international fame. To learn more about the real Margaret Brown—who never was called Molly—see Chapter Two, page 36.

Horace and Baby Doe

Another Leadville mining millionaire, Horace Austin Warner Tabor, also became a prominent Denverite. One of Leadville's first silver barons, he was elected as Colorado's lieutenant governor in 1878 and moved to Denver. He eventually became governor and then the U.S. Senator from Colorado. He also created some of Denver's most impressive buildings, such as the Tabor Block and the lavish Tabor Grand Opera House. Earlier, when he'd struck it rich, he divorced his frumpy wife Augusta and married pretty young Elizabeth Bonduel McCourt, who he called his "little baby doe."

Unfortunately, their lives would end in tragedy. The Tabors lived extravagantly in Denver, spending money as fast as it rolled in from their Leadville mines. Then in 1893, the federal government stopped supporting the price of silver. Denver went on the skids and the Tabors lost their fortune. The penniless Tabor died of a ruptured appendix in

1899. Baby Doe returned to Leadville, where she moved into the tool-house of one of their now worthless mines called the Matchless. She froze to death there during a harsh winter in 1935. (For more on the Tabors, see Chapter Thirteen, pages 206 and 208.)

Ironically, the silver panic that ruined Tabor and nearly destroyed Denver became the basis for J.J. Browns' fortune. As superintendent of Leadville's Ibex Mining Company, he devised a method of shoring up the shafts of the Little Jonny Mine, allowing the miners to keep digging until they struck gold. The company rewarded him with stock and he began buying and operating other mines.

One of Denver's most interesting early characters was Jefferson Randolph "Soapy" Smith. He didn't affect the town's overall economy although he conned many of its citizens out of their paychecks. The son of a Southern attorney, he headed west after the Civil War had ruined his family's fortunes. He worked as a cowboy, became proficient as a con artist and arrived in Denver via Leadville in 1886. He opened his Tivoli gambling club on Larimer Street and began fleecing Denver's citizens. He earned his odd nickname because he also peddled bars of soap, a few of which were wrapped with $20 to $100 dollar bills. He sold the soap bars for $5 each, although only his shills wound up with bars wrapped in currency. He eventually was run out of town, and in 1897 wound up in Skagway, Alaska, lured by the Yukon Gold Rush. He and a gang of con artists ran the town for a year until he was confronted by a deputized citizen named Frank Reid. They fired their weapons at one another, and both eventually died.

Lessons in survival

Denver survived the silver panic, as it had survived the fizzle of the Cherry Creek gold strike, the bypassing of the transcontinental railroad, the great fire and flood, Indian wars and Soapy Smith. A major gold strike at Cripple Creek in 1894 reaffirmed the city's position as a provisioning and commercial center.

In fact, it has survived so well that the rest of its history isn't really that exciting. It coasted into the twentieth century, endured the Depression and became a military center during and after World War II. President Dwight D. Eisenhower used Lowry Air Force Base as his summer White House, partly because his wife Mamie's mother was a Denver resident. The base was closed during military cutbacks, although a site between Denver and Colorado Springs was chosen as the setting for the U.S. Air Force Academy. The federal government also decided, during the Cold War, to build an atomic-bomb proof operations center deep in the bowels of nearby Cheyenne Mountain.

The energy boom of the 1970s brought new wealth to the Mile High City. Ironically, much of the action—oil drilling and coal mining—was in neighboring Wyoming, although many of the energy companies built new skyscrapers in Denver. Cheyenne never did become "the queen city of mountain and plain."

The real queen city survived the energy crunch of the eighties, then in the nineties, it caught the wave of a new kind of energy, becoming a mile-high version of Silicon Valley. With the coming of the new millennium, Denver has settled into a comfortable role as a city of diversified economies, serving the commercial needs of an area larger than Europe. It's enjoying yet another boom; its population has increased by twenty-three percent since 1990.

The city that was started in the wrong place by a claimjumper obviously has learned well the lessons of survival.

THE TEN BEST DENVER SUPERLATIVES
Gleaned mostly by Rich Grant, Communications Director
Denver Metro Convention and Visitors Bureau

1 *A SUNNY DISPOSITION* • According to U.S. Weather Bureau statistics, Denver has an average of 310 days of sunshine a year, more than San Diego or Miami.

2 *THINK THIN* • Denver's citizens are physically fit. A study by the Coalition for Excess Weight Risk determined in a 1996 study that Denver had the thinnest residents of America's thirty-three largest cities. Only twenty percent of its citizens are overweight, compared with a national average of fifty percent.

3 *CULTURE VULTURES* • The Denver Performing Arts Complex is the nation's largest under one roof and it's the second largest in total seating, after Lincoln Center. The complex has eight individual performance halls, hosting everything from classic symphony music to *avant garde* theater.

4 *GET SMART* • According to the U.S. Census Bureau, Denver has a higher percentage of high school graduates (92.1) and college graduates (35 percent with bachelor degrees) than any other major American city.

5 *TAKE A HIKE* • Denver has the nation's largest public park system, with more than 200 parks within the city limits and 20,000 acres of city-owned mountain parks in the nearby Rockies. The forty-seven mountain parks include everything from a ski resort to alpine tundra to the grave of Buffalo Bill.

6 *PLAY BALL!* • Denver is the smallest city in America to support all four major league teams. They are—count 'em—football's Denver Broncos (where have you gone, John Elway?), baseball's Colorado Rockies, basketball's Denver Nuggets and hockey's Colorado Avalanche.

7 *AN OCEAN ON THE PLAINS?* ● The new Ocean Journey aquarium is the largest between Chicago and the West Coast. The million-gallon facility traces the Colorado River from the Rockies to the Sea of Cortez—finally putting Denver in touch with salt water.

8 *BOOKWORMS* ● More than half of Denver's citizens hold library cards, and that's the highest percentage of any urban area in the nation. The Denver Public Library is one of the country's largest, with five million items on forty-seven miles of bookshelves. Further, the Tattered Cover bookstore's two outlets have nearly half a million titles, making it one of the largest retail book outlets in America.

9 *MAKE MINE SCRAMBLED* ● Because Denver is a mile above sea level, it takes four minutes to boil a three-minute egg.

10 *BEER HERE!* ● People of the Denver area brew—and possibly consumes—more beer than in any other region in America. Coors, the world's largest brewery, is in nearby Golden, where it produces seventeen million gallons a year. Denver has nearly a dozen microbreweries, including America's largest, Wynkoop Brewing Company. Denver's Great American Beer Festival—the nation's largest, with more than 300 brewers participating—is held every October.

Denver is the natural halting place for tourists and visitors, by reason of its extended connections with...pleasure resorts, its excellent hotel accommodations, and its size, prominence and general attractions. It is the finest and most enterprising city of the New West.

— Denver resident Frank Fossett in 1879

Chapter two

DOING DENVER...

...AS A TOURIST

Denver has sufficient attractions to occupy a visitor for several days. It is not a city to be glimpsed briefly and then abandoned in favor of the nearby Rockies, despite their great outdoor appeal. In fact, the Mile High City has many outdoor appeals of its own—the largest public park system in America and miles of walking and cycling trails, particularly along Cherry Creek and the South Platte River.

This is a city rich in both culture and tourist curiosities, with an outstanding aquarium, art museum and science museum; an historic district brimming with fine restaurants and shops, an excellent zoo, a remarkably interesting botanical garden and—for the kids—an amusement park that's practically downtown. (Speaking of kids, middle to late May is field trip season for Denver schools, when students—under the loose control of teachers and volunteer parents—swarm through every museum and attraction in town and even invade the Sixteenth Street Mall and the Larimer Square historic district.)

A visit to Denver must include Golden, just a few miles west. Some of the area's top attractions and activities are in or near this charming little foothill town, such as the Coors Brewery tour, Colorado Railroad Museum, Red Rocks Amphitheatre and Buffalo Bill's Grave and Museum. These attractions are covered at the end of this chapter under "A Golden opportunity," since they can be visited on a loop driving tour from Denver.

GETTING THERE: Each listing in *The Best of Denver and the Rockies* includes detailed driving directions, which you can apply to a city map to find your way about. To provide consistent points of reference, all directions begin either from downtown or from one of the major freeways. A detailed Denver map will be extremely helpful in following these directions.

☺ **KID STUFF:** This little grinning guy marks attractions that are of particular interest to pre-teens.

PRICING: Since prices frequently change, we use dollar sign codes to indicate the approximate cost of adult admission to various attractions and activities: **$** = under $5; **$$** = $5 to $9; **$$$** = $10 to $14 ; **$$$$** = $15 to $19; **$$$$$** = $20 or more. And you already know that prices are almost always less for seniors and kids.

THE TEN VERY BEST ATTRACTIONS

In most of our Ten Best lists—with a few exceptions—we start with the very best, and then follow with the rest in alphabetical order. Thus, we have no losers in *The Best of Denver and the Rockies,* only winners and runners up. Our ten favorite Denver attractions are a mixed bag, reflecting the diversity of this Mile High City.

1 OCEAN JOURNEY • *700 Water St.; (303) 561-4450. (www.oceanjourney.org) Weekdays 9 to 6:30 and weekends 9 to 8 Memorial Day through Labor Day; daily 10 to 6 the rest of the year; $$$$, plus parking. GETTING THERE: From I-25, take exit 211 (23rd Avenue) and go northeast on Water Street. If you're downtown, follow Fifteenth Street about a mile northwest and cross the South Platte River at Confluence Park. Turn left on Platte, pass the large REI store, cross under the Speer Street Bridge and blend onto Water Street; the aquarium is on the left and parking is on the right. ☺*

Well, of course there was an ocean here—sixty-five million years ago. Using that premise and the fact that the Colorado River ultimately reaches the Sea of Cortez, a private non-profit group has created Denver's best attraction and one of the finest aquariums in the land. To give it more dimension, they peered through the globe and found another river directly opposite Colorado, which also starts in the mountains and ends in the sea—the Kampar in tropical Indonesia. Thus, this Ocean Journey takes visitors along rivers with two completely different personalities. The museum uses detailed topographical models, often full dimensional, to create realistic settings for these river journeys.

The Colorado River journey takes visitors from its source in the high Rockies, across the arid Colorado Plateau where it has carved fantastic canyons and finally to the Sea of Cortez. River "pools" along the route—held in place by thick Plexiglas panels—contain live otters and the types of fish one might encounter along the way. The river and its followers then enter a deep canyon with simulated bones of prehistoric fish and reptiles that thrived in Colorado when it was the shoreline of a shallow sea. At the Sea of Cortez, the visitor sees real shorebirds and reefs busy with tropical fish. And one is reminded that, because of excessive upstream water diversion, the river's ecology has been changed dramatically and only a tiny trickle now reaches its mouth.

The Kampar lures its river-runners through a lush rainforest, where graphics point out that it is born of torrential rains, not of snowmelt. A free-flying aviary and tiger lair are special features of this damp, tropical exhibit. At river's end are large deep-sea aquariums where visitors may see divers feeding the fishes. The large aquarium complex also has a sea otter cove, touchy-feely exhibits, docent presentations a restaurant with views of the South Platte River, and a gift shop. Ocean Journey has more than 15,000 fish, mammals and birds, representing about 300 species.

2 *COLORADO HISTORY MUSEUM • 1300 Broadway; (303) 866-3682. (www.coloradohistory.org) Monday-Saturday 10 to 4:30 and Sunday noon to 4:30; $. GETTING THERE: The museum is just below the Civic Center on the southeast side of downtown, corner of Thirteenth and Broadway.*

This is Colorado captured in a basement. Although the museum building looks rather stern outside—other than it's attractive mural-frieze—it's delightful from within. The permanent displays are downstairs, while changing exhibits on the main level, provide excuses for repeated visits. Like any progressive museum, this one features interactive displays, videos and oral histories. The main exhibit begins with an appealingly cluttered Colorado timeline, tracing the state from 1800 when this land was ceded by Spain to France and was then included in the Louisiana Purchase. The timeline continues through settlement, conflicts with native peoples, the 1876 "Centennial Statehood" and into the last century, ending with 1949, where the preparators apparently ran out of wall space.

The rest of the museum is decidedly uncluttered, featuring full-size items such as a plains Indian teepee, a complete Conosoga wagon and an impressive mockup mining and ore stamp mill operation, called "Out of the Earth." An extensive display covers cowboying in the west, starting with a life-sized cutout of Roy Rogers in his movie costume, to show what real cowboys *didn't* look like. The exhibit focuses on Black cowboys, who made up a fair percentage of the West's steer punchers. Another display, *La Gente*, features Hispanics of Colorado, from *con-*

quistadores to *vaqueros*. Much of our Western attire—wide-brimmed hats, chaps, lariats and saddles with horns—came from the *vaquero* or Mexican cowboy.

The most interesting Denver exhibit is a large, detailed tabletop model of the city in the 1860s. Other displays trace its development from the discovery of gold on Cherry Creek to its establishment as a provisioning, business and shipping center—the role it continues to this day. Particularly interesting is 1914 Fritchle electric car built by a Denver inventor and entrepreneur. A video traces its history and follows a recent cruise around the city.

3 *COLORADO STATE CAPITOL* • *200 E. Colfax Ave.; (303) 866-2604. (www.state.co.us) Open weekdays 7 to 5:30; free tours every forty-five minutes from 9 to 2:30. Dome open 7 to 3:30. GETTING THERE: The capitol is just southeast of downtown, between Lincoln and Grant streets. To pick up a visitor's pamphlet or to take a tour, use the north entrance at Colfax and Sherman; a visitor information desk is just inside.* ☺ *(Kids will like the capitol dome climb)*

State capitol buildings are considered tourist attractions almost by default, although Colorado's—modeled after the nation's capitol—is particularly appealing. It's one of the few capitols in America whose dome is open to the public, at least to those willing to climb ninety-three steps. And this dome, in fact, is gold plated.

Those who eschew the long climb will find many items of interest in the lower reaches, including not just one but two mile-high markers on the west side steps. The original marker is on the eighteenth step, proclaiming this point to be exactly one mile above sea level. After a more precise measurement in 1969, a brass survey marker was placed three steps higher. Step inside to admire its off-white marble floors and distinctive rose onyx wainscotting, mined at the Beaulah quarry in Colorado and used in no other building. You can ascend to the second floor and peek into the elaborate senate and assembly chambers, then climb to the third level and step into their visitor galleries when they're in session. Also worth a peek on the third level is a gallery of portraits of every American President.

Should you choose to make the assault on the dome, the long climb begins on the west side of the third floor. A third of the way up, you can take a break at an interesting small museum featuring photos, architectural drawings and anecdotes concerning the capitol's construction. (See "The Ten Best Museums" farther along in this chapter, on page 37.) Once you've reached the dome, you can—assuming you aren't troubled by vertigo—step outside and stroll around the circular Observation Balcony. You'll enjoy grand views of the city, the nearby Rockies and the endless prairie.

4 DENVER ART MUSEUM • *100 W. Fourteenth Avenue Parkway; (303) 640-4433. (www.denvermuseum.com) Tuesday-Saturday 10 to 5 (until 9 Wednesday), Sunday noon to 5; closed Monday; $. Free to Colorado residents on Saturdays. Extra fees for some special exhibits. GETTING THERE: The museum is just below Civic Center Park near downtown, at the corner of Bannock between Thirteenth and Fourteenth, beside the Denver Public Library.*

Never mind that the building resembles a modernistic urban prison, with its tall gray walls and tiny windows. Within that structure is one of the finest art museums in the nation. Even cultural clods will enjoy this splendid repository, with its impressive collections of artifacts, videos and "Art Stops" where docents let patrons handle replicas of museum objects. (These action stations are on weekends only.) If you have kids, take them to the "Just For Fun Family Center" in the basement. And if art makes you hungry, Palettes Restaurant and Palettes Express serve quite tasty food. There are several lounges within this seven-story museum where patrons can relax, watch videos, read material related to the exhibits and even activate CD roms to study art works of the great masters. Incidentally, as the largest art museum between Kansas City and the Pacific, it hosts major traveling exhibits.

The term "art museum" is a bit understated. Although its walls are hung with paintings, including those multiple colored blobs that pass for modern art, this is more of a social history museum, with artifacts from cultures around the globe. It has the finest collection of native peoples art and artifacts in America, covering nearly every major tribal group. Particularly imposing is the Northwest collection, with brilliantly colored totems, carved panels and the entire carved wall of a longhouse. Other museum floors cover pre-Colombian and Spanish Colonial art, with some splendid *santos* (small carved wooden saints) and religious paintings from South America; Asian art ranging from Buddhist images to classic Chinese to contemporary Japanese art forms; and European and American art.

The top floor is devoted to Art of the American West, from fine cowboy bronzes to those splendidly romanticized Nineteenth Century paintings of Western scenery. When you reach this level, look through a glass door to a really cute "Cowboy and Indian Shootout" on the roof, sculpted of aluminum and Fiberglas by artist Red Grooms.

5 DENVER BOTANIC GARDENS • *909 York St.; (303) 331-4000. (www.botanicgardens.org) Wednesday-Friday 9 to 5 and Saturday-Tuesday 9 to 8 from May through September; then daily 9 to 5 the rest of the year; $. GETTING THERE: Go east from downtown about 1.5 miles on Colfax Avenue, then south half a mile on York Street.*

Even if you have a black thumb and wouldn't know a peony from a parsnip, add the Botanic Garden to your list of things to see in Denver. More than a patch of plants, it's a huge complex of twenty-three different theme gardens, plus the domed 14,000 square foot Boettcher Memorial Conservatory that resembles a habitat from a distant planet. Indeed, the interior is alien to Denver, for it's a lush tropic jungle of more than 800 varieties of tropical plants. One section is a-bloom with gorgeous orchids. A centerpiece disguised as a banyan tree offers a nice overview of this mile high rainforest. Out in the gardens, you can stroll shady paths, relax in quiet patios beside trickling waterways and smell blooms to your heart's content. The large Japanese garden is particularly attractive, and ritualistic tea ceremonies are held periodically in its teahouse.

This is one of America's largest horticultural gardens, covering twenty-three acres and nurturing 15,000 species of growing things. Its botanical centerpiece—certainly appropriate to Denver—is the Rock Alpine Garden, crowned with 500 tons of rock and featuring thousands of varieties of high altitude plants from thirty countries.

The Botanic Garden's personnel are considerably more active than the plants they nurture. They sponsor periodic lectures, classes, spring and fall plant sales and even summer evening jazz concerts.

6 *DENVER MUSEUM OF NATURE & SCIENCE* • *In City Park at 2001 Colorado Blvd.; (800) 925-2250 or (303) 370-6357. (www.dmnh.org) Sunday-Wednesday 9 to 5 and Thursday-Saturday 9 to 7 Memorial Day through Labor Day; daily 9 to 5 the rest of the year; $$. Extra charge for IMAX theater, which shows current wide-screen films; combination museum and IMAX tickets available. GETTING THERE: Go east on Colfax Avenue about 2.5 miles from downtown, turn left onto Colorado Boulevard and follow it north about half a mile alongside City Park. Go left into the park on 22nd Avenue, then left again for the museum parking area.*

Known until recently as the Denver Museum of Natural History, this rivals Ocean Journey as the city's finest attraction. The name change is appropriate, since it deals extensively with human science as well as natural history. Our favorite is the Hall of Life, a sophisticated, interactive look at the human condition and what we can do about it. By picking up a "Life Card" you can answer questions about your lifestyle on a computer (honestly, please), then take fitness tests at several stations to see how you shape up—literally.

Another fine exhibit is the Prehistoric Journey. It begins with a brief video about the origins of life, then takes you through Colorado's primordial past when it was a sea and then a swamp. Fine exhibits show the progression of life from single-celled blobs to the tyrant king lizard, *tyrannosaurus rex* and mastodons. All of these creatures had their moments on what is now the great prairie of Colorado and neighboring Kansas. The dinosaur exhibit features several fully constructed skeletons.

The Explore Colorado exhibit features dozens of well-done life-sized dioramas populated by stuffed critters from hereabouts. Then, like Ocean Journey, the museum jumps to the other side of the globe for a detailed look at Botswana. Although most of these exhibits are static, they've been modernized with video touch screens and other interactive devices. Other displays focus of North American Indians and wildlife of Australia and the South Pacific.

7 **DENVER ZOO** • *In City Park, off 23rd Avenue; (303) 376-4800. (www.denverzoo.org) Daily 10 to 6 April-September and 10 to 5 the rest of the year; $$. GETTING THERE: Go east on Colfax Avenue about 2.5 miles from downtown, turn left onto Colorado Boulevard and follow it north half a mile alongside City Park. Turn left into the park on 22nd Avenue and then right to the zoo parking area.* ☺

Constantly improving, the Denver Zoo is taking its place as one of America's better zoological parks. And it's *huge*, so bring your walking shoes or buy an all-day pass to a tram that visits the zoo's key points. The generously landscaped park covers thirty-five acres and houses about 600 species, with a total critter count topping 3,000. This thoroughly modern zoo uses walled enclosures only for climate control of temperature sensitive inmates; most of the animals are in open air enclosures. The current star attractions are several komodo dragons. The dwell in the new Tropical Discovery Center, 22,000 square feet of rainforest under glass. Another impressive complex—probably not favored by creationists—is the seven-acre Primate Panorama, with twenty-nine species of our closest animal kin. It includes exhibits about our linkage to these folks whose knuckles drag the ground. Occupants range from 600-pound gorillas to marmosets weighing just a few ounces.

Since the Rocky Mountain bighorn is the state's official quadruped, the zoo has an elaborate fake mountain complex for these and other high-altitude sheep and goats of the world. About the only old fashioned compound is the Monkey House, built in 1908, probably more interesting to historians than the monkeys still dwelling therein.

8 **SIX FLAGS ELITCH GARDENS** • *2000 Elitch Circle; (303) 595-4FUN. (www.sixflags.com) Daily 10 to 10 June through Labor Day weekend (closes at 8 some days); shorter hours from late April through May and September-October; closed in winter; $$$$$. Admission includes all rides. Pikes Peak climb and carnival games are extra. GETTING THERE: Take Speer Boulevard northwest, cross over a railyard, then turn left onto Elitch Circle, opposite the Pepsi Center. From downtown, take Fifteenth Street through LoDo and turn left onto Little Raven Street.* ☺

This amusement park began in 1890 when John and Mary Elitch created a ballpark and picnic area in their apple orchard on the edge of Denver. It gradually evolved into an amusement park, theater and dance pavilion that drew luminaries such as the Dorsey brothers and Lawrence Welk. Then in 1995, Denver's old fashioned amusement park moved to a space alongside the Platte River, and it became a Six Flags property in 1999. Under the Six Flags Banner, the old fashioned park has taken a decidedly modern turn. Yet it retains its yesterday heritage with a Main Street-style entrance reminiscent of early Denver and old fashioned carnival rides like the Tilt-a-Whirl, carousel, bumper cars and Ferris wheel. However, most of the kids head for wild and wet rides like the Tower of Doom free fall, Twister wooden roller-coaster, Boomerang looping reverse rollercoaster and a ten-acre water park. At Shipwreck Falls, riders and a lot of innocent bystanders are guaranteed to get wet.

The park also features live bands, a Looney Tunes theme musical, songs and dances from Broadway shows and a Batman and Robin action show.

9 SIXTEENTH STREET MALL • *Downtown, between Cleveland and Blake streets. GETTING THERE: The mall begins just northwest of Civic Center Park and the state capitol building. Several all-day parking lots are in this area, mostly along Fifteenth near Cleveland.*

Developed during the Eighties, the nicely landscaped Sixteenth Street Mall is the shopping and dining heart of downtown Denver. Curiously, most guidebooks give it only brief mention, and one even suggests that it's lined mostly with tourist shops. Hardly. It's lined with highrise office buildings and some of Denver's better stores and restaurants. Far more residents than tourists embrace this mile-long walkway. Hundreds of them spill from their offices to catch lunch at a dozen or more outdoor restaurants. Others do the brown bag thing at the mall's many benches and tables, or they buy their nourishment from one of several lunch carts. This is a happening place on warm days, where kids splash through street-level fountains and street musicians entertain passersby.

The area is secure day and night, since it's patrolled by horseback-mounted policemen. (Their mounts apparently are mall-broken, since we rarely saw evidence of their passing.)

Our only complaint about Sixteenth Street is that it isn't quite a pedestrian mall. Cross streets cut through at every block, and shuttle buses run the mall's length. These free buses certainly are convenient for shoppers and the foot-weary. However, they're a disruption for folks who just want to stroll and relax—particularly since they run as frequently as every ninety seconds. One needs to stay alert when crossing from one side of the mall to the other.

10 WINGS OVER THE ROCKIES AIR & SPACE MUSEUM

10 *WINGS OVER THE ROCKIES AIR & SPACE MU-SEUM • Academy Boulevard near Rampart Way.; (303) 360-5360. (www.dimension-al.com/~worm) Monday-Saturday 10 to 5 and Sunday noon to 5 mid-May through mid-September; closes at 4 the rest of the year; $. GETTING THERE: Head east on Colfax Avenue about 2.5 miles, then go south on Monaco two miles and east (left) on Alameda. After half a mile, you'll pass through a traffic signal at Quebec Street; continue east briefly and you'll enter a roundabout. Spin off to the north onto Rampart Way and you'll see the museum's hangar ahead; turn right for the parking area. ☺*

Featuring more air than space, this museum in Hanger One at the former Lowry Air Force Base has about two dozen aircraft on display. They're mostly World War II and post-war fighters and bombers, plus an interesting collection of civilian "kit planes" that are dwarfed by the military hardware. Even though the hangar is huge, the largest exhibit doesn't fit; a B-52 Stratofortress sits out front. Although the museum's collection isn't large, it includes aircraft rarely seen on public display. The star of the show is a big, bold and black 150-foot-long 1960s era B-1 bomber, the third prototype built and the second to fly.

A craft that's never been airborne—except in flights of fancy—is a full-scale mockup Jedi X-Wing fighter from the *Star Wars* series. It's made mostly of Plexiglas and plastic. One of the few space displays is a mock-up core module for a space station, although more exhibits may be added as the museum expands. Another interesting exhibit is a re-creation of the "Eisenhower Room" that once was part of the Lowry Air Force Base Officers' Club. President Eisenhower often used it as a summer White House. Mamie's mother was a Denver resident and the room was furnished with her dining table and dish cabinets.

THE NEXT TEN BEST ATTRACTIONS

Denver has so many lures that they don't all fit in one list. If you have time left after visiting the top ten, check out these attractions.

1 FOUR MILE HISTORIC PARK

1 *FOUR MILE HISTORIC PARK • 715 S. Forest St.; (303) 399-1859. Wednesday-Friday noon to 4 and weekends 10 to 4 April through September, then weekends only noon to 4 the rest of the year; $. GETTING THERE: Go southeast from downtown on Speer Boulevard, which blends into First Avenue after about 2.5 miles. Follow it 1.5 miles east to Colorado Boulevard, go south less than a mile to Leetsdale (Highway 83) and turn left. Go southeast just under a mile to Forest Street, go right (south) a few blocks and then right again onto Exposition. ☺*

Wedged between Cherry Creek and spreading Denver suburbia, this farm once was four miles from the city and thus the name. Four Mile Park's centerpiece is an intriguing eighteenth century home that reflects three early building styles—rough squared log, board and batten and finally sturdy brick. Costumed docents take visitors through the home, starting with the oldest section. It served as a stage stop on the Cherokee Trail that linked early Denver to the rest of the country. Although the exterior is prim board and batten, the inn's interior was been return to its original chink-log look, when it was built in 1859. From there, visitors step through a doorway and into another era—a middle class late eighteenth home that was added by later owners.

The surrounding park covers twelve acres, all that remains of the original 600 acre farm; the rest has been absorbed by the growing city. The park has several outbuildings, conostoga wagons, corrals with assorted farm animals and old farm equipment. Note the beautifully restored stage coach that hauled visitors from the stage stop to downtown Denver. The park's role is to "preserve and interpret the Western rural heritage of Colorado and America." It sponsors frequent living history programs and old fashioned holiday celebrations. It's particularly popular with kids. A gift shop featuring folk crafts and souvenirs occupies one of the board and batten buildings.

2 BUCKHORN EXCHANGE • 1000 Osage St.; (303) 534-9505. Noon to late evening, serving lunch through dinner. GETTING THERE: From downtown, go west on Colfax and then south (left) on Osage just before you reach a viaduct. Follow Osage about half a mile to Tenth.

Although it's a saloon and restaurant, this historic establishment belongs on any list of Denver attractions, since it's also a museum of Western lore. The Buckhorn is the oldest saloon in Colorado, opened in 1893 and holding state liquor license number one. It has survived the degradation of an old industrial area and now finds itself sandwiched between a housing development and a light rail facility. The two-story weathered brick building is easy to spot, standing alone as a holdout from yesterday. A longtime favorite of Denverites, the Buckhorn has become the darling of the tourist set. Folks flock by the hundreds to see its eclectic collection of old posters, antique signs, Western regalia, weapons and more than 500 hunting trophies.

Original owner Shorty Zeitz supposedly was a friend to Buffalo Bill and a hunting guide who hosted such luminaries as Teddy Roosevelt on his shoots. Some of the trophies date from that era. Wild game—not the same ones—is a menu feature. For more on dining at the Buckhorn, see Chapter Three, page 74. Even if you aren't hungry, stop by for a look at its eclectic collection. The upstairs bar, built in Germany in 1857, is a good place to keep out of waitress traffic while admiring the regalia and morosely staring game heads.

3 *BUTTERFLY PAVILION & INSECT CENTER • 6252 W.*
104th Ave., Westminster; (303) 469-5441. (www.butterflies.org/) Daily
9 to 5; MC/VISA; $$. GETTING THERE: The butterflies and bugs are in
Westminster, north of Denver. Take I-25 north about seven miles, then
go northwest on Highway 36, following Boulder signs. After about seven
miles, take the Church Ranch/104th Avenue exit, go right briefly, turn
right again opposite the Westin Hotel, then left into the parking lot. ☺

Your kids may go "ugh!!!" and perhaps you will too, when you see
the live palm-sized tarantulas and giant cockroaches. And that makes
this unusual museum all the more fun. It's devoted to the invertebrates
among us. You'll learn about sexual dimorphism (in which some in-
sects make arbitrary choices about their gender) and you can watch
busy bees in a cut-away hive. You can get up close and impersonal
with deadly black widows, scorpions (safely behind glass) and big ugly
black rhino beetles. These are part of the "Crawl-a-see-em" portion of
the museum.

Considerably more charming—if less titillating—is the butterfly
section, an appealing glass-roofed conservatory housing multi-colored
butterflies from around the world. Bring your binoculars for closer
looks at these winged creatures, although most of them don't hold still
for very long. You'll see more than butterflies in here; the conservatory
is lush with tropical flora. If you have the patience, you can sit and
watch pupae hatch into butterflies and moths. "Butterfly releases" are
scheduled daily at 12:30 and 3:30 to introduce new members to the
conservatory.

Outside, you can stroll through the Butterfly Garden, where local
butterflies are drawn to their favorite blooms. The garden path merges
into a half-mile nature trail that wanders through the riparian foliage
of Big Dry Creek, which is quite wet most of the year. This pleasing fa-
cility also has an invertebrate-oriented gift shop, several aquarium
tanks, a snack bar and picnic tables.

4 *BYERS-EVANS HOUSE • 1310 Bannock St; (303) 620-*
4933. (www.coloradohistory.org) Tours 11 to 3 daily except Monday; $.
GETTING THERE: The house sits at the corner of Bannock and Thir-
teenth Avenue on the southern edge of downtown.

This house—now surrounded by growing downtown Denver—has
a interesting history, since it was owned by two of the city's most influ-
ential families. It was built in 1883 for *Rocky Mountain News* founder
William Byers, then sold in 1889 to William Gray Evans, the son of
Colorado's first territorial governor. The house remained in the Evans
family until 1981, when it was donated to the Colorado Historical So-
ciety, and nearly everything inside is original. It has been restored to
the 1912-1924 period, when the Evans family acquired most of its cur-

rent furnishings. They're an eclectic mix of things gathered by family members as they traveled about the globe. The home has that dark and gloomy look typical of this era. Only a couple of the upstairs rooms and a sun porch exhibit much cheer.

Visits are by guided tour only, and while the docents certainly know their stuff, the tour is too protracted for anyone not fascinated by old houses or Denver history. Perhaps more interesting is a nicely done twenty-minute video chronicling the history of Denver as it was shaped by the Byers and Evans families.

5 BLACK AMERICAN WEST MUSEUM AND HERITAGE CENTER • *3901 California St.; (303) 292-2566. (www.coax.net/people/lw/bawmus.html) Daily 10 to 5 May through September; Wednesday-Friday 10 to 2 and Saturday-Sunday noon to 5 the rest of the year; $. GETTING THERE: From downtown, follow one-way Stout Street about a mile northeast, turn right onto 31st and then right again onto California. The museum is at the corner, in a three-story brick house.*

You never saw this in Hollywood horse operas, but about a third of the cowboys on the Western frontier were Black and another third were Mexicans. White cowpunchers were in the minority. This small museum tells the story of the westward migration by Blacks, particularly after the Civil War. Because of racist Jim Crow laws in the South, tens of thousands of freed slaves joined the westward movement. They formed their own wagon trains, established frontier towns, mined for gold and silver, and many of them became cowpunchers. The museum was established in 1971 by Paul W. Stewart, who has spent much of his life collecting artifacts and seeking information about Blacks during this era. Appropriately, it's housed in the former home of Dr. Justina L. Ford, Denver's first Black doctor and one its first woman physicians. Artifacts, historic photos and other exhibits focus on Black explorers, cowboys and miners, the Black Cavalrymen that the native people called "Buffalo Soldiers" and more contemporary people such as the all-Black fighter pilot squadrons of World War II and current Colorado business and professional leaders.

6 CHILDREN'S MUSEUM OF DENVER • *2121 Children's Museum Dr.; (303) 433-7444. (www.cmdenver.org) Tuesday-Friday 9 to 4 and Saturday-Sunday 10 to 5; closed Monday except on school holidays; $$ plus a parking fee; additional charges for snowboarding and rollerblading. GETTING THERE: From I-25, take exit 211 (23rd Avenue) and go northeast on Water Street. Turn right onto Seventh Street just short of Ocean Journey, then right again onto Children's Museum Drive. If you're downtown, follow Fifteenth Street about a mile northwest and cross the South Platte River at Confluence Park. Turn left on Platte, pass the large REI store, cross under the Speer Street Bridge and blend onto Water Street; go past the aquarium and turn left onto Seventh Street.* ☺

Curiously, it costs as much to use the parking lot as it does to visit this museum. But never mind that; this is an exceedingly nice and cleverly done archive for visitors with kids in tow. Housed in a bright green building topped by a purple pyramid, the Children's Museum of Denver is busy with interactive exhibits and activities designed to stimulate kids' celebration of life. For a reality check, they can shop at a mock-up grocery store, or they can revert to the fantasy of the Three Bears' House. Kids can learn inline skating, or even schuss down a year-around bunny hill on snowboards. An outdoor playground and picnic area are adjacent.

7 DENVER FIREFIGHTERS MUSEUM • *1326 Tremont Place; (303) 892-1436. (www.firedenver.org) Monday-Saturday 10 to 2; $. GETTING THERE: The museum is just south of downtown between Thirteenth and Fourteenth streets.* ☺

Housed in a former firehouse built in 1909, this small museum recalls Denver's flame-battling history, starting with the formation of its first volunteer fire department in the 1860s. Kids—and adults for that matter— can climb into the driver's seat of a 1928 American La France. The rest of the old equipment is to be admired only. The collection includes early hand-drawn hose carts and pumpers, an 1880s steam-powered pumper and lots of old firefighting apparatus. A time line chronicles Denver's worst fires, from the great conflagration of 1865 to the 1970s.

8 DENVER MUSEUM OF MINIATURES, DOLLS & TOYS • *1880 Gaylord St.; (303) 322-1053. Tuesday-Saturday 10 to 4 and Sunday 1 to 4; $. GETTING THERE: The museum is at Gaylord between Eighteenth and 20th avenues, near City Park. Take Colfax Avenue east from downtown and go north (left) on Gaylord about four blocks.*

Located in the historic Pearce-McAllister Cottage, this small museum is busy with antique dolls, doll houses, toys, and remarkably detailed miniatures. It's also a workshop, offering classes for adults and youngsters in making dolls, toys and miniaturized arts and crafts. The building itself is worth a look—a two-story Dutch Colonial revival structure dating from 1899, with handsome period décor within.

9 LAKESIDE AMUSEMENT PARK • *I-70 at Sheridan Blvd.; (303) 477-1621. Daily 10 to 11 June through Labor Day weekend; weekends only in May. Gate admission $; unlimited ride ticket $$$$. GETTING THERE: From the I-70/I-25 interchange, travel west on I-70 about 3.5 miles and take Sheridan Boulevard exit 271-A.* ☺

If you'd like to reminisce about old fashioned amusement parks, or if you're on a budget and have small kids in tow, stop by friendly old

Lakeside Amusement Park. Considerably cheaper—although more modest and less flashy—than Six Flags Elitch Gardens, if offers the kinds of rides you remember as a kid. Climb aboard—or toss your kids aboard—the Tilt-a-Whirl, Octopus (called the Spider at Lakeside), flying swings, the Ferris wheel and merry-go-round. Lakeside also has a couple of rollercoasters, a lakefront kiddie train ride and a special section of low G-force toddler rides.

Gate admission, which includes parking, costs only small change and you can buy individual ride tickets or all-day passes. Rides prices begin at less than $1 and don't rise much beyond that. The place is a bit worn at the edges but well-kept. A large park and picnic area provides a pleasant tree-shaded centerpiece. The management doesn't permit booze or loud radios, so it's a nice family-outing place.

10 MOLLY BROWN HOUSE MUSEUM • 1340 Pennsylvania St.; (303) 832-4092. (www.mollybrown.org) Monday-Saturday 10 to 4 and Sunday noon to 4 from June through August; closed Mondays the rest of the year; $. GETTING THERE: The home is between Thirteenth and Fourteenth avenues, just southeast of downtown. Tour tickets are sold in a gift shop behind the main house.

Visitors will discover much about the real Margaret Tobin Brown (see box) in this rough-cut stone home. Well informed docents spin true tales of Denver's most famous woman while guiding people through her former residence. It isn't a mansion, but a three-story house with rather small, cluttered although immaculately restored rooms. It's overly decorated in the fashion of the 1890s, with an eclectic mix of colors, patterns and styles. The house was very modern for its time—one of the first in Denver to have electricity, a bathroom and telephone.

Although the furnishings are appropriate to the period, only a few are original. Margaret Brown (don't call her Molly) was a world traveler and art collector, although her possessions were auctioned off when she died in 1932. Also, she didn't spend a lot of time here in her later years, but lived most of her later life in the East, when she wasn't traveling abroad. (See page 36.)

THE TEN BEST OVERLOOKED ATTRACTIONS

These attractions often are missed by visitors for various reasons. Some are a few miles off the beaten tourist path, yet worth a short drive of discovery. Others are small museums or attractions that may be omitted from other guidebooks. And some, such as the Auraria Campus, aren't regarded as tourist attractions, yet they offer considerable appeal.

1 MUSEUM OF OUTDOOR ARTS • *7600 E. Orchard Rd., Room 160-N, Englewood (Greenwood Village); (303) 741-3609. (www.fine-art.com/museum/moa.html) Outdoor art may be viewed any time; office open weekdays 8:30 to 6; free. GETTING THERE: Go twelve miles south on I-25 and take East Orchard Road (exit 198) west. After less than a mile, pass through a traffic light at Greenwood Plaza Boulevard and take the next left into Harlequin Plaza. Park in the north lot and you'll find the museum office in a modern glass office building. Go through the front entrance, walk to the rear (around central elevator shafts) and go downstairs; the office is to the right.*

This unusual "museum" consists of more than fifty sculptures—mostly bronzes—placed about the extensive Greenwood Plaza business park south of Denver. You can pick up a map of the complex and the art sites in the museum office in Harlequin Plaza, one of several office parks on either side of Orchard Road. If the office is closed, you can find art works around Harlequin Plaza, in Carrara Place to the south, Samson Park to the southeast, and The Triad, north of Harlequin Plaza across East Orchard Road. Our favorite is the "Alice in Wonderland" series in Samson Park, between Greenwood Plaza Boulevard and Fiddler's Green Circle. These wonderful sculptures of the Mad Tea Party, the Magic Mushroom, the Cheshire Cat, the Mad Queen and Tweedle Dum and Tweedle Dee are based on the original sketches in Lewis Carroll's book.

2 AURARIA CAMPUS • *Just west of downtown, alongside Speer Boulevard. GETTING THERE: Most roads into the campus have been converted into pedestrian paths, and parking is limited, particularly during the school year. We suggest parking nearby and walking into the campus.*

It's hard to miss that great swatch of green lawns and brick buildings lawns just west of downtown alongside Cherry Creek, but what is it? It resembles a college campus and in fact it's home to three higher learning institutes—Community College of Denver, Metropolitan State College of Denver and the University of Colorado at Denver. It also has historical significance, for this was the site of Auraria, the first mining camp established alongside Cherry Creek in 1858. The odd name—based on *aura*Latin for "gold"—comes from an earlier mining town in Georgia, from whence those prospectors came. Two years later, Auraria, Highland and Denver City merged into the City of Denver.

Auraria offers much of interest for visitors, since it's fashioned as a large park, with patios, fountains and great patches of lawn between the many campus buildings. The complex also contains a pair of historic churches and a student union, where you can pause for refresh-

MOLLY BROWN: THE UNSINKABLE MYTH

Margaret Tobin Brown was one of the most misrepresented, fictionalized women in American history. While this five-foot-eight redhead was flamboyant, she was not the country bumpkin portrayed in the The Unsinkable Molly Brown. Nor was she the slang-slinging matron depicted in the film *Titanic*. She and her husband James Joseph Brown weren't social outsiders, as the Broadway musical indicated. According to a local newspaper, "they were not ostracized by Denver society—they *were* Denver society."

Molly wasn't even her nickname, according to Kristen Iversen, author of *Molly Brown: Unraveling the Myth.* She was known as Margaret and sometimes Maggie, but mostly—in accordance with custom of the day—Mrs. J.J. Brown. "Molly" was the creation of writer Richard Morris, who collaberated with Meredith Willson in the Broadway musical that became a movie. He simply decided that the name Molly fit the lyrics better. And J.J. wasn't called "Leadville Johnny." That was the nickname of John F. Campion, a partner in the mining firm that Brown managed. Nor did Brown discover the Little Jonny mine that helped make him rich; he didn't even own it.

So what's the real story of Colorado's most famous and most fictionalized couple? They were both children of poor Irish immigrant families, and both wound up in Leadville during its silver mining boom. J.J. was born in Pennsylvania and headed west in the 1870s to seek his fortune. Margaret was born in Mark Twain's hometown of Hannibal, Missouri. She accompanied her sister to Leadville 1886, although she never worked in a saloon, as the *Unsinkable* plot portrays. She met James Brown at a Catholic church picnic and they were married within a few months.

Hard work, not luck

Hard working J.J. eventually became superintendent of Leadville's Ibex Mining Company. His wealth came gradually, although it was accelerated by a government decision which—ironically—nearly ruined the town. In 1890, Congress voted to stop supporting the price of silver and its value plummeted. To avoid bankruptcy, Ibex officials decided to sink a deeper shaft in its Little Jonny silver mine, hoping to find gold. A slippery overburden of dolomite sand made digging difficult, so J.J. devised an ingenious combination of timbers and hay bales to shore up the shaft. They struck gold and Brown was rewarded with 12,500 shares of company stock.

In 1894, the family moved to Denver and bought what is now the Molly Brown House Museum. Margaret became active in local charities and was a strong crusader for women's rights, a cause with which her husband did not agree. She also championed the rights of children, and worked with local judge Ben Lindsey to create America's first juvenile court system. The Browns traveled abroad extensively, although Molly enjoyed it much more than J.J.

The truth is more interesting than the fiction

Eventually, for reasons ranging from his infidelity to their personal and political differences, they were separated, although their strong Catholicism prevented them from getting a divorce.

During an overseas trip in 1914, she received word by wire that her grandson was ill, so she cut her trip short to be with him. As luck would have it, she booked the maiden voyage of the *Titanic* for her return home and the legend began.

When the ship began sinking after hitting an iceberg, she became so preoccupied with assisting women and children that crew members had to literally throw her into a lifeboat. However, she did not force other lifeboat passengers to row at gun point and she certainly didn't lead them in song. One of the *Titanic's* crewmen was in charge of the lifeboat. Margaret simply grabbed an oar along with the others. They rowed mostly to keep warm in the freezing cold of the North Atlantic. When they were rescued and taken to New York, she helped look after the other survivors for several days before returning to Denver. She later returned to present medals to the crew of the ship *Carpathia* that had rescued them.

Honored as a heroine and not shy about publicity, she became a national figure and remained in the limelight for much of the rest of her life. She campaigned for safety at sea laws and even ran unsuccessfully for the U.S. Senate.

J.J. died of a heart attack in 1922 in a New York hospital at age sixty-eight. Margaret and her children Helen and Lawrence became locked in a bitter legal battle over his extensive holdings. Although she was embittered and her fortune was diminished, she soon bounced back, resuming her travels and her upbeat lifestyle. By coincidence, she also died in New York, in 1932 at age sixty-five, of complications from a brain tumor.

ments. One section of the campus, called Ninth Street Park, is lined with some of Denver's oldest surviving houses, how used as offices and activity centers. For a detailed walking tour of Auraria Campus, see Chapter Ten, page 152.

3 *CAPITOL DOME MUSEUM* • *Colorado State Capitol, 200 E. Colfax Ave.; (303) 866-2604. (www.state.co.us) Dome and museum open weekdays 7 to 3:30; closed weekends. GETTING THERE: The capitol is just southeast of downtown, between Lincoln and Grant streets. The dome and its museum are accessible from the third floor.* ☺

Many people puffing up the ninety-three steps to the dome of the Colorado statehouse tend to plod right past this small, very appealing museum. Set among steel girders and masonry trusses, it has an interesting assortment of old photos, architectural drawings and other exhibits relating to this noble building's construction. The Colorado Assembly passed legislation in 1883 to build a capitol, with two stipulations: That it face west toward the mountains and that it cost not more than $1 million. Although they got their directional wish, by the time this elaborate structure was finished in 1904, the price tag had risen to nearly $4 million. The dome initially was covered with copper, but it soon turned green and officials decided to cover it with gold plate in gleaming salute to the area's mining history. Because of weathering, it has been regilded three times.

4 CASA BONITA • 6715 W. Colfax Ave.; (303) 232-5115.

Mexican restaurant serving lunch and dinner daily; wine, beer and margaritas. Major credit cards; $ to $$. GETTING THERE: Take Colfax west from downtown four miles and turn right on Newland into JRS shopping center just beyond Sheridan Boulevard. ☺

Is it an attraction, a restaurant or both or neither? And should it be included in this list, or remain overlooked? Casa Bonita is the mother of all tourist gimmicks—an excessively decorated Mexican restaurant featuring cliff divers, old West shootouts, strolling mariachis, magicians and puppet shows. The dining area is terraced steeply above a landscaped pool into which a thirty-foot waterfall and occasional cliff divers splash. Or you may see the sheriff shoot it out with Black Bart, or a "hilarious puppet show" or dancing monkeys in costume. To enter this "Beautiful House," you much purchase a meal by getting into a queue line and placing your order. Within a minute or so, the food pops out from a little hole in the wall—presumably prepared in a kitchen and not a surplus inflight meal from Aero Mexico. You then carry your booty to a maitre 'd station, where you're assigned to a table. We found the food to be plentiful, cheap and inferior. My nacho salad consisted of cold, wilted lettuce over a soggy, lukewarm heap of hamburger meat and shredded cheese, into which shards of tortilla chips had been jabbed. The lettuce was too warm, the beef was too cold and the tortilla chips were too soggy.

Kids may like the place because they're usually easy to please, as long as the food comes with entertainment and free drink refills. The menu lists three very inexpensive "little amigo" meals, such as the Piñata Plate which—like a real piñata—probably should be beaten with a stick.

5 DENVER PUBLIC LIBRARY • 10 W. Fourteenth Avenue

Parkway; (303) 640-6200. (www.denver.lib.co.us/) Open Monday-Wednesday 10 to 9, Thursday-Saturday 10 to 5:30 and Sunday 1 to 5. GETTING THERE: The library is just south of the Civic Center between Bannock and Broadway.

Libraries aren't normally regarded as tourist attractions, although this one is a notable exception. It's one of the nation's largest and most dramatically styled library buildings. More than 2,000 visitors a day come to marvel at the 540,000 square foot interior, and to access its font of information from forty-seven miles of bookshelves and 200 computer and internet terminals. It's built in an atrium style, with two of its seven floors balconied over the spacious ground floor area. The library even has a retail store, which sells used and new books, note cards and other paper goods.

The library's most impressive feature is the Western History and Genealogy Department, occupying most of the fifth floor. It's the world's largest study center devoted to the American West. Further, it's a virtual museum, with paintings and bronzes by Frederic Remington, William Russell and other early Western artists. It also displays memorabilia from Buffalo Bill's Wild West Show and historic photos chronicling the great westward movement. An architectural focal point is a monumental hexagonal oak structure called "Spirit of the West," which dominates the Western History Reading Room. When we asked what it represented, a smiling librarian said: "A tipi, or maybe an oil derrick. Whatever you'd like it to be."

6 *FORNEY TRANSPORTATION MUSEUM* • *4303 Brighton Blvd.; (303) 297-1113. (www.forneymuseum.com) Monday-Saturday 9 to 5, closed Sunday; $. GETTING THERE: The museum is about 2.5 miles from downtown, near the Denver Coliseum. Go northeast on Market, fork to the left onto Brighton and go about two miles.* ☺

The Forney Transportation Museum isn't exactly an overlooked attraction; it a displaced one. The museum, featuring a collection of one-of-a-kind vehicles, occupied the old Denver Tramway Power Company building from 1968 until 1999, when the structure was purchased by REI; see below. It has moved to a site near the Denver Coliseum, although it hadn't reopened when this book went to press. The phone number and web site are still active, so you can check on its progress. Among its exhibits are a Kissel car owned by Amelia Earhart, a huge steam locomotive, an early-day McCormick reaper and Prince Aly Khan's Rolls-Royce.

7 *HUDSON GARDENS* • *6115 S. Santa Fe Dr., Littleton; (303) 797-8565. (www.hudsongarden.org) Daily 9 to 5 May-September and 10 to 2 October-April; $. A small shop sells garden-oriented gifts and books on gardening. GETTING THERE: Head south on I-25, take the Santa Fe Drive exit and continue south for about eight miles to Littleton. The gardens are on the right, about half a mile south of the major intersection of Littleton/Bowles in downtown Littleton.*

Overlooked by many visitors yet certainly worth the short drive from Denver, this quiet retreat near the South Platte River is a complex of sixteen gardens that rim green parklands and lakes. Most are rather informal, planted with flowers, shrubs and trees of Colorado. Plantings are so varied that there's almost always something in bloom. Paths meander from one garden to the next; benches and picnic tables invite strollers to linger. Particularly appealing are the Wildflower Meadow, busy with blooms in spring and early summer; the Water Garden with a lily pad pond; the Rose Garden built around a reflection pool and fountain; and the sweetly-scented Fragrance Garden. Our favorite is the Railroad Garden, a landscaped mound where toy trains chug through tunnels and across trestles. Hudson Gardens is a good bird watching place, since its wetlands and pools attract migrating and resident shorebirds. Several Canadian Honkers apparently have taken out American citizenship for they've become permanent residents.

If you walk northwest toward the river, you'll encounter a great place to relax—a snack bar called Mr. D's Oasis on the Platte, which serves light foods and fruit smoothies. You can carry your snack to a patio table near the river and watch cyclists and skaters glide by on the adjacent Mary Carter Trail. Mr. D's best creation, incidentally, is a thick, lush Mocha Shivver.

8 *MIZEL MUSEUM OF JUDAICA* ● *560 S. Monaco Parkway; (303) 333-4156. (www.mizelmuseum.org) Weekdays 11 to 4, Saturday 11 to 1:30 and Sunday noon to 4; free. GETTING THERE: Take Colfax Avenue 4.5 east miles to Monaco Parkway, then go right (south) 2.5 miles to the Jewish center. It's on the left, opposite Washington High School. Drive just past the center, turn left onto Center Street and go to the rear of the complex, where you'll find parking and the entrance to the museum.*

Part of a large Jewish community center and school complex, the Mizel Museum's mission is to create "Bridges of Understanding" through exhibits, tours and outreach programs. It's the only Jewish heritage museum in the Intermountain region. The main exhibit hall features changing shows that range from Jewish artifacts to contemporary art exhibits. The main corridor to the right of the gallery is lined with display cases with exhibits concerning the history and culture of Judaism, including some striking antique silver *Hanukkah* lamps, plus shields, crowns and finials used to enhance and protect the Torah, the sacred books of Moses. As part of its "Bridges of Understanding" theme, the corridor contains displays of religious and folk art of native Americans, Muslims, the Asian-Pacific, African Americans and Hispanic-Latin. The museum's most moving artifact is an old Torah in a display case just to the left of the main gallery entrance. It was discovered in a Polish warehouse, where it had lain neglected for forty years after the Holocaust.

9 *MUSEO DE LAS AMÉRICAS* • *861 Santa Fe Dr.; (303) 571-4401. (www.museo.org) Tuesday-Saturday 10 to 5; $$. GETTING THERE: The museum is southwest of downtown between Eighth and Ninth avenues. Since Santa Fe is one way northbound, go southeast on Champa, then south on Klamath as you cross Colfax Avenue. After several blocks, go left on Seventh to Santa Fe and then left again (north) to the museum.*

Most visitors miss this little museum unless they're looking for Mexican food along Santa Fe Drive, which is the heart of Denver's Hispanic community. As its name implies, the "Museum of the Americas" is multi-cultural, like the city's *Latino* population. It covers not only the Mexican culture, but that of Central and South America. This fine storefront museum is only one of its kind in the Rocky Mountain region. Its permanent collection consists mostly of excellent examples of centuries-old paintings, crucifixes, reliquaries, polychrome sculptures and other religious objects of Mexico and South America. The collection also features contemporary works by Mexican-American artists, including a mural of the ancient Aztec "lake city" of Tenochtitlan and a beautifully detailed replica of the 1479 Aztec Sun Stone, made of eighty-four different kinds of wood. The museum mounts a variety of special exhibits, ranging from pottery and textiles to contemporary art.

10 *REI DENVER FLAGSHIP STORE* • *1416 Platte St.; (303) 756-0272. GETTING THERE: Take Fifteenth Street about a mile northwest from downtown and cross the South Platte River at Confluence Park. Turn left on Platte Street and you're at the store.*

When is a store a tourist attraction? When it's one of the largest outdoor stores in America, and it's located in a grand brick building at the confluence of the South Platte River and Cherry Creek, with a "coffee deck" offering great views of downtown Denver. Opened in 2000, this is the second largest store of the REI chain, after the Seattle flagship. It's housed in the brick 1901 Denver Tramway Power Company building. A Starbuck's Coffee outlet has a sunny deck, where one can watch folks play in the river and enjoy a fine view of Denver's highrises. We like to relax over a caffé latte here before starting a stroll along the river or the creek. Inside this great brick building, outdoor fanatics will find their mecca; see Chapter Nine, page 144.

THE TEN BEST THINGS TO DO

We've certainly established that Denver is an active city, with 200 public parks and miles of walking and biking trails. It also offers several interesting tours and other activities. Here are our ten favorite mile high things to do.

1 CATCH A ROCKIES GAME OR TOUR THE BALLYARD

• *Coors Field, 2001 Blake St.; (303) ROCKIES. (www.colorado-rockies.com) Public tours available when the Rockies aren't playing, at 10, 10:30, 12, 12:30, 1, 2, 2:30 and 3; $$. Advance reservations aren't needed for tours but call to confirm their availability. For game and tour tickets, call the number above or stop by the ticket windows near Gate C at the foot of 21st Street. There's a special window for tours on the right. You also can get game tickets from most local ticket vendors; check the Yellow Pages under "Ticket sales—entertainment & sports." GETTING THERE: Coors Field is at Nineteenth and Blake, an easy walk from downtown or LoDo. If you're driving, go northwest on 20th or 21st streets or northeast on Wazee Street and you'll see several parking lots around the stadium.* ☺

If it weren't for the tall light standards sticking above its brick façade, Coors Field could be mistaken for one of LoDo's old buildings. That, of course, was the idea. The completion of the 50,381-seat ballpark in 1995 helped accelerate LoDo's redevelopment. Tours lasting more than an hour take visitors throughout the facility, with stops at the concession area, luxury boxes, press boxes (the best seats in the house), dugout and finally onto the field, which is twenty-one feet below street level. The field faces northwest, offering Rocky fans a view of the Rockies, particularly from the right field seats. And if you want to sit exactly a mile high in salute to Denver's overdone elevation gimmick, ask for a seat in the purple row; it rims the entire stadium.

You learn as you tour that $215 million can buy a lot of ballyard. Coors Field amenities include a full service restaurant, baseball's only brewpub (Chapter Seven, page 122), climate-controlled indoor batting and pitching cages, and an international food court. A landscaped fountain in center field shoots water forty feet high whenever a Rocky hits a homer. If you're among the economically privileged, you can rent a twelve-seat luxury box for a mere $81,000 to $120,000 per season, which comes to $1,000 or more a game. (Of course you get twelve seats for that, plus your own TV, wet bar and other amenities.) At tour's end, visitors conveniently exit through the club's large logo and souvenir shop. One of the nicest things about this tour is that its net proceeds go to youth charities.

2 SEE HOW THEY MAKE A MINT

• *Denver Mint tour, West Colfax at Cherokee St.; (303) 405-4761. (www.usmint.treas.gov) Weekdays 8 to 2:45; half-hour tours depart every twenty minutes; free. GETTING THERE: The Denver Mint is just south of downtown and west of Civic Center Park, and the visitor entrance is on Cherokee Street. No cameras are allowed inside. The tour is particularly popular in summer; to avoid long waiting lines, go early in the morning.*

This tour is probably more interesting for what you learn than for what you see. What you see—from an observation gallery—is ranks of high-speed presses stamping out small change, everything from pennies to the new gold-colored dollars. The presses themselves are inside blue metal housings to muffle the noise of the stamping, so you see only glittering coins spilling out into collection buckets. The tour begins in a small numismatic museum, where you can view exhibits on the history of money while waiting for your guide to show up. It's an interesting exhibit if you're into numismatics, with displays on ancient coinage, penny piggie banks, coin purses and items that—through history—have been used as currency, including Club Med pop-beads.

What you don't see is an estimated $100 billion in gold bullion stored in the basement; this is America's second largest repository after For Knox. Originally, the tours included a peek at six gold bars, but the display had been eliminated when we last passed through.

What you learn is that the Denver Mint produces about half the coins in the country. The other half comes from the Philadelphia Mint, while the San Francisco Mint produces only collector coins and medallions. The Denver Mint runs twenty-four hours a day, and sometimes seven days a week, producing an average of fifty-two million coins a day. Why so many? Because there's an average of $50 in loose change in every American household. Some coins are deliberately collected while others are just casually accumulated or perhaps lurking beneath the cushions of couches. "We need to make about three new coins a day for every man, woman and child in the country," our guide pointed out.

The tour concludes at an exhibit concerning the "State Quarters" program honoring all fifty states with commemorative coins. Started in 1999, the program will continue at the rate of five new coins a year until 2008, with states being honored in the order they were admitted to the Union. Delaware was first and Coloradans will have to wait until 2006 to see their commemorative coins. From the State Quarters exhibit, visitors are steered to a gift shop that sells mint coin sets, collector albums and coinage souvenirs.

3 SADDLE UP WITH BLAZING SADDLES ● *Blazing Saddles, 1432 Market Street; (303) 534-5255. (www.blazingsaddles.com) GETTING THERE: The place to get saddled with a bike is between Fifteenth and Sixteenth streets in the LoDo area.* ☺

The creators of Blazing Saddles have more or less reinvented the concept of rental bikes. They not only offer the latest model street and mountain bikes, they provide detailed directions for five suggested cycling routes. Four of them start near the shop and a fifth is a challenging mountain bike run in the nearby Rockies. The Denver runs follow the city's most popular bike paths, including Clear Creek and the South Platte River. The detailed cycling directions slip into a little see-through packet on the handlebars, so they're easy to follow. Each bike also has a computer to calculate mileage, speed and total distance. Thus, you'll know if you're getting a good workout.

4 **GET CULTURALLY CONNECTED BY TROLLEY** • *The Cultural Connection Trolley runs daily from mid-May through Labor Day Weekend. Call (800) 366-RIDE or (303) 299-6000 for transit information. (www.rtd-denver.com)*

A special trolley operated by the Regional Transportation District links many of Denver's major museums and other attractions, and you can buy an all-day ride pass for a modest fee. It's available from transit drivers or at transit centers. The pass allows you to hop on an off the trolleys as often as you choose.

The Cultural Connection Trolley has two different loop routes. The Green Route runs from 9:30 to 5:30, starting at the Colorado Convention Center at Fourteenth and California downtown. It criss-crosses the Sixteenth Street Mall, then stops at the State Capitol, the Denver Museum of Nature and Science near the Denver Zoo, Denver Botanic Garden and Molly Brown House. The Red Route also starts at the convention center and runs from 10 to 6. Its stops include the Denver Art Museum, Denver Public Library, Cherry Creek Shopping Center and Colorado History Museum. The various stops are marked by special red or green Cultural Connection Trolley signs.

5 **GET GROCERIES FROM GROWERS** • *Cherry Creek Farmers Market, Saturdays 7:30 to 12:30, May through October; and Wednesdays 8 to 1, June through September. The market is held on the Cherry Creek Shopping Center's west side parking lot at First Avenue and University; (303) 394-2903. GETTING THERE: Follow Speer Boulevard southeast about three miles along Cherry Creek. Turn right onto University and then left into the Cherry Creek west parking lot.*

A group called Colorado Fresh Markets sponsors several farmers markets in Denver from spring into fall. The most popular is held twice at Cherry Creek. You can get produce, fruits, specialty foods and other edibles directly from the growers, plus potted plants and a few arts and crafts. Most of the markets also have food courts where you can sample and buy a variety of breads, croissants, quiches, cookies, sausages and even popcorn.

Sunday is farmers' market day in the City Park Esplanade by East Denver High School, 9 to 1, June through September. To reach it, go east from downtown on Colfax Avenue for nearly two miles, then turn left (north) into the Esplanade below the park.

A Thursday market is held at Southwest Plaza Mall in Littleton south of Denver. It's at Bowles Avenue and Wadsworth Boulevard, June through September from 9 to 1. To get there, follow I-25 about three miles south from central Denver, take exit 207-B and continue south on Santa Fe Avenue (Highway 85) for about 6.5 miles to Bowles Avenue in Littleton. Go west three and a half miles to Southwest Plaza at Wadsworth.

6 **BROWSE FOR BARGAINS** ● *Mile High Flea Market; I-76 and 88th Ave.; (800) 861-9900 or (303) 289-4656. Saturday, Sunday and Wednesday 7 to 5. GETTING THERE: Go five miles north of Denver on I-25, then five miles northeast on I-76 and take the 88th Avenue exit briefly east. The market is on your left.*

If you're a bargain hunter, you'll want to check out America's third largest flea market, held three days a week ten minutes northeast of Denver. More than 700 booths are set up each day, with more than 2,000 vendors taking turns spreading out their booty. The site covers about eighty acres and it is said that if you walk past each booth, you'll cover more than three miles. That should work up an appetite and—fortunately—the market also has dozens of food vendors. They sell everything from roast chicken legs and Hawaiian shaved ice to roast corn on the cob and hot dogs.

7 **HANG OUT AT CONFLUENCE PARK** ● *At the confluence of the South Platte River and Cherry Creek just northwest of the city center. GETTING THERE: Take Fifteenth Avenue from downtown, cross the Platte and find a place to park along Platte Street. ☺*

Confluence Park is our favorite place to sit and do nothing. It has elements on both sides of the Platte, where it's joined by Cherry Creek. The city side of the park has grassy slopes and concrete risers that terrace down to the edge of the Platte. Across the river, reached by pedestrian/bike bridges, are more terraces, including Shoemaker Park, which extends right into the stream. The park also marks the convergence of the Platte River Walkway and Cherry Creek Trail, the city's two most popular walking and cycling paths. It is thus a nice place to sit and watch the cyclists and walkers, or become one. A fifteen-minute walk up the Cherry Creek Trail will deliver you to the LoDo historic district and Sixteenth Street Mall. Or cross to the west bank and stroll to the huge REI store, Ocean Journeys aquarium and the Children's Museum of Denver. Meanwhile, back at Confluence Park, you may see kayakers playing in the brief cataracts created by a diversion dam, or kids and their dogs splashing in the streams.

8 **TAKE A RIVERSIDE TROLLEY RIDE** ● *Platte Valley Trolley, 2785 N. Speer Blvd., (303) 458-6255. Daily 11 to 4 in summer, with half-hour and one-hour narrated tours along the South Platte River. Departures every half hour; reduced schedule in the off-season; call* for specific times. GETTING THERE: The trolley departs from a stop near REI on the Platte River walkway. Take Fifteenth Street northwest from downtown and cross the South Platte River. Or go north on I-25, take exit 23 and follow signs to Ocean Journey on Water Street, then continue around to your left onto Platte Street; there's two-hour meter parking on Platte and nearby streets. ☺

This jolly little trolley runs along the North Platte River, several miles upstream past Ocean Journey and the Children's Museum. Riders in the open air trams enjoy nice views across the Platte to the Denver skyline and Six Flags Elitch Gardens, while the conductor entertains them with bits of history and early Denver anecdotes. Hour-long trips follow former interurban trolley tracks to Lakewood Gulch.

9 LEAVE THE DRIVING TO THEM • *Colorado Sightseer, 6780 W. 84th Circle, Suite 60, Arvada, CO 80003; (800) 255-5105 or (303) 423-8200. (www.coloradosightseer.com) Major credit cards; $$$$$. GETTING THERE: You don't have to; the firm makes pickups at major hotels.*

If you don't want to drive or fuss with your own itinerary, Colorado Sightseer has a variety of tours in Denver and beyond. Among its offerings are half-day tours of historic Denver with stops at the capitol, Molly Brown House and other sites; and Western Foothills tours to Coors Brewery, Buffalo Bill Museum and Red Rocks Park. Full-day tours head south for the U.S. Air Force Academy, Colorado Springs, Garden of the Gods and the Pikes Peak Cog Railway; west to the Mount Evans Wilderness, the old mining town of Idaho Springs and the Phoenix Gold Mine; and north to Rocky Mountain National Park. Tours include all entrance fees and snacks.

10 TAKE A MILE HIGH HIKE • *"The Mile High Trail" booklet is available at visitor centers for a modest fee. For details, call the Denver Metro Convention & Visitors Bureau at (303) 892-1505.*

This isn't really a trail. It's a compilation of interesting walking routes through the heart of Denver. A booklet called *The Mile High Trail* outlines six easy loop walks that will help you become acquainted with the city. The "Sixteenth Street Mall Tour" takes you the length of this twelve-block pedestrian mall. The "Civic Center Park and Museum Tour" hits the highlights of the Civic Center and state capitol complex and their various museums. The "Performing Arts and Auraria Tour" winds through the Performing Arts Complex and then crosses Cherry Creek for an exploration of the Auraria Campus, home to three universities. For a neck-craning look at Denver's downtown highrises, take the "Business and Financial District Tour." History buffs will want to take the "Lower Downtown Tour" and the "Historic Hotel, Home & Church Tour."

The walking tour booklet was jointly produced by the Denver Metro Convention & Visitors Bureau, Downtown Denver Partnership, Greater Denver Chamber of Commerce and the Mayor's Office of Economic Development.

A GOLDEN OPPORTUNITY

The Ten Best things to see and do in and around Golden are listed in their order of appearance, in a loop driving tour from Denver. Plan on two days to catch all of these lures, perhaps spending one night in Golden and then continuing on to Red Rocks Amphitheatre, the Buffalo Bill Museum and other lures the next day. Note in the list below that some of the attractions are closed on Sunday, so schedule your trip accordingly.

With a population of only 13,000, Golden is as small and quaint as Denver is big and bustling. It's tucked into the foothills—locals like to call this area the "Front Range"—about fifteen miles west of the Mile High City. Bypassed by major freeways, it has thus been bypassed by the Denver growth bug. Downtown Golden has retained its old fashioned eighteenth century look. It wasn't always a back burner town, however. Golden was founded in 1859—just a year after Denver—when gold was discovered in Clear Creek. It thrived briefly as a lively mining camp and served as the territorial capitol from 1862 until 1867, when Denver citizens snatched it away. The gold ran out and the town soon went to sleep. Then in 1873, a young Prussian immigrant named Adolph Kors was drawn here by the area's natural spring water. Soon he was creating gold of another sort—a fine amber colored beer. He Anglicized his name to Coors you know the rest of the story.

To learn more about this attractive little town, contact the Greater Golden Chamber of Commerce, 1010 Washington St., Golden, CO 80401; (800) 590-3113 or (303) 279-3113. (www.goldenchamber.org; E-MAIL: info@goldenchamber.org) It's open weekdays 8:30 to 5 and weekends 10 to 4. A helpful assistant there can mark a map showing the location of area attractions, including those on the list that follows.

GETTING THERE: To begin this Golden tour, head west from Denver on I-70 and take exit 265 (Highway 58), and go right onto McIntyre. Take a quick left onto West 44th Avenue and follow signs to your first stop, which comes up in about a mile:

1 **COLORADO RAILROAD MUSEUM** • *17155 W. 44th Ave., Golden; (303) 279-4591. (www.crm.org) Daily 9 to 5 (until 6 June through August); $. Steam train runs on weekends from June through September.* ☺

Rail buffs will want to spend a good part of a day here. While not a professionally done museum, it exhibits a wealth of railroading lore in its depot-style museum building, and a grand array of old locomotives and rolling stock on its sprawling grounds. Volunteers of the Colorado Railroad Historical Foundation—many of them retired or active rail workers—are doing a remarkable job of workin' on this railroad, running their non-profit museum and restoring historic trains and cars. One of the most appealing exhibits is an elaborate model railroad layout in the museum's basement. In addition to the usual webwork of tracks, it features three detailed turn-of-the-century towns and some cutaway mines. You can set one of the trains in motion for a quarter and follow it through this labyrinthian layout. If you'd like to see the entire system rolling, come by on "Operating Night," the first Thursday of each month from 7:30 to 10.

Out in the railyard, you can climb into cabs of several ancient trains, walk through a post office car where workers once sorted mail as the train rolled across the country, and explore a once luxurious private car that's undergoing restoration. The museum's most unusual exhibits are three "Galloping Geese," 1930s short-haul rail motorcars with truck chassis and powered by V-8 gasoline engines. They resemble elongated Model "A's."

NEXT STOP: From the Colorado Railroad Museum, continue westward on 44th Avenue, which becomes Tenth Street as it enters Golden. You'll soon pass the 3.5-mile-long Coors Brewery, a massive complex that more resembles an industrial facility. However, your nose will tell you that there's beer here. Immediately past the brewery, turn left onto Ford Street, go two blocks to Thirteenth Street and go left again into the parking lot.

2 COORS BREWERY TOUR • *Thirteenth and Ford streets, Golden; (303) 277-BEER. (www.coors.com) Monday-Saturday 10 to 4; closed Sunday. Tours depart every few minutes; free.*

What started as a struggling venture more than a century ago has become America's third largest beer producer, and it's still run by the founding family. This facility is the world's largest individual brewery, producing 1.5 million gallons of suds a day. Coors makes its own cans and bottles, contracts with a thousand growers for its barley and still draws from Adolph's original springs, with thirty well sites on the property. The tour covers the basic process from malting the barley to brewing to packaging the beer. Visitors are given a "beer break" at mid-tour, and offered samples of Coors or Coors Light (which is seventy percent of the firm's market). At tour's end, participants are turned loose in a comfortable hospitality center, where they can try glasses of most of the Coors' line. Free soft drinks are available for the kids. The final stop—of course—is a large gift shop.

Naturally, tour guides like to regale visitors with Coors superlatives. About 300 rail cars and 2,400 trucks leave the firm's breweries each week to quench the nation's thirst. An average rail car can hold 7,200 cases of twelve-ounce cans and if you drank a six-pack a day, it would take seventy-nine years to consume a carload.

This would be quite a challenge. Since the legal drinking age in most states is twenty-one, you'd have to live to age 100 to accomplish this feat. Your liver would never make it.

NEXT STOP: From the brewery, follow Thirteenth Street two blocks to Washington Street in the heart of downtown. It's busy with galleries, gift shops and restaurants, housed in handsomely restored brick and masonry buildings. If you'd like to pick up some visitor information, turn right onto Washington and drive or walk three blocks to the Chamber of Commerce. It's just across Clear Creek near the corner of Tenth Street. You can pick up a walking tour map that will take you past most of the town's attractions. These are our three favorites:

3 ASTOR HOUSE MUSEUM • *822 Twelfth Street at the corner of Arapahoe; (303) 278-3557. (www.web-span.com/fastpart/astor-house.html) Tuesday-Saturday 10 to 4:30; $.*

This is one of the best small museums in the Denver area. The cut-stone Astor House was opened in 1867 as "the handsomest as well as the most substantial hotel building in Colorado," according to its builder Seth Lake. It functioned through various owners as a hotel and boarding house until 1952. Listed on the National Register of Historic Places, it has been restored and furnished as a typical turn-of-the-last-century hostel. Visitors are permitted to move through at their own pace instead of following a tour guide who might become too enraptured with the finer details of a lamp shade, or dwell on century-old gossip concerning its owners. Those who seek more information can push buttons at several audio stations and hear detailed descriptions or interesting bits of history. One can enter most of the furnished rooms and peek from doorways into the rest. The beautifully attired parlor-dining room is particularly attractive.

4 GOLDEN PIONEER MUSEUM • *923 Tenth Street at Cheyenne Street; (303) 278-7151]. (www.henge.com/~goldenpm) Monday-Saturday 10 to 4:30; free, donations appreciated.*

There's not much interpretation in this rather large museum although it has lots of interesting stuff, including nineteenth century furnishings. Among its exhibits are a velvet covered piano, an antique galvanized bath tub, rows of apothecary jars, a large Indian doll collection, the usual native pottery and projectile points. A rather morbidly fascinating display is an embalming table (also known as a cooling table), with graphics describing in vivid detail the embalming process.

5 COLORADO SCHOOL OF MINES GEOLOGY MUSEUM

● *Sixteenth and Maple on the school campus; (303) 273-3823. Daily 9 to 4 Monday-Saturday and 1 to 4 Sunday during the school year; closed Sunday in summer; free.*

The Colorado School of Mines has more than 50,000 minerals, fossils and artifacts in its collection and most of them seem to be displayed in its museum. As you enter, your eyes will be drawn to a striking strawberry colored mineral called *rhodochrosite*, gleaming in a small spotlighted case. From here, you can peruse a large collection of minerals and crystals from around the world, walk through a mockup gold mine, study mining equipment and learn about the earth's geological history. A timeline features small fossil examples from each of the major geological eras. A large exhibit of gemstones is particularly interesting, showing them in the rough, and then after they've been cut and polished.

Other Golden lures

The 1913 **Foss General Store** a combined mercantile, museum, pharmacy, souvenir shop and liquor store at Thirteenth and Washington, open 8 to 9 Monday-Friday and 10 to 3 Sunday; (303) 279-3373.

Clear Creek History Park, just north of the visitor center alongside Clear Creek, Wednesday-Sunday 11 to 4 mid-May to mid-October; (303) 278-3557.

Rocky Mountain Quilt Museum, downtown in Golden Center at 1111 Washington Avenue, Monday-Saturday 10 to 4; 277-0377.

If you'd like to visit the "second largest brewery in Golden," stop by the tiny **Golden City Brewery** on Cheyenne between Eleventh and Twelfth; (303) 279-8092. Open Monday-Saturday 11:30 to 6:30, it offers free samples of its hearty brews, and sells beer by the glass, plus light snacks. Coors probably spills more beer than this place makes.

Our favorite Golden meal stop is **Old Capitol Grill**, occupying the former territorial legislative building at Washington and Twelfth Street. It's handsomely attired in Victorian décor and serves lunch and dinner daily, with full bar service; (303) 279-6390.

NEXT STOP: After you've finished with Golden, head east on Washington Street, go right on Nineteenth for a few blocks, then go left (east) on Sixth Avenue, which is U.S. Highway 6. After about a mile, turn right onto Heritage Road opposite the Jefferson County Administration Center, and follow it south. It will soon blend into Highway 40 (Colfax Avenue), which takes you south to an I-70 interchange. Go under the freeway, swerving slightly to the left to blend onto State Highway 26. After about a mile, turn right near a traffic separator and follow a winding road through dramatically tilted red sandstone strata to one of the area's most noted landmarks.

6 *RED ROCKS PARK & AMPHITHEATRE* • *12700 W. Alameda Parkway, Morrison; (303) 697-8935 for the park and trading post and (303) 640-2637 for the amphitheatre. Free to the public when there isn't a scheduled event. Trading post open daily 9 to 5:30. (www.red-rocks.com)* ☺

Red Rocks is one of the most dramatically situated amphitheaters on the globe—a great terrace of sloping seats wedged between 400-foot-high tilted red sandstone strata. This 9,000-seat theater hosts frequent concerts and other special events, including an Easter sunrise service and spectacular Fourth of July fireworks show. Even if nothing is happening on stage, there's much to see here. Enjoy an awesome panorama of the Denver Basin with the city's skyscrapers rising from the plains, and the sculpted drama of the surrounding sandstone formations. The amphitheatre is part of a 640-acre Denver city and county park, and you can follow roads and hiking trails that provide assorted views of the city and surrounding prairie. Stroll or drive down from the amphitheatre to the rustic adobe style Trading Post, one of the area's oldest curio shops. Just above the turnoff to the trading post, follow signs up a steep winding road to a picnic shelter and geological marker. A display here discusses the geology of the area and points out the peaks, ridges and other features of the Rockies' Front Range.

Red Rocks Amphitheatre was built by the Civilian Conservation Corps during the late 1930s and dedicated in 1941. The huge facility has sixty-nine seating rows ranging from 138 to 231 feet wide, with a 100-foot stage far below.

NEXT STOP: Exit Red Rocks Park and drive straight across the junction, following Highway 26 as it sweeps up and around a brushy, wooded rise called Dinosaur Ridge. Within a mile, watch on your right for your next stop.

7 *DINOSAUR RIDGE VISITOR CENTER* • *16831 W. Alameda Parkway (Highway 26), Morrison; (303) 697-3466. (www.dinoridge.org) Monday-Saturday 9 to 4 and Sunday noon to 4; may be open until 5 in summer; free.* **NOTE:** *The parking lot gate is locked shortly after the visitor center closes, so if you plan to follow the "dinosaur trail" and it's near closing time, park your car outside.*

The word "Morrison"—the name of a nearby town—is familiar to every paleontologist and geologist. In 1877, local school teacher Arthur Lake made the world's first discovery of large dinosaur bones near here. The site was named Dinosaur Ridge and the Jurassic sandstone strata in which the fossils were found is called the Morrison Formation. Lake's discovery started a "dinosaur rush" and dozens of other sites have been found in Western America. Exhibits at the small visitor center focus on Lake's find, with fossils and displays concerning the adjacent "Jurassic Park" ridge. The facility also has a small picnic area, and volunteers conduct periodic field trips.

Our favorite attraction here is linear. Two "dinosaur trails"—one a continuation of the other—take strollers through geologic time to several discovery sites. Trail maps are available at the visitor center. The combined paths—a two-mile round-trip—travel along the shoulder of the highway. To begin, follow painted dinosaur tracks out of the visitor center parking lot and go right toward Dinosaur Ridge. The first section, about a quarter of a mile long, is a 300-million-year "Walk Through Time." Informational signs are placed every few yards to mark a progression back in the earth's geological history. Each sign describes a different era. The second trail begins at the end of the first, taking you up and around Dinosaur Ridge. It leads past several sites where dinosaur tracks, fossils and other geologic formations such as petrified sand riffles can be seen. Seventeen specific sites along the route are marked with informational signs. The trail ends at Lake's 1877 discovery site, not far from the entrance to Red Rocks Park. You can drive this route, although you'll miss most of the marked sites, since only a few have parking areas.

If you'd like to see more fossil sites, informational signs at four park-and-ride lots at the freeway interchange point to other finds. Each of the lots is named for a prehistoric critter.

NEXT STOP: Retrace your route on Highway 26 to the I-70 interchange. Go under the freeway—not onto it—turn left onto U.S. Highway 40 and head west. The original route through the Rockies, it's now an oversized frontage road to the freeway. Within a mile, you'll see a sign directing you to the right for the next stop:

8 **MOTHER CABRINI SHRINE** ● *20189 Cabrini Blvd., Golden. (www.den-cabrini-shrine.org) Daily 7 to 8 in summer and 7 to 5 the rest of the year. Mass in the nearby chapel at 7:30 daily, and 7:30 and 11 Sunday.*

The Missionary Sisters of the Sacred Heart of Jesus must be in pretty good shape if they pay frequent homage to the imposing Mother Cabrini Shrine. It's a 22-foot statue of Jesus, standing atop a pedestal reached by climbing 366 steps from a parking lot. This is a popular pilgrimage for area Catholics since there are two Stations of the Cross alongside the steps and another surrounding the monument. For the rest of us, it's an opportunity to view an impressive religious sculpture and to enjoy a dramatic panorama of the Denver Basin and Great Plains to the east and a slice of snowcapped peaks of the Continental Divide to the west.

The shrine was erected in 1954 in honor of Mother Francesca Maria Cabrini, who worked among early-day Denver's poor and became the first American to be canonized a saint.

NEXT STOP: Return to Highway 40 and continue west. After just over two miles, turn right up Lookout Mountain Road and begin winding steeply upward through the trees. After about 1.5 miles, turn left onto Colorow Road for the first stop:

9 LOOKOUT MOUNTAIN NATURE CENTER & BOETTCHER MANSION • *900 Colorow Road, Golden; (303) 526-0594 for the nature center and (303) 526-0855 for the mansion. (www.mansion.co.jefferson.co.us) Nature Center open Tuesday-Sunday 10 to 4. Mansion open Monday-Friday 8 to 5; closed to the public during special events.* ☺

This rustically handsome nature center was erected in a pine grove near the crest of Lookout Mountain in 1997. It features exhibits on the flora and fauna of the area, and rangers here conduct frequent nature programs. An outdoor deck provides nice views, although the best vistas of far-below Denver and Golden are across the highway, at a trailhead with a bench and picnic table. There's an extensive network of hiking trail in the area and you can pick up brochures at the center. This facility is run by the Jefferson County Open Space Foundation.

Nearby Boettcher Mansion, an imposing cross-timbered and stone structure, was built in 1917 as a summer home for wealthy Coloradan Charles Boettcher. It's now operated by the Jefferson County Board of Commissioners and can be rented for special events. When it's not in use, visitors can follow a self-guiding tour through it's nicely renovated interior. They'll encounter a mix of early twentieth century "Arts and Crafts" and contemporary furnishings. Exhibits focus on the history of the home and its builder.

NEXT STOP: A woodsy one-mile trail leads from the nature center to the Buffalo Bill memorial, with some nice views of Denver and Golden along the way. We describe the hike in more detail in Chapter Ten, page 154. You can drive there—most people do—by returning to Lookout Mountain Road from the nature center and following signs.

10 BUFFALO BILL GRAVE & MUSEUM • *Lookout Mountain Road, Golden; (303) 526-0747. Daily 9 to 5 May through October and Tuesday-Sunday 9 to 4 the rest of the year; $.* ☺

He was one of the West's most colorful characters—a frontier scout, Pony Express rider and self-promoting showman, known internationally for his "Wild West" show. A conservationist he wasn't. William Frederick Cody earned his nickname for killing buffalo to help feed railroad workers. Buffalo Bill wasn't a longtime area resident, but just before he died at his sister's home in Denver in 1917, he asked to be buried on Lookout Mountain, a vista point he'd often admired. Folks from Cody, Wyoming—a town he founded—and North Platte Nebraska—where he lived for many years—kicked up a mighty fuss about his being buried in Colorado. Fearing a kidnapping, the state once sent a National Guard tank up to protect the grave. In 1921, his foster son and show manager Johnny Baker built a museum near the gravesite and thus was born one of Colorado's most popular attractions. When Baker and his wife died, the museum and gravesite were given to the city of Denver.

Baker's original museum, in a rustic wooden structure called the Pahaska Tepee, is now a large gift shop and snack bar. A new museum is bunkered into a nearby slope and it features a complete retrospective of the great showman's life. Begin by watching a short video that recaps his life and the development of the memorial. It includes some rare film footage of his wild west show. Then stroll by professionally done exhibits that track his life from an early friendship with Wild Bill Hichcock to his creation of his internationally-traveled Wild West Show. You'll see some of his original beaded and buckskin costumes, lots of show memorabilia, Western America paintings, antique firearms, saddles and other regalia of the old west. A special exhibit focuses on early tourism in Colorado. In a Kiddie Corral, youngsters can try on boots and Stetsons and other cowboy regalia.

The grave is a short walk away, under sheltering pines, offering that view of the great American prairie over which the old showman had roamed.

NAVIGATIONAL NOTE: If you haven't time to take our "Golden opportunity" tour and want to see the Buffalo Bill grave and museum, head west from Denver on I-70, take exit 256 and follow signs uphill.

...and back to Denver

To complete the loop tour, go left out of the Buffalo Bill memorial and begin spiraling downhill on Lookout Mountain Road. Completed in 1913 to provide access to the mountain top—and later to the Buffalo Bill grave and museum—it drops dramatically and quickly into Golden. There are several hairpin turns in this route, and we wouldn't recommend it for large RVs or trailer rigs. Several viewpoints along the way provide motorists with an opportunity to pull over and enjoy the vista.

The route becomes Nineteenth Street in Golden. Turn right onto Sixth Avenue (Highway 6) and head back toward Denver. You can make a half left after about a mile, following signs to I-70 east. Or stay with U.S. 6, which becomes a freeway and hits I-25 just below Denver.

Part of the secret to success in life is to eat what you want and let the food fight it out inside.
— **Mark Twain**

Chapter three

A DINING GUIDE

THERE'S MORE HERE THAN DENVER OMELETS

The Zagat Survey's *Rocky Mountain Top Restaurants* recently came up with an interesting fact. The Intermountain West has for the past four years experienced the highest per capita restaurant growth in America. And much of this action is happening in Denver, which is cultivating its own signature chefs such as Kevin Taylor, while attracting others from California, New York and New Mexico. High-end restaurant chains such as Morton's of Chicago and McCormick's from the Northwest have opened shop here in recent years.

While the Mile High City isn't a dining mecca to rank with New York, New Orleans, Chicago or San Francisco, it is certainly far and beyond any other city in the Rocky Mountain West. No other can match the number and variety of restaurants.

Leading the legions of new Denver diners are several restaurants once called American *nouveau* and now defined as contemporary American. Local foodies talk of Rocky Mountain cuisine or Colorado cuisine, which means contemporary American with a focus on beef, trout or game. Buffalo meat also is popular and—to our thinking—

highly overrated. It's so lean and low in fat that it's rather bland—good for the body but not for the taste buds. We tried and failed to find a buffalo burger as tasty as a good old greasy beefburger. Another local specialty is the Rocky Mountain oyster, which we feel is eaten more as a dare than a delicacy.

Denver's dining scene reflects the informal attitude of the city itself. Folks here prefer blue jeans to blue serge and only a few restaurants request coats and ties for the gentlemen. (Why is it they never set apparel standards for the ladies?)

One of the best aspects of the Denver dining scene is its rich mix of Hispanic restaurants. While most Western cities have multiple Mexican cafés, Denver offers a much broader *Latino* culinary base. The mix includes traditional Mexican, Tex-Mex, Santa Fe style Southwestern, South and Central American and a surprisingly good selection of Hispanic takeouts. Because of Denver's variety of *Latino* diners, we've created a Ten Best Hispanic list further down this chapter.

Denver doesn't have a large Asian population nor does it have a great number of Oriental restaurants. It has the ubiquitous Chinese restaurants, of course, but no Chinatown. The most concentrated Asian community is along Federal Boulevard, south from Alameda Avenue, and these folks are mostly latter-day Vietnamese arrivals. A dozen or more Vietnamese restaurants are scattered for a couple of miles along this "Little Vietnam" stretch, interspersed with a few Chinese, Thai and Mexican cafés.

The Denver dining scene is focused in three areas—along the Sixteenth Street Mall downtown, in LoDo and the Cherry Creek area. Because of the city's sunny weather, outdoor dining areas are very popular, particularly along Sixteenth Street Mall. With a couple of notable exceptions, Denver has few grand hotels and thus few grand hotel restaurants. The city's many Hispanic restaurants are scattered rather widely, although there are several along Santa Fe Drive, a *Latino* area just south of downtown.

PRICING: In our listings, we use simple strings of dollar signs to indicate the price of a typical dinner with entrée, soup or salad, not including drinks, appetizers or dessert: *$* = less than $10 per entrée; *$$* = $10 to $19; *$$$* = $20 to $29; *$$$$* = "Did you say you were buying?"

THE TEN VERY BEST RESTAURANTS

With hundreds of restaurants in Denver, how can one possibly select the very best? Obviously, by being quite arbitrary. We dined anonymously at each of our "Ten Very Best" selections, paid the check, left a reasonable gratuity and departed, like true phantom diners.

Our choices reflect current Denver dining trends, tilted toward contemporary American. However, our overall winner might be described as French with an American accent.

1 **PAPILLON** • *250 Josephine St.; (303) 333-7166. French with nouveau accents; full bar service. Lunch weekdays; dinner nightly. Major credit cards; $$ to $$$. GETTING THERE: It's in the Cherry Creek shopping area, between Second and Third avenues. From downtown, follow Speer Boulevard southeast. Shortly after it blends into First Avenue, go left (north) one block on Josephine*

Writers of insiders guides are reluctant to follow the crowds. However, the crowds—local food critics, national food critics and faithful patrons—kept leading us to this smartly modern butterfly. The Zagat survey gave it the highest rating of any Colorado restaurant. The look of Papillon is sleek and clean—with dark furniture accented by white nappery, brocaded booths, burgundy accents and modern art. Soft music adds a final touch of relaxed elegance. A shaded patio rimmed by flower planters is particularly inviting on warm days. The fare might best be described as French with pan-Asian accents. Some examples from a current menu—which changes frequently—were rosemary charbroiled salmon; pork with Thai curry, apples, spinach and raisins; trout grilled with charbroiled vegetables; sweetbreads with a Tamarind glaze; and a seafood fricassee of scallop, shrimp and lobster in a Newburg style sauce with white sherry.

2 **AUBERGINE CAFÉ** • *225 E. Seventh Ave.; (303) 832-4778. Mediterranean-Italian; wine and beer. Dinner Tuesday-Sunday. Major credit cards; $$$. GETTING THERE: Head south from downtown on Broadway, then go left (east) four blocks; it's between Grand and Sherman streets.*

The look of this cozy café is simple French country or perhaps seaport bistro, with mustard colored walls, brown paper table coverings and dried herbs hanging in the windows. Yet this is one of Denver's most elegant and certainly most popular restaurants. The menu hops merrily about the Mediterranean, yet it has a decidedly American *nouveau* accent in many of its dishes. It changes frequently, so you may or may not find some of these entrées—grilled ribeye steak with rosemary hash browns, Hawaiian tuna with asparagus, and sea scallops with bacon and shiitake mushrooms. *Aubergine* is French for eggplant, and that humble vegetable is crafted into a savory, full flavored roasted entrée, topped with eggplant purée. A Sunday special—hopefully on the menu when you're in town—is herb-roasted chicken. Aubergine has an excellent wine list to match its eclectic offerings.

3 **THE FORT** • *19192 Highway 8, Morrison; (303) 697-4771. American; full bar service. Dinner nightly. Major credit cards; $$$ to $$$$. GETTING THERE: The Fort is about twelve miles southwest of*

Denver. *The fastest all-freeway approach is to go west on U.S. 6, which blends into I-70 after about eight miles. Continue west briefly then go south at exit 260 on Highway 470 for five miles. At the interchange with U.S. 285, go southwest (toward Fairplay) about a mile, take the Highway 8 exit (Morrison) and the restaurant is immediately on your right.*

The area's most contrived tourist restaurant is worth the drive from Denver. Despite the gimmickry of a reconstructed adobe fort built around a quadrangle, the food is excellent. Even the often-skeptical Zagat review gives it high marks, as do local restaurant critics. Dinner is served in one of several dining areas in the large "Eating House." Menu items when we last dined included bison steak, teriyaki marinated charbroiled quail, elk medallions with huckleberry sauce, rack of venison with port wine and blackberry sauce, and applewood bacon-wrapped trout.

The Fort is one of the area's more pricey restaurants. If you're unwilling to part with $70 to $100 for dinner for two, at least drive out for a look. The place is busy with museum-quality artifacts, rare Edward Curtis photos of native people and Old West regalia. The central courtyard is rather pleasant, with a crackling campfire and votive candles set in old fashioned lanterns. The adjacent "Trading Post" offers a good assortment of Western artifacts and gift wares. Find time before or after dinner for a drink on a large deck outside the main restaurant, where you'll catch a slice of greater Denver between foothills. The Fort is particularly pleasant after dark, with that courtyard fire and the twinkling lights of distant Denver.

4 HIGHLANDS GARDEN CAFÉ ● *3927 W. 32nd Ave.; (303) 458-5920. Contemporary American; wine and beer. Lunch Tuesday-Friday, dinner nightly. MC/VISA; $$ to $$$. GETTING THERE: It's in Denver's Highland Park area northwest of downtown, between Osceola and Perry streets. Follow Speer Boulevard about two miles, then fork to the left on 32nd Avenue and go six blocks west. The restaurant is on your right, near Perry Street.*

This distinctive restaurant shares two Victorian homes which have been joined, and it spills onto a a pair of landscaped patios. The intimate dining rooms feature early American décor, cozy candle lit tables with white nappery and brick walls adorned with murals or framed watercolors. The landscaped patio gardens are particularly popular in summer. The menu changes frequently, even between lunch and dinner, depending on what the chefs have found fresh at the markets. So you may or may not find entrées such as pan seared tuna with Asian dipping sauce, grilled mahi mahi with fruit salad, roasted leg of lamb with sun-dried tomatoes, roasted duck with sherry port sauce, or chipotle glazed chicken breast with guacamole. This elegant little retreat also was chosen as one of Denver's most romantic restaurants; see Chapter Eight, page 130.

5 *KEVIN TAYLOR* ● *In the Teatro Hotel at 1100 Fourteenth St.; (303) 820-2600. Contemporary American; full bar service. Dinner nightly. Major credit cards; $$$ to $$$$. GETTING THERE: It's on the edge of LoDo at the corner of Fourteenth and Market.*

Denver's best known signature chef has installed two restaurants in the Teatro Hotel and immodestly named one for himself. His prices also are immodest; Kevin Taylor is one of the most expensive restaurants in town. Foodies say it's worth it as they reverently delve into beautifully presented creations such as poached chicken with porcine flan and Madeira sauce, seared duck breast with confit, beef sirloin with potato puree and green peppercorn, and potato crusted halibut with endive and shiitake mushrooms. Taylor also offers two rather pricey *prix fixe* tasting menus. The look is as elegant as the food presentations, with lace curtains, light wood paneling, selected artwork on the walls and several vases bursting with flowers. It is at once cheerful yet subdued. The hotel's second Taylor restaurant, Ju Ju, is less formal and equally cheerful, serving breakfast through dinner.

6 *PALACE ARMS* ● *In the Brown Palace at 321 Seventeenth St.; (303) 297-3111. (www.brownpalace.com) Continental; full bar service. Lunch weekdays, dinner nightly. Major credit cards; $$$$. GETTING THERE: The legendary downtown hotel is cradled by Seventeenth, Broadway and Tremont.*

Like the rest of "The Brown," the Palace Arms exudes continental class and extravagance, from its almost painfully opulent old European décor to its tuxedo-clad waitstaff and certainly its prices. It's one of the rare Denver restaurants that asks gentlemen to dress the part; not in tuxedos but at least in jacket and tie. Food is served on collector china and the wine list is one of the best on either side of the Rockies. The entrées are rather straightforward without a lot of *nouveau* trappings of air-dried beef or raspberry purée. Among selections when we lasted visited were grilled catch of the day, duck l'orange, beef Wellington for two, rosemary crusted rack of lamb, lobster tails, grilled elk and fillet of buffalo.

7 *STRINGS* ● *1700 Humboldt St.; (303) 831-7310. Contemporary American; full bar service. Lunch and dinner Monday-Friday with a Saturday brunch; dinner only Sunday. Major credit cards; $$ to $$$. GETTING THERE: Go east from downtown on Seventeenth Avenue to Humboldt Street; the restaurant is on the northeast corner.*

One of several cafés along an emerging Seventeenth Avenue restaurant row, Strings seems to be almost effortlessly trendy. It's cheery look of white walls with geometric splashes of color, contemporary art and mobiles and its sunny outdoor tables attract the kind of people that make it a see-and-be-seen place. Two generations ago, the clientele would be called yuppies; today they're called upwardly mobile and they're still driving Beamers. The place lends itself to camaraderie, with its cathedral ceiling main dining room and a smaller loft above. The changing menu is trendy as well, featuring lightly done fish crusted in interesting spices, crab cakes, in-house cooked pastas, and curiously seasoned steak, chop and chicken dishes. All are artfully presented by a waitstaff noted for attentiveness and attention to detail. One local foodie really went overboard, saying service was "caring and kind, sometimes in a deeply human way." We're not sure what that meant. Our waitress certainly had a cheery smile, although she didn't offer any counseling.

8 **TANTE LOUISE** • *4900 E. Colfax Ave.; (303) 355-4488. French, wine and beer. Dinner Monday-Saturday; closed Sunday. Major credit cards; $$$ to $$$$. GETTING THERE: It's about three miles east on Colfax, on the corner of Eudora Street.*

This charming tree-shaded cottage restaurant sits in a curious transition zone, with the busily commercial Colfax Avenue on one side and an older, well-kept neighborhood on the other. The transition is pleasantly abrupt, as you step from the buzz of traffic into a quiet haven with its dark wainscotting, floral wallpaper, lace curtains and fireplaces. The sound of Colfax is muffled and you're somewhere in the south of France. The menu is more contemporary—French with some American *nouveau* accents. You may find—the menu changes several times a year—roasted rack of lamb with caramelized potatoes, grilled veal chops with porcine mushrooms and garlic sauce, or classic French style sweetbreads. The kitchen also offers a few pastas and vegetarian dishes. All of this is supported by an extensive wine list. Plan on arriving early and adjourn to a pretty garden to sip an aperitif before dinner.

9 **VESTA DIPPING GRILL** • *1822 Blake St.; (303) 296-1970. (www.vestagrill.com/dip) Eclectic menu; full bar service. Lunch and dinner daily. Major credit cards; $$$. GETTING THERE: It's in LoDo between Eighteenth and Nineteenth streets.*

To dine is to dip at this new Denver hotspot. Restaurants generally offer sauces with their entrées; Vesta gives you choices. Each dish comes with a selection of three "dipping sauces," which can be selected from a list of at least thirty-five. Choices range from fruity purées and spicy dips to gentle chutneys, fiery salsas and piquant curries. Some examples are roasted red pepper salsa, apple salsa, Rasta tri-pepper chutney, sweet chili ginger sauce, peanut sauce and honey soy sauce. Go with one or more friends and have fun dipping back and forth. The entrées are generous and well-prepared, including grilled chicken, ginger chili-seared tuna, thick cut garlic-soy pork loin, glazed salmon, and brown sugar smoked duck breast. To widen your dipping variety further, order the sampler appetizer—wedges of pita bread with five sauces. Vesta is installed between rough brick walls in one of LoDo's grand nineteenth century buildings. Designers have done what should be done to these fine old structures—as little as possible. The ceiling has been shored up with heavy, rough beams, and tables, chairs and a bar have been installed below.

10 **ZENITH AMERICAN GRILL** • *815 W. Seventeenth St.; (303) 293-2322. Contemporary American with Southwestern accents; full bar service. Lunch and dinner daily. Major credit cards; $$ to $$$. GETTING THERE: This apex of restaurants is downtown, between Champa and Stout streets.*

Another Kevin Taylor creation, Zenith is one of Denver's most attractive restaurants. It's installed in an old bank lobby, with a lofty ceiling held up by fluted columns. Large, wonderfully whimsical Mardi Gras jester scenes dominate the high walls. The main restaurant is rimmed by a dark wood planter, with more intimate dining areas tucked into corners. The menu is predictably trendy, preoccupied with sun-dried tomatoes and caramelized sauces. Taylor's creations have been cited in *Gourmet* and *Bon Appétit*. His menu changes frequently, although one might find such fare as roasted chicken with chipotle, garlic roast pork with posolé corncakes and tomatillo chutney, or macadamia crusted sea bass with Thai red curry.

How ARE THINGS IN GUACAMOLE?
THE TEN BEST HISPANIC RESTAURANTS

As we noted above, Denver has a large Hispanic population and this is reflected in its restaurant choices. Our favorites range from high end trendy to mom and pop basic. Selections include Brazilian, Argentine, Tex-Mex and Southwestern restaurants.

1 **CANYON CAFÉ** • *2500 E. First Ave.; (303) 321-2700. Southwestern; full bar service. Lunch and dinner daily. Major credit cards; $$ to $$$. GETTING THERE: The restaurant is near the corner of First and University. From downtown, follow Speer Boulevard southeast about three miles along Cherry Creek. It blends onto First Avenue and the café is on the right, just short of Cherry Creek Shopping Center.*

Handsome Canyon Café earns the top spot in our list because the food is quite tasty and the fare represents a broad Hispanic cross section, from Tex-Mex to Mex-Mex to Southwestern. The menu's write-up about the mythical *kokopelli*—which the café uses as a symbol—is inaccurate, but never mind that. People are drawn to Canyon for its good looks and tasty food, not to learn about the mischievous Pueblo Indian spirit. Examples from the Southwestern side of the menu are barbecued salmon in corn husk, Yucatan chicken breast with achiote glaze, and chili-rubbed shrimp skewers. The kitchen also serves the usual Mexican and Tex-Mex tacos, quesadillas, flautas and such. It's a comely café with *faux* adobe, peeled log beam ceilings, Navajo style tapestries and New Mexican pottery. The large restaurant's dining room is divided into several cozy seating areas.

2 *THE ARMADILLO • 2401 Fifteenth St.; (303) 477-5880. Mexican; full bar service. Lunch and dinner daily. Major credit cards; $$. GETTING THERE: Take Fifteenth Street about a mile northwest from downtown and cross the South Platte River at Confluence Park. The restaurant is on your right, at the corner of Platte Street.*

There are six family-owned Armadillo's in the region and this is the most appealing, mostly because it's installed in one of those great old riverfront brick buildings. The menu isn't particularly innovative although it's tasty, featuring ample versions of flautas, burritos, chimichangas and such. The kitchen does depart from convention with specials like *bistek con rajas* which translates as beef with ranchero sauce, and crab enchiladas. Designers wisely left most of the attractive interior undisturbed, with its raw brick walls and pressed tin ceilings. A few bright serapes are draped around thick columns and a cheerful fountain burbles in the middle of the dining area.

3 *BREWERY BAR II • 150 Klamath St.; (303) 893-0971. Mexican; full bar service. Lunch and dinner Monday-Saturday; closed Sunday. MC/VISA, DISC; $. GETTING THERE: Head south from downtown on one-way Klamath for about a mile and a half. The restaurant is in a small beige and aqua building on your left, near Second Avenue.*

The only thing Hispanic here is the menu, and that's quite enough. Despite the name, it's not a *gringo* brewpub, although its décor consists primarily of neon beer signs. The food is spicy hot Mexican and this place is a mob scene during the weekday lunch break. Get here as soon as the doors open at 11 a.m., or come for a more relaxing late lunch or evening meal. The best things here are the huge super burritos that arrive drowned in red or green chile sauce. Another special is the Brewery Bar chili relleno, available in crispy chicken or beef versions. The kitchen also issues the usual tacos, enchiladas and tostados and they're *very* spicy. Consider ice tea with your meal, since your glass is never permitted to go dry and you'll need plenty to cool the piquant fare.

4 *BLUE BONNET CAFÉ* ● *457 S. Broadway; (303) 788-0147. Mexican; wine, beer and margaritas. Lunch and dinner daily. MC/VISA; $. GETTING THERE: Follow Broadway about two miles south of the Civic Center. Blue Bonnet is your right near the corner of Virginia Street, on the edge of a large shopping center parking area.*

Like Brewery Bar, Blue Bonnet doesn't have an Hispanic name and the look is a mix of art deco and modern diner, although the menu is definitely from south of the border. The kitchen issues the usual burritos, tacos, tostados and chimichangas, plus specials such as *carne tampiquena* (beef strips with refried beans and rice) spicy broiled Mexican steak, a vegetarian tamale dinner, and *menuedo* (tripe stew with hominy). It's a bright and airy place; the main dining room is open to the fresh air, with an outdoor patio beyond.

5 *CHIPOTLE MEXICAN GRILL* ● *Several Denver area locations. Those closest to downtown are at 745 Colorado Boulevard near Eighth Avenue, (303) 333-2121; 333 E. Alameda Avenue between Logan and Grant Streets, (303) 733-1331; and 550 Broadway near Sixth Avenue, (303) 866-0725. Mexican; wine, beer and margaritas. Lunch through dinner daily. MC/VISA; $.*

Although Chipotles are fast-food takeouts, they're quite attractive and the food is several notches above Taco Bell. This earns them a spot on our Ten Best Hispanic list. Most have appealing outdoor dining patios. The featured attractions here are huge burritos, large enough to sink your boat, so don't drop one on your foot. Another specialty is *baracoa*, a flour tortilla with shredded beef, cilantro, rice, sour cream and tomatillo green chili salsa.

6 *EL NOA NOA RESTAURANT* ● *722 Santa Fe Drive; (303) 623-9968. Mexican; full bar service. Late breakfast through dinner daily. Major credit cards; $ to $$. GETTING THERE: It's near the corner of Seventh Avenue. Santa Fe is one-way northbound, so to reach the area from downtown, drive south on Klamath, then go left on Seventh to Santa Fe.*

This pleasantly old fashioned Mexican restaurant is popular for its well-prepared food at modest prices and its appealing patio. Although the restaurant has a few comfortable booths inside, most patrons head for its dining garden unless it's howling cold outside. Sheltered from the street by an ornate brick wall, this refuge is thickly landscaped and accented by a cheerful fountain. Noa Noa features mariachi music indoors and out Thursday, Friday and Sundays. The menu lists the typical range of tacos, burritos, chimichangas and beyond. Its specialty is *tanamos mariscos*—Mexican style seafood dishes.

7 *LOS CABOS II* • *1512 Curtis St.; (303) 571-0007. Peruvian-Chinese; full bar service. Lunch and dinner daily. Major credit cards; $$. GETTING THERE: It's in LoDo, off Sixteenth Street Mall near the corner of Fifteenth Street.*

Chinese and Peruvian food in a restaurant with a Mexican name? Denver's Hispanic dining scene reaches its eclectic peak at this attractive LoDo café. Los Cabos—which translates as "the capes" or "rocky promontories"—features tasty Peruvian fare with Spanish accents, plus a separate Cantonese menu offering *kung pao* shrimp and chicken, almond chicken and *lo mein*. This isn't as odd as it sounds, since Peru has a large Chinese population, which has influenced its cuisine. The *Latino* side of the menu offers interesting fare such as *jalea de mariscos* (breaded deep-fried fish, octopus and scallops), *kau kau de mariscos* (seafood stew in light curry), *polo la braza* (spiced chicken with fries and salad) and *aji de gallina* (shredded chicken in Parmesan nut sauce). Indicative of the Chinese influence, many of the Peruvian entrées are served with white rice instead of the more spicy *arroz*. The look of the place is eclectic as well, with a rather contemporary light wood décor accented by both Peruvian and Chinese artifacts.

8 *RODIZIO GRILL* • *Eighteenth and Wynkoop, near Union Station in LoDo; (303) 294-9277. Also at C-470 and Quebec Street, (303) 346-5556; and West Quincy at Wadsworth in Littleton, (303) 972-0808. Brazilian churrascaria; full bar service. Lunch and dinner daily. Major credit cards; $$. (www.rodizio.com)*

This appealing restaurant occupying one of LoDo's grand old brick warehouses brings to Denver the Brazilian dining tradition of *churrascaria*. Assorted meats, fowl and fish are seasoned, skewered and cooked over wood fires. Then waiters dressed in *gaucho* garb carry the still warm spits about the dining room, carving off chunks as requested by patrons. This is augmented by appetizer trays and a serve-yourself salad bar with thirty-five items. The restaurant has a simple two-price policy: A sampler with two meats and unlimited salad and appetizers; or the more expensive "full Rodizio" with unlimited everything. Protein selections include several types of seasoned beef, chicken drumsticks, lean turkey, pork loin, Brazilian sausage and skewered catch of the day. If you can't handle all of this, sandwiches are available or you can order salad or appetizers only. Of the area's three Rodizios, the LoDo location is the most attractive, with raw brick walls and high thick beam ceilings with exposed heating ducts.

9 *SEÑORITA'S CANTINA* • *1700 Wynkoop Street at the corner of Seventeenth in LoDo; (303) 298-7181. Mexican; full bar service. Lunch weekdays and dinner nightly. Major credit cards; $$.*

This is hardly a typical family Mexican café. It's the creation of *gringo* restaurant designers and we wish they'd given it a more original name. It makes our Ten Best Hispanic list for two good reasons—we like some of the creative entrées including several vegetarian dishes, and the place is quite attractive. It's installed one of those high ceiling masonry buildings in LoDo, decorated with Mexican folk pottery and paintings. Among the more interesting menu items are grilled chicken breast with roasted corn relish, butterfly shrimp with a plantain crust, and chili-glazed quail. Of course, one can get the usual things wrapped in tortillas; fajitas are a specialty.

10 *TOSH'S HACIENDA* • *3090 Downing Street at the corner of 31st Avenue, (303) 295-1861; and 5071 S. Syracuse Parkway near Belleview Avenue, (303) 770-8980. Mexican; full bar service. Lunch and dinner daily. Major credit cards; $ to $$.*

One of Denver's oldest still active restaurants, the original Tosh has been sitting in the same place for more than half a century. It's 1.5 miles north of Colfax Avenue on Downing Street, in an old multi-ethnic neighborhood that's starting the regenerate. Don't be put off by the scruffy look of the building; you'll find a cozy Spanish *hacienda* inside with floral-painted walls, ceiling fans and Mexican artifacts. The newer Tosh, several miles south of I-25 and Bellevue, is more contemporary. "Tosh," incidentally, refers to MacIntosh, since the founding family was Mexican-Scottish. No kippers here, however; the menu is typical Mexican, with the usual things wrapped in tortillas. Tosh's also features tasty specials such as tequila lime shrimp, spicy seafood Mazatlan and halibut with lobster-chili sauce.

THE TEN BEST OTHER ETHNIC RESTAURANTS

Denver's ethnic cuisine scene tilts mostly toward Europe and the Mideast. We've also discovered a fair selection of Oriental restaurants even though, as we noted above, the Mile High City doesn't have a major Asian community.

Ethnic authenticity tends to be modified by new environments. The proper ingredients may not be available locally, and recipes are sometimes altered to cater to American tastes. In choosing the Ten Best ethnic places, we focused mostly on family-owned or chef-owned cafés that haven't strayed too far from their culinary roots. They range from upscale restaurants to mom and pop diners.

1 *CHINESE: Imperial Chinese Seafood Restaurant* • *431 S. Broadway; (303) 698-2800. (www.imperialchinese.com) Full bar service. Lunch and dinner Monday-Saturday, dinner only Sunday. Major* *credit cards; $$ to $$$. GETTING THERE: Follow Broadway about two miles south of the Civic Center; it's at the corner of Dakota Street, on your right.*

This establishment has earned its rather imperious name, having won numerous local dining awards. It's a large, elegant restaurant decorated with selective Chinese artifacts, with beamed ceilings and lacquered furnishings. Particularly striking is a large and ornate shield at the dining room entrance. The seafood side of the menu is excellent, featuring lightly steamed and subtly flavored fish, fried dungeness crabs, and dish of shrimp, scallops and crabmeat called Velvet Seafood Delight. Beyond the sea, the menu dances from mildly spiced Cantonese to peppy Szechuan and Mandarin dishes. The *moo shu* entrées— shrimp, chicken, pork or vegetables served with a plum sauce and wrapped in crepes—are particularly tasty. If you like lamb with an attitude, try the spicy *Yue Shang* or Genghis Kahn's lamb.

2 **FRENCH: Tante Louise** • *4900 E. Colfax Ave.; (303) 355-4488. Wine and beer. Dinner Monday-Saturday; closed Sunday. GETTING THERE: It's about three miles east on Colfax, on the corner of Eudora Street, opposite a Rite Aid pharmacy.*

A lushly landscaped cottage between busy Colfax Avenue and a quiet residential area shelters this charming French country style restaurant. Although the menu tilts toward American *nouveau*, some of its best dishes are frankly French, such as sweetbreads, grilled veal chop and roasted rack of lamb over porcine mushrooms. Denver's finest French restaurant also is one of its Ten Best restaurants overall; see above on page 60.

3 **GERMAN: Café Berlin** • *2005 E. Seventeenth Ave.; (303) 377-5896. Wine, beer and schnapps. Lunch weekdays, dinner nightly. MC/VISA, DISC; $$. GETTING THERE: The restaurant is about a mile east of downtown on one-way Seventeenth, near the corner of Race Street.*

This little restaurant is almost too quaint to be a *Berliner*. Sitting on a tree-lined street, it seems more a German village café. The interior is bright and cheerful without the heavy carved woods of many German restaurants. Light walls are embellish with large splashes of contemporary art and a few decorative plates. Café Berlin also has an attractive sidewalk dining area. The menu is certainly typical, featuring such Germanic staples as *jäger schnitzel* (breaded veal cutlet), *cordon bleu* (veal cutlet with ham and Swiss cheese) and *rouladen* (beef rolls stuffed with onions, bacon, pickles and mustard.) Don't try to pronounce *hühnerbrust mit frischen kräutern*; just ask for breast of chicken with fresh herbs. Meals are hearty and hefty, arriving with choices of boiled potatoes, spätzle, red cabbage, potato dumplings or sauerkraut. Finish your feast with *schnapps*, a strong, subtly flavored multiple-distilled drink similar to gin, but more assertive.

4 **INDIAN: Delhi Darbar** • *1514 Blake St.; (303) 595-0680. Wine and beer. Lunch and dinner daily. Major credit cards; $$ to $$$. GETTING THERE: The restaurant is in LoDo, between Fifteenth Street and the Sixteenth Street Mall.*

This cozy little Indian café focuses on *tandoori* (charcoal oven-baked) meats, poultry and seafood, richly flavored with curries, turmeric, coriander and other spices of the Sub-continent. Some savory examples are *tandoori murgh* (chicken marinated in yogurt, spices and lemon juice), the traditional spiced lamb *shish kebab* and *murgh ticca masala* (tandoor baked boneless chicken with a tomato onion cream sauce). A specialty is cubed lamb and potatoes in a hot curry sauce. The menu also lists several vegetarian dishes so hearty and generously spiced that diners won't miss the meat. Delhi isn't a typically garish India restaurant draped with baubles and beads. The décor is pleasingly simple, with curtained booths and a few woven tapestries on the walls. The restaurant serves an inexpensive lunch buffet.

5 **IRISH: Fadó** • *1735 Nineteenth St.; (303) 297-0066. GETTING THERE: Fadó is in the old Union Pacific building between Nineteenth and Coors Field, immediately north of downtown.*

In Ireland, a pub is a proper place to eat as well as to drink and Denver's best Irish pub serves typical fare from the *auld sod.* Stop by for a pint o' Guinness and accompany it with corned beef and cabbage, fish and chips, shepherd's pie (ground sirloin and vegetables in gravy, baked in a crust) or "boxty straws." They're fried potato pancakes served with a rich sauce. Our Fadó favorite is Irish *rollóg*—corned beef, cheddar cheese, lettuce and horseradish, wrapped in a boxty and served with coleslaw. The kitchen also serves several American dishes such as peppered salmon, tenderloin of pork in a honey and clove sauce and charbroiled New York strip steak in a peppercorn sauce. We also selected Fadó as one of Denver's Ten Best drinking establishments; see Chapter Seven, page 112.

6 **ITALIAN: Maggiano's Little Italy** • *500 Sixteenth Street Mall; (303) 260-7710. Full bar service. Lunch and dinner daily. Major credit cards; $$. GETTING THERE: The restaurant is in the ground level of the Denver Pavilions, between Glenarm and Tremont.*

Our favorite Denver Italian restaurant looks older than its age, and that's intended as a compliment. Designers have created the aura of a venerable, long established Italian family diner within the modern confines of the Denver Pavilions. Wooden floors, milk glass light fixtures and red checkered tablecloths suggest an aged mom and pop trattoria, albeit a large one. Maggiano has several dining areas and an inviting outdoor patio. The kitchen issues many good things Italian, from a dozen or so pastas to the typical Parmesan, scallopines and saltimboccas. Our favorite is chicken *giardiniera*—crusted breast of chicken swamped with spicy vegetables, onions, green olives and capers. Maggiano also offers several steaks, rosemary lamb chops and fresh seafood. Try to find space for a tasty, generous slab of sensuously rich tiramisu.

7 *JAPANESE:* **Domo** • *1365 Osage St.; (303) 595-3666. Saké and beer. Lunch and dinner Thursday-Saturday. MC/VISA; $$ to $$$. GETTING THERE: Go west on Colfax Avenue, then turn left (south) onto Osage just before you reach a viaduct. The restaurant is two long blocks south, in a beige brick building on your right.*

There are several things strange about Denver's best Japanese restaurant. It's in a square-shouldered old brick building between an industrial area and a low cost housing development, far from the nearest restaurant row. It's open only three days a week, and it doesn't do a lot of sushi. Within this building—whose windows are closed to the world by bamboo strips—diners find a rustically elegant Japanese inn with stone-topped tables, fabric covered tree stump chairs and folk art. There's an appealing Oriental dining garden outside. Domo shares the building with the Nippon Kan cultural center, and offers access to a fine folk museum. The restaurant serves traditional and perfectly prepared Japanese cuisine. The rather small menu features yellowfin tuna *sashimi, tojimono* (sautéed meat or seafood with onions, shiitake mushrooms, *wakame* seaweed and carrots), several teriyaki variations and *nabenomo,*, a tasty vegetarian dish of sesame-flavored braised tofu, carrots, yam cake, bamboo shoots and shiitake mushrooms. Although the menu is small, diners have a choice of thirty different sakés. *Domo* is the word preceding *arigato,* meaning "thank you," and you'll certainly want to say it after dining here.

8 *MIDEASTERN:* **Fettoush** • *1448 Market St.; (303) 820-2554. Full bar service. Lunch and dinner daily. Major credit cards; $ to $$. GETTING THERE: It's in LoDo, between Fourteenth and Fifteenth streets.*

The menu is Lebanese, eastern Mediterranean and beyond, although the look of this bright and cheerful bistro is *art moderne* hip. It's painted in maroons, mauves and burgundies, with contemporary art and sleek designer furniture. For a sampler of Middle Eastern fare try the *mezze mix of hummus* (mashed chickpeas), *baba ghanoush* (spiced eggplant), *dolmas* (stuffed grape leaves), *falafel* (spiced chickpea patties) and other small plate savories. Dinner entrées include *sha-warma* (broiled filet of beef or chicken), *kafta kabob* (charbroiled chunks of beef, chopped onion and fresh parsley) or spiced lamb shanks. The busy menu also lists pizzas and calzones. An outdoor seating area is popular with the downtown lunch crowd.

9 THAI: Busara • *1435 Market St; (303) 893-2884. Wine and beer. Lunch through dinner daily. Major credit cards; $$. GETTING THERE: It's in LoDo, midway between Fourteenth and Fifteenth streets.*

Although LoDo offers a good mix of international cafés, many focus more on food than décor. The Busara look is quintessential LoDo with rough brick walls, old fashioned chandelier fans and a gorgeous pressed tin ceiling. Little here suggest Thailand except the menu, which features classic fare with a few *nouveau* accents. Some examples are red curry coconut chicken, spicy "drunken noodles," wok-sautéed chicken or beef with basil and garlic, and catfish in green curry sauce with eggplant. A favorite dish with a great name is "Sea of Love"— wok-sautéed lobster, squid and shrimp with shallots, shiitake mushrooms and roasted chili sauce. If you enjoy *al fresco* dining, Busara has both a sidewalk patio and a roof garden with umbrella tables and heat lamps.

10 VIETNAMESE: T-Wa Inn • *555 S. Federal Blvd; (303) 922-4584. Full bar service. Lunch through dinner daily. Major credit cards; $$. GETTING THERE: Go west on Colfax Avenue about two miles to Federal, turn left and go south just over two miles to Custer (passing broad Alameda Avenue); the restaurant is on your right.*

Denver's first Vietnamese restaurant is still its best. T-Wa Inn opened in the "little Vietnam" section of Federal Boulevard in 1984. It has won numerous local awards for its well-prepared fare, served in generous portions. The kitchen issues a wide assortment of inexpensive rice noodle bowls and rice plates, plus several complete entrées, priced from under $10 to the mid teens. Among its specials are curried lamb, hot and spicy seafood, stuffed quail and spicy pork. In addition to offering good, inexpensive food, the place is remarkably cute, with Asian artifacts in brick-arch niches, and golden fans and Asian prints on the walls. It's one of the few small Asian restaurants in "little Vietnam" with full bar service. An attractive cocktail lounge is adjacent to the dining room.

THE TEN BEST SPECIALTY RESTAURANTS

Most of our specialty selections concern the type of food served, although we have a couple of visual categories at the end of this list. Our choices are listed in no particular order.

1 **THE BEST BREAKFAST CAFÉ: Eggshell & Incredibles Café** • *1520 Blake St.; (303) 623-7555. Breakfast through lunch daily. MC/VISA, AMEX; $. GETTING THERE: It's egg-zactly (sorry about that) midway between Fifteenth and Sixteenth streets in LoDo, a short walk from Larimer Square.*

The look of this popular breakfast parlor is stereotypical LoDo, with raw brick walls, exposed heating ducts and drop lamps. The large breakfast menu features the full range of wake-up fare—pancakes, waffles, cereals, and eggs in just about every form imaginable, from Spanish style *huevos rancheros* (omelet with salsa) and breakfast burritos to eggs Benedict. A Zagat review called the restaurant "A hangover's best friend." It's as much a lunch parlor as a breakfast bistro, drawing crowds of downtown workers for its roast beef, grilled cheese, gyros, avocado and chicken tenders and other luncheon specials. Naturally, we tested the restaurant by ordering a Denver omelet. It was *huge*, filled with the requisite diced ham and green peppers and laden over with melted cheese. The heavy-duty omelet was accompanied by a tasty pile of skins-on French fried potatoes.

2 **THE BEST SUNDAY BRUNCH: Baby Doe's Matchless Mine** • *2520 W. 23rd Ave.; (303) 433-3386. American; full bar service. Brunch Sundays 10 to 2, lunch weekdays and dinner nightly. Major credit cards; $$. GETTING THERE: Take exit 211 from I-25 north of downtown and go left onto Twenty-third; it's immediately on the left.*

This place is a rustic kick. Roundly ignored by other travel writers, who apparently lack our sense of humor, Baby Doe's is a big, rambling, barnboard frontier museum thinly disguised as a restaurant. Although it's designed like a mining operation and stamp mill, complete with a mockup mine shaft entrance, it's all pretend. The real Matchless Mine was in Leadville, where Horace A.W. Tabor and his young wife Baby Doe made their fortune in silver. (See Chapter Thirteen, pages 206 and 208.) However, it's fun to dine among the museum relics in one of the many dining rooms and enjoy views—sliced horizontally by the freeway—across to the Denver skyline. In addition to basic Western grub for lunch and dinner, Baby Doe serves the most complete Sunday brunch in town—a spread that equals those of Las Vegas casino resorts. It includes assorted salads, crab legs and shrimp, breads, a large desert section, the full range of breakfast fare plus hot entrées such as chicken cacciatore, beef stew, swordfish and vegetable lasagna.

3 **THE BEST DELI CAFÉ: Market on Larimer Square** • *1445 Larimer St.; (303) 534-5140. Deli fare; wine and beer. Breakfast through dinner daily. Major credit cards; $. GETTING THERE: This deli delight is between Fourteenth and Fifteenth streets.*

Although cleverly disguised as a deli, the Market is more of a café and one of Denver's most popular eating and greeting places. Scores of tables crowd into a handsome old brick building and spill out onto the street, where happy diners nosh on muffins, bagels, croissants, blintzes, lox, salads, sandwiches, soups, pastries and tarts. Display counters and shelves are lined with obligatory deli items such as olive oil, jars of dry pasta, bulk teas and spicy specialty foods. The Market offers a good selection of cheeses, spiced meats and prepared salads, along with designer coffees and interesting coffee blends. If your tooth is sweet, check out the display case of caramel chocolate myrtles, sweet pretzel sticks and truffles.

4 **THE BEST BURGERS** ● There are two kinds of burgers in and about Denver—beef and buffalo, so this is a dual listing. Colorado is the home where the buffalo still roam, mostly on ranches that supply meat to restaurants and markets. Although buffalo originally were wild—as we all were—the meat doesn't have that strong gamy taste. It is in fact rather mild, so order your hamburger medium rare or it'll be rather chewy and tasteless. If it's properly cooked, you can detect the slightest hint of game flavor. Overdone, it has the flavor of a sautéed artgum eraser. Buffalo is much leaner than beef, about ninety-seven percent fat free, and it's lower in cholesterol. Of course it's the fat that gives beef burgers their flavor. The result: buffalo burgers are healthier; beef burgers are tastier. And the winners are:

BUFFALO BURGERS: Denver Buffalo Company ● *1109 Lincoln St.; (303) 832-0880. Full bar service. Lunch and dinner daily. (www.denverbuffalocompany.com) GETTING THERE: It's at the corner of Lincoln and Eleventh Avenue, just south of downtown. Take one-way Broadway south and then cross over to Lincoln.*

The company that's trying to make buffalo "the meat of the Twenty-first century" serves the best buffalo burgers in town. Which is no surprise, since it probably sells more buffalo meat than all other outlets combined. This is no hamburger joint; it's a first class restaurant with a connecting Buffalo Express Deli, a fresh meat market and a Western-theme gift shop. Patrons are greeted by a bronze buffalo out front and—rather corny—a mannequin of a buffalo hunter and his faithful Indian companion near the maitre 'd desk. A stuffed buffalo stands guard between the restaurant and deli. Otherwise, the décor is rather nicely done and all reminiscent of the Old West.

The buffalo burger is primarily a luncheon feature here. It doesn't even appear on the dinner menu, which focuses on assorted buffalo steaks, cow steaks, plus pasta, fresh fish, chicken and prairie oysters if you dare. However, you can get a burger in the evening if you ask nicely. And ask for it medium rare to capture what little flavor this rather lean meat offers. The burger is huge—sufficient for two. It arrives on a toasted sesame seed bun with lettuce, tomato and red onion slices on the side, along with a generous portion of excellent seasoned thick-cut fries.

Meanwhile, back at the buffalo ranch, will this become the meat of the Millennium? Not unless producers can lower their prices. Filets at the company's meat market were more than $25 a pound and tenderloin topped $20 when we last window-shopped the meat case. "They're expensive to raise," our waitress explained, "because they're free range. We don't use growth hormones or feedlots." Obviously, prices were cheaper before we white folks came, when the range really was free. There were several million buffalo on the hoof, instead of about 80,000 on ranches and game preserves.

BEEF BURGERS: Denver Chop House and Brewery ● *1735 Nineteenth St.; (303) 296-0800. Full bar service. Lunch and dinner daily. Major credit cards. GETTING THERE: It's in the old Union Pacific Building at the corner of Nineteenth and Wynkoop, immediately north of downtown.*

We have found, in researching this and other guidebooks, that places specializing in hamburgers don't usually serve the best ones. They're either too budget-minded or they become preoccupied with gadget burgers with avocado and other strange toppings. The best straightforward beefburger we found in town was at the Denver Chop House. Since this firm specializes in steak, it follows that the kitchen is capable of producing a first-rate burger. Its Chop House Burger is made of ground chuck, charbroiled with light seasoning and a bit of olive oil. It's served on a toasted onion roll, accompanied by excellent skins-on thick-cut fries. A wedge of dill pickle, plus lettuce, tomato and a red onion slice are served on the side to avoid cooling the meat before your first bite. And it will take many bites to finish it, for this thing is *huge*.

5 **THE BEST PIZZA PARLOR: Wazee Lounge and Supper Club** ● *1600 Fifteenth St.; (303) 623-9518. Full bar service. Lunch through late evening daily; $. GETTING THERE: It's in LoDo at the corner of Fifteenth and Wazee.*

Housed in old LoDo brick, the Wazee is really more of a bar than a lounge or supper club and it's not really a pizza parlor, yet it serves the best pizza in town. These are not designer pizzas with cute names and curious ingredients. They're straightforward pizza pies built to your specs. The most adventurous variety available is the Pacific Rim with ham and pineapple. Regular patrons generally go for the more conventional pepperoni-ham-sausage combo, which arrives piled high with goodies in a rich sauce over a crunchy crust. Designate your choice of toppings, then order a drink and wait a bit, since preparation from scratch takes time.

6 *THE BEST SEAFOOD RESTAURANT: McCormick's Fish House & Bar* • *In the Oxford Hotel at 1659 Wazee St.; (303) 825-1107. Full bar service. Lunch weekdays, dinner nightly and Sunday brunch. Major credit cards; $$ to $$$. GETTING THERE: McCormick's is in LoDo, on the corner of Wazee and Seventeenth Street.*

The Northwest's most famous fish house has come to Denver and brought with it an imposing variety of fresh seafood. The list is so long that it contains some sea creatures we've never heard of. The daily-changing menu offers more than a dozen freshly flown-in entrées such as Atlantic salmon, trout, halibut, jumbo shrimp and less common selections like monkfish, monchong and tombo. Most are simply prepared—lightly grilled in lemon butter, although you can order more contemporary entrées with sun-dried tomatoes, basil pesto or salsa. Those who aren't fans of finny things can order New Zealand lamb, thick pork chops, shiitake-crusted chicken or several steaks. All of this is served in an attractive environment of brick walls, dark wood wainscotting, brass rod café curtains, Tiffany style chandeliers and coffered ceilings. It's an extensive complex, with two large dining rooms.

7 *THE BEST STEAK HOUSE: Morton's of Chicago* • *1710 Wynkoop St.; (303) 825-3353. Full bar service. Dinner nightly. Major credit cards; $$$ to $$$$. GETTING THERE: Morton's is in LoDo, opposite Union Station.*

Most Morton's are regarded as clubby places, although the Denver version has rather soft touches, with light walls accented by Leroy Neiman artwork and framed photos of stars and regular patrons. With its white nappery and candle-lit tables, it makes our list as one of the Mile High City's most romantic restaurants; Chapter Eight, page 131. A cozy mahogany bar off the main dining room has more of a typical Morton's men's club look. In this era of raspberry puree, sun-dried tomatoes and air-dried beef, the Morton fare is simple, straightforward and perfectly prepared. And it is not inexpensive, since perfection has its price. Of course it's primarily a steak house, so beefeaters can choose filet mignon, porterhouse, New York strip, ribeye or a spicier Cajun ribeye. Other offerings on the rather brief menu include veal chops, broiled swordfish steak, lamb chops, whole baked Maine lobster and Chicken Christopher in garlic *beurre blanc* sauce.

8 *THE BEST PAN-ASIAN RESTAURANT: Roy's Cherry Creek* • *Cherry Creek Shopping Center, 3000 E. First Ave.; (303) 333-9300. (www.roysrestaurant.com) Full bar service. Lunch and dinner daily. Major credit cards; $$ to $$$. GETTING THERE: Follow Speer Boulevard southeast three miles along Cherry Creek; it blends into First Avenue, which crosses the front of the shopping center.*

One of a growing number of signature chefs to join Denver's dining scene, Roy Yamaguchi opened his first restaurant in Honolulu in 1988. He blends Japanese, Thai, Chinese, Polynesian French and Italian fare into a kind of tropical polyglot that some foodies call Pacific Rim or Pan-Asian fare. His restaurants are spreading as quickly as a *tsunami* and he has won an impressive number of culinary awards. The James Beard Foundation picked him as "Best Chef in the Pacific & Northwest" in 1993, his Honolulu restaurant received Hawaii's highest Gault Millau rating and Roy's Kahana Bar & Grill was picked as Maui's most popular restaurant by the Zagat Survey.

Since Denver is a long way from the Orient and the town is rather weak on creative Asian fare, Roy's arrival should be welcome news to local food enthusiasts. Some of examples of his fare at Cherry Creek are lemon grass chicken breast, Mongolian grilled rack of lamb, blackened ahi with soy mustard butter sauce, and roasted banana pork loin. Should you choose to dine inside, you'll find a pleasing space with a light wood modern Japanese look.

9 **THE BEST TOURIST CAFÉ: Hard Rock Café** • *500 Sixteenth Street Mall; (303) 623-3191. American; full bar service. Lunch and dinner daily. Major credit cards; $ to $$. GETTING THERE: It's on the mall near Glenarm Place.*

When cafés Hard Rock were first created several decades ago, they were the rage of teenyboppers, who lined up to admire the rock star memorabilia, listen to raucous rock blasting from speakers the size of mini-vans and eat hamburgers and babyback ribs. They've become more of a tourist staple of late. Although they still appeal mostly to the younger set, it's common to see thirty-somethings proudly wearing their Hard Rock T-shirts from Toledo, Tokyo or Denver. We suspect the cafés sell more logo items from their souvenir shops than burger patties from their grills. In fact the Denver Hard Rock logo shop keeps longer hours than the restaurant. When you do step inside the café, you'll see that the rock décor has been somewhat localized, with lots of memorabilia collected by Denver concert promoter Barry Fey. You'll also find that the Hard Rock menu has changed to appeal to its broader audience. In addition to the usual burgers, it offers more contemporary fare such as grilled marinated chicken breast, jambalaya penne pasta and Caribbean pork tenderloin.

10 **THE BEST WESTERN STYLE RESTAURANT: Buckhorn Exchange** • *1000 Osage St.; (303) 534-9505. Full bar service. Lunch weekdays; dinner nightly. Major credit cards; $$ to $$$. GETTING THERE: From downtown, go west on Colfax and then south (left) on Osage just before you reach a viaduct. Follow Osage about half a mile to Tenth.*

Is it a saloon, a restaurant or an old West museum? Certainly. Dating from 1893, the Buckhorn is Colorado's oldest saloon. It's also a restaurant specializing in wild game and it's something of a museum, a-clutter with yesterday artifacts and more than 500 game trophies. It is said that some of the them date back to the turn of the last century, when original owner Shorty Zeitz guided hunting parties, including one hosted by Teddy Roosevelt. Wild game—not the same—is found on the menu as well. The Buckhorn specializes in farm-raised buffalo, elk, quail and duck. If you want to step into a very interesting dish, try the rattlesnake with chipotle pepper cream cheese. Is it farm-raised? Not on my farm, Charlie! (Should you wonder, rattlesnake tastes a bit like chicken.) For more on the museum aspects of the Buckhorn, see Chapter Two, page 30.

DINING AL FRESCO:
THE TEN BEST OUTDOOR CAFÉS

Since it doesn't rain much and heat lamps drive away the chill, *al fresco* dining is quite popular in the Mile High City. Most of the open air dining venues are along the Sixteenth Street Mall downtown and most of the dining happens at noon when clerks and office workers head for their favorite cafés.

1 *MARLOWE'S* • *501 Sixteenth Street Mall at Glenarm. American; full bar service. Lunch and dinner Monday-Saturday, dinner only Sunday. Major credit cards; $$ to $$$.*

A recent *Denver Post* poll named Marlowe's as the city's best overall restaurant. We won't go *that* far, although we will agree with a 1999 Zagat Survey comment: *The best sidewalk dining viewing in Denver.* Marlowe's has been a see-and-be-seen place for several decades; it has survived the deterioration of downtown to thrive as Sixteenth Street Mall's best sidewalk restaurant. Marlowe's is appealing indoors as well, with a typical wood and brass trim steak and chop house look. A large bar suggests that this is a serious drinking establishment, and it's noted particularly for its martinis and good beer selection. The menu is American eclectic, bouncing from buffalo burgers to contemporary fare such as chicken chipotle pasta and almond-crusted salmon. It also offers several steaks and it was named one of America's top ten steak houses by an obscure source—*Steakout*, the newsletter of the American Beef Lovers Association.

2 *BRAVO!* • *In the Adam's Mark Hotel at 1550 N. Court Place; (303) 893-3333. (www.adamsmark.com) Italian; full bar service. Lunch and dinner daily. Major credit cards; $$$. GETTING THERE: The hotel* *is on the southeastern edge of downtown between Court and Tremont; the restaurant fronts on the Sixteenth Street Mall.*

Although many restaurants spill onto the Sixteenth Street Mall, this is one of the few linked to a hotel. It can be your choice if you like both *al fresco* dining and Italian food. The menu features such traditional fare as chicken breast saltimbocca layered with prosciutto, veal scaloppine piccata, veal osso buco and assorted pastas. The kitchen also departs from tradition to create entrées such as pork chops with caramelized pear, and tenderloin of beef with roasted garlic mashed potatoes.

3 *FADÓ IRISH PUB* • *1735 Nineteenth St.; (303) 297-0066. Irish; full bar service. Lunch through dinner daily. Major credit cards; $$. GETTING THERE: Fadó is in the old Union Pacific building between Nineteenth and Coors Field, immediately north of downtown.*

This popular drinking establishment has a shaded outdoor deck off traffic-free Wynkoop Plaza, so patrons are spared auto noise and exhaust. And they have a nice view of LoDo and downtown highrises just beyond. Fadó is a handy pre-game stop; you can walk from here to Coors Field faster than you can slam back a Guinness Stout. The fare is typical for an Irish pub, including corned beef and cabbage and Irish stew, plus some Americanized dishes. We also chose this as Denver's best Irish restaurant (above, page 67) and one of its Ten Best drinking establishments (Chapter Seven, page 112).

4 *EL NOA NOA RESTAURANT* • *722 Santa Fe Drive; (303) 623-9968. Mexican; full bar service. Breakfast through dinner daily. Major credit cards; $ to $$. GETTING THERE: It's near the corner of Seventh Avenue. Santa Fe is one-way northbound, so to reach the area from downtown, go south on Klamath from Colfax Avenue. After several blocks, go left on Seventh to Santa Fe.*

This popular restaurant's brick-walled, landscaped garden patio provides a pleasant refuge for diners in Denver's Hispanic district. It's one of the city's few restaurants with an outdoor dining area that's completely sheltered from the street. Cheerful fountains and lush vegetation add nice touches. For more, see the Ten Best Hispanic restaurant list above, on page 63.

5 *PALOMINO EURO BISTRO* • *1515 Arapahoe Street on the Sixteenth Street Mall; (303) 534-7800. Mediterranean-American; full bar service. Lunch and dinner daily. Major credit cards; $$ to $$$.*

A cool curving design with warm colors is the trademark of this deliberately *chic* restaurant, which originated in Seattle and is spreading to other major cities. Denver's version also has spread onto the Six-

teenth Street Mall. Sitting under the sun, you can order curiously creative fare such as grilled chicken breast with apricot cilantro sauce,
honey peppercorn chicken, paella roast garlic prawns and designer pizzas. Applewood rotisserie roasting is a specialty here. Should you
choose to dine within, you'll be greeted by orange, salmon, hot pink
and other Indian summer colors, contrasted by black, white and rose
marble table tops.

6 PARAMOUNT CAFÉ • 511 Sixteenth Street Mall between
*Glenarm and Welton; (303) 893-2000. American; full bar service. Lunch
and through late evening daily. MC/VISA; $ to $$.*

Next door to Marlowe's, the Paramount has a similar outdoor dining area, aided and abetted by a canopy and heat lamps. In menu,
décor and attitude, it appeals more to a younger crowd, with a menu
featuring hamburgers, buffalo burgers, quesadillas, chicken fingers
and such. A specialty here is Kentucky bourbon pecan pie. The Paramount also is popular with after-theater crowds since the kitchen is
open late and it's just around the corner from the splendidly restored
Paramount Theater. In fact, this was the theater's original entrance,
and the terrazzo tile floor and handcrafted gilt work are still in place.

7 PIZZA COLÓRES • Fifteenth and Larimer in Writer Square;
*(303) 534-6844. Italian; wine and beer. Lunch and dinner daily. Major
credit cards; $ to $$.*

While Bravo! (listed above) features more elaborate Italian fare,
Pizza Colóres should be your choice if you seek something simple under the sun. This small café has a large *al fresco* seating area in Writer
Square, removed from the traffic of surrounding streets. It features a
good choice of three-cheese pizzas, plus the usual pastas, and chicken
or veal Parmigiana and a rather good vegetarian lasagna.

8 RIALTO CAFÉ • 934 Sixteenth Street Mall (Curtis); (303)
*983-2233. American-Mediterranean; full bar service. Lunch through din-
ner daily plus weekend brunch. Major credit cards; $$ to $$$.*

Historic in name—it occupies the site of the old Rialto Theater—
but modern in menu, this locally popular restaurant spills onto the pedestrian mall when weather permits. It's a gathering spot for business
lunches and pre-theater crowds. The Rialto is adjacent to the Downtown Courtyard by Marriott and can be reached through its lobby, although it's not part of the hotel operation. It serves creative American
fare with Mediterranean accents, such as grilled salmon with ginger
chutney, spicy chicken breasts, and tuna with white beans, plus sturdy
American steaks and some good pastas. The large, handsome bar is a
late night hangout for downtowners, often featuring live music.

9 ROY'S CHERRY CREEK • *Cherry Creek Shopping Center at 3000 E. First Ave.; (303) 333-9300. Polynesian eclectic; full bar service. Lunch and dinner daily. Major credit cards; $$ to $$$. GETTING THERE: From downtown, follow Speer Boulevard southeast about three miles along Cherry Creek; it blends into First Avenue, which crosses the front of the center. Roy's is just to the right of the valet entrance.*

The view isn't much—mostly of a parking lot, although Roy's outdoor dining patio just off the entrance to Cherry Creek Shopping Center is pleasant and the food is excellent if you like fare with tropical accents. It's a good place for people watching as shoppers hurry in with their credit cards and hurry away with their treasures. For more on Roys, see page 73.

10 WILLIE G'S • *1585 Lawrence Street on the Sixteenth Street Mall; (303) 575-9000. Seafood and steaks; full bar service. Lunch weekdays and dinner nightly. Major credit cards; $$$.*

Although this is one of our favorite outdoor dining venues, you may be tempted to nosh within and enjoy the old fashioned, clubby dark wood interior, with its wainscotting and mounted fish trophies. If you choose to dine *al fresco*, several tables are alongside the Sixteenth Street Mall. Willie G's menu is as pleasantly old fashioned as interior look. Don't expect raspberry purée, sun-dried tomatoes or air-dried beef. (Or is it the other way around?) The menu is rather straightforward, offering simply prepared fresh fish, prime rib and a good selection of steaks. The mixed seafood grill—available either fried or broiled—is one of our favorites. Willie also offers a few pastas.

I wasn't born in a log cabin, but my family moved to one as soon as they could afford it.
— **Melville D. Landon**

Chapter four

PROUD PAUPERS
A BUDGET GUIDE

Denver is a relatively inexpensive vacation destination when compared with most other major American cities. Of course, a downtown hotel room will cost $100 or more a night and you can easily go through another $100 for dinner for two at a designer diner. However, you also can find more modest-priced lodgings—usually motels at freeway interchanges or in suburban communities. And Denver has scores of moderately priced restaurants.

This chapter is for folks on a budget, who are seeking the *really* inexpensive places to play, dine and sleep. It begins with freebies—the city's Ten Best attractions that cost not a penny. We aren't just talking about public parks or pathways.

FRUGAL FUN:
THE TEN BEST FREE ATTRACTIONS

You already will have encountered some of these attractions in Chapter Two. Other Ten Best freebies are a mixed bag, ranging from some of the Mile High City's more interesting parks to our favorite creekside walk. The choices also include next-door Golden.

☺ *KID STUFF:* The little grinning guy indicates attractions that are of particular interest to pre-teens.

79

1 CONFLUENCE PARK AREA • At the confluence of the South Platte River and Cherry Creek just northwest of the city center. GETTING THERE: Take Fifteenth Avenue from downtown and find a place to park on either side of the river. ☺

More than any other landmark, Confluence Park personifies Denver, for it is both the city's historical and recreational focal point. The first two settlements that became Denver—Auraria and Denver City—were established near here, on opposite banks of Cherry Creek. However, its primary appeal is more contemporary than historic. This merger of the South Platte and Cherry Creek is one of the city's favorite gathering places. Elements of the park are on both sides of the river, and they hug the banks of the creek.

Folks come here to picnic, snooze on the grassy slopes and play in the two streams. Kayakers splash down a brief brace of rapids created by a diversion dam in the river; kids and their dogs wade in the shallows of the creek. The city's two most popular recreational paths—Cherry Creek Greenway and the South Platte River Trail—converge here, so it's a gathering spot for cyclists, walkers and skaters. The views from here are grand—of the Denver Skyline, Elitch Gardens and the distant Rockies. The new REI Denver Flagship Store sits just above the park and its Starbucks outdoor deck is a fine spot for sitting and enjoying the views. The park is within walking distance of the Ocean Journey aquarium, Children's Museum of Denver and LoDo with its many shops and restaurants.

2 CHERRY CREEK GREENWAY • From Confluence Park southeast to Cherry Creek Reservoir. GETTING THERE: See above.

If you enjoy hanging out at Confluence Park, a natural next step—many steps, in fact—is to stroll along the Cherry Creek Greenway. Although it brushes past the edge of downtown, it's as close to peaceful as urban gets, since the path and creek are sunk about fifteen feet below street level. The path follows both banks in the lower part of the creek, separating cyclists and skaters from walkers. Occasional benches along the way invite you to relax and stare idly into the slow-flowing stream.

If you'd like to explore LoDo or the Sixteenth Street Mall, the greenway provides pleasant access. Walk about half a mile, then exit to street level at a creekside plaza marked by several Southwest native graphic designs; it's beside the urban campus of the University of Colorado at Denver. You'll emerge onto Larimer Street, which forms the border between LoDo and the downtown highrise area. Sixteenth Street Mall is a short walk away. If you're feeling ambitious, the creek provides a sheltered path all the way to Cherry Creek Shopping Center, about four miles from Confluence Park. It continues beyond to Cherry Creek Reservoir State Park, about twelve miles away, although that's more of a bike run than a walk. For more on the pathway, see Chapter Ten, pages 149 and 155.

3 **CITY PARK** • *Just east of downtown. GETTING THERE: Go east on Colfax Avenue about 2.5 miles to Colorado Boulevard, turn north (left) for half a mile then turn left again into the park on Montview Boulevard or 22nd Avenue.* ☺

Established in 1881, this is one of Denver's largest, oldest and most versatile public parks. It's home to the Denver Zoo and Denver Museum of Nature and Science. They have admission fees of course. However, it costs nothing to walk or bike the park's miles of paths and traffic-free roads, enjoy a picnic beneath century old trees, follow an asphalt path around Ferrill Lake and poke about the recently restored City Park Pavilion. For a small fee, you can rent a paddleboat and play on the lake. Other park features include tennis courts, horseshoe pits and a rose garden. In summer, free public concerts are presented at a bandstand on Ferrill Lake's west shore.

4 **COLORADO SCHOOL OF MINES GEOLOGY MUSEUM** • *Sixteenth and Maple on the school campus; (303) 273-3823. Daily 9 to 4 Monday-Saturday and 1 to 4 Sunday during the school year; closed Sunday in summer. GETTING THERE: See directions to Golden and the geology museum in Chapter Two, page 50.*

This is the best free museum in the greater Denver are and one of the best in the state. Don't be put off by the scholarly name. This isn't a commonplace collegiate collection of rocks. It's a nicely done museum featuring some brilliant gem and minerals, mining gear, fossils and other geologic exhibits from around the world. For more, see Chapter Two, page 50.

5 **COLORADO STATE CAPITOL & CAPITOL DOME MUSEUM** • *200 E. Colfax Ave.; (303) 866-2604. (www.state.co.us) Open weekdays 7 to 5:30; free tours every forty-five minutes from 9 to 2:30. Dome open 7 to 3:30. GETTING THERE: The capitol is just southeast of downtown, between Lincoln and Grant streets. To pick up a visitor's pamphlet or to take a tour, use the north entrance at Colfax and Sherman; a visitor information desk is just inside.* ☺

Most things are free here, except for the tax laws passed by Colorado's legislators. You can take free public tours or stroll about the handsome marble-walled capitol on your own, admiring exhibits and statuary. Then climb ninety-six steps up to the dome for a grand view of the city. Pause part way for a look at the unusual Capitol Dome Museum, which has exhibits on the construction of this statehouse. For more on the capitol and its museum, refer to Chapter Two, pages 23 and 37.

6 *COORS BREWERY TOUR* • *Thirteenth and Ford streets, Golden; (303) 277-BEER. (www.coors.com) Monday-Saturday 10 to 4; closed Sunday. Tours depart every few minutes. GETTING THERE: See directions to Golden and the Coors Brewery in Chapter Two, page 48.*

Not only is this tour of the world's largest brewery free; you'll also get free drinks. Adults can sip samples of Coors beers and kids are offered gratis soft drinks.

7 *DENVER MINT TOUR* • *West Colfax at Cherokee St.; (303) 405-4761. (www.usmint.treas.gov) Weekdays 8 to 2:45; half-hour tours depart every twenty minutes. GETTING THERE: The Mint is just south of downtown and west of Civic Center Park, and the visitor entrance is on Cherokee Street. No cameras are allowed inside. The tour is particularly popular in summer; the shortest lines are early in the morning.*

See how the Denver Mint stamps out fifty-two million coins every twenty-four hours in this fortress-like building. This facility produces half of America's coin supply, with the other half coming from the Philadelphia Mint. Curiously, sixty percent of the coins are pennies, although you can't get much for a penny these days. For more details on the tour, see Chapter Two, page 42.

8 *LOOKOUT MOUNTAIN AND BUFFALO BILL'S GRAVE* • ***Nature Center*** *and* ***Boettcher Mansion*** *at 900 Colorow Road, Golden; (303) 526-0594; (www.mansion.co.jefferson.co.us) Nature Center open Tuesday-Sunday 10 to 4. Mansion open Monday-Friday 8 to 5; closed to the public during special events.* ***Buffalo Bill Grave and Museum*** *is just beyond on Lookout Mountain Road; (303) 526-0747. Museum open daily 9 to 5 May through October and Tuesday-Sunday 9 to 4 the rest of the year.*
GETTING THERE: Head west from Denver on I-70 for about twenty miles, take exit 256 and follow signs uphill. You'll first fork to the left for the nature center, then signs will direct you from there to Buffalo Bill's Grave and Museum. ☺

There's much to see and explore on Lookout Mountain, a thickly wooded peak rising above Golden and Denver, and many of its attractions are free. The fine Lookout Mountain Nature Center has exhibits on the area's flora and fauna, and the historic Boettcher Mansion can be toured when it isn't booked for special events. Several hiking trails weave through the area, and one leads through the woods to the Buffalo Bill Museum and grave. Or you can drive there. There's a small admission fee for the museum, although it costs nothing to visit the grave site or explore the historic Pahaska Tepee, which was the site of the original museum.

9 **MUSEUM OF OUTDOOR ARTS** • *7600 E. Orchard Rd., Room 160-N, Englewood (Greenwood Village); (303) 741-3609. (www.fine-art.com/museum/moa.html) Outdoor art may be viewed any time; office open weekdays 8:30 to 6; free. GETTING THERE: Go twelve miles south on I-25 and take East Orchard Road (exit 198) west. After less than a mile, pass through a traffic light at Greenwood Plaza Boulevard and take the next left into Harlequin Plaza. Park in the north lot and you'll find the museum office in an adjacent modern glass office building.*

This "museum" is a collection of fine bronzes dispersed through several office parks in Englewood south of Denver. You can pick up a locator map at the museum office (see above), them prowl about on your own. Particularly delightful are several life-sized bronzes of *Alice in Wonderland* characters. For specifics, see Chapter Two, page 35.

10 **RED ROCKS PARK & AMPHITHEATRE** • *12700 W. Alameda Parkway, Morrison; (303) 697-8935 for the park and trading post and (303) 640-2637 for the amphitheatre. Trading post open daily 9 to 5:30. (www.red-rocks.com) GETTING THERE: See directions in Chapter Two, page 51.* ☺

It costs nothing to explore this dramatically situated showplace between performances. It's part of a Denver City and County Park, set among a wonderland of sculpted red rocks and offering grand views of the Denver Basin and Great Plains beyond. In addition to the imposing 9,000-seat amphitheatre, the park has several miles of hiking trails, an historic trading post and several marked geological sites.

THE TEN BEST CHEAP ATTRACTIONS

A five dollar bill doesn't buy much these days, although five dollars or less will get you into some of Denver's better attractions. Here are our favorites, with page references to their main listings, which all are in Chapter Two.

1 **COLORADO HISTORY MUSEUM** • *1300 Broadway; (303) 866-3682. (www.coloradohistory.org) Monday-Saturday 10 to 4:30 and Sunday noon to 4:30. GETTING THERE: The museum is just below the Civic Center on the southeast side of downtown, corner of Thirteenth and Broadway.*

One of Colorado's best museums, it relates the story of the state and the Mile High City with very creative exhibits, including a Colorado timeline, large exhibit on "real" cowboys and a tabletop model of 1860 Denver. And it's a bargain to boot. See page 24 for details.

2 ASTOR HOUSE MUSEUM • *822 Twelfth Street at the corner of Arapahoe, Golden; (303) 278-3557. (WEB: www.web-span.com/fast-part/astorhouse.html) Tuesday-Saturday 10 to 4:30.*

This carefully restored small boarding house is perhaps the area's best small museum. See page 49 for details and directions.

3 BLACK AMERICAN WEST MUSEUM & HERITAGE CENTER • *3901 California St.; (303) 292-2566. (WEB: www.coax.net/people/lw/bawmus.html) Daily from 10 to 5 May through September; Wednesday-Friday 10 to 2 and Saturday-Sunday noon to 5 the rest of the year. GETTING THERE: From downtown, follow one-way Stout Street about a mile northeast, turn right onto 31st and then right again onto California. The museum is at the corner, in a three-story brick house.*

This interesting little archive tells you something you never learned from those old Roy Rogers movies—about a third of America's cowboys were Black. Another third were Hispanic, so Roy and Dale were minorities. See Chapter Two, page 32.

4 BUFFALO BILL MUSEUM • *Lookout Mountain Road, Golden; (303) 526-0747. Daily 9 to 5 May through October and Tuesday-Sunday 9 to 4 the rest of the year. GETTING THERE: Head west from Denver on I-70 for about twenty miles, take exit 256 and follow signs up-hill.* ☺

This professionally done museum dedicated to the great showman of the West is part of a Denver city and county park, with just a token admission price. See Chapter Two, page 53.

5 COLORADO RAILROAD MUSEUM • *17155 W. 44th Ave., Golden; (303) 279-4591. (www.crm.org) Daily 9 to 5 (until 6 June through August). Steam train runs on weekends from June through September.* ☺

This extensive railroad exhibit includes lots of choo-choos, railroading memorabilia and an elaborate model train layout. See page 47 for details and directions.

6 DENVER ART MUSEUM • *100 W. Fourteenth Avenue Parkway; (303) 640-4433. (www.denvermuseum.com) Tuesday-Saturday 10* to 5 (until 9 Wednesday), Sunday noon to 5; closed Monday. Free to Colorado residents on Saturdays. Extra fees for some special exhibits. GETTING THERE: The museum is just below Civic Center Park near downtown, at the corner of Bannock between Thirteenth and Fourteenth, beside the Denver Public Library.

One of the great art museums of the West isn't just a building stuffed with paintings and statues. It features artifacts from cultures around the world, including America's best native peoples exhibit. See page 25.

7 DENVER BOTANIC GARDENS • 909 York St.; (303) 331-4000. (www.botanicgardens.org) Wednesday-Friday 9 to 5 and Saturday-Tuesday 9 to 8 from May through September; then daily 9 to 5 the rest of the year. GETTING THERE: Go east from downtown about 1.5 miles on Colfax Avenue, then south half a mile on York Street.

It doesn't cost much to stop and smell the flowers at this extensive botanical complex and tropic conservatory. See page 25.

8 FOUR MILE HISTORIC PARK • 715 S. Forest St.; (303) 399-1859. Wednesday-Friday noon to 4 and weekends 10 to 4 April through September, then weekends only noon to 4 the rest of the year. GETTING THERE: Go southeast from downtown on Speer Boulevard, which blends into First Avenue after about 2.5 miles. Follow it 1.5 miles east to Colorado Boulevard, go south less than a mile to Leetsdale (Highway 83) and turn left. Go southeast just under a mile to Forest Street, go right (south) a few blocks and then right again onto Exposition. ☺

One of Denver's earliest roadhouses and homes has been preserved in this large historic park. See page 29.

9 MOLLY BROWN HOUSE MUSEUM • 1340 Pennsylvania St.; (303) 832-4092. (www.mollybrown.org) Monday-Saturday 10 to 4 and Sunday noon to 4 from June through August; closed Mondays the rest of the year. GETTING THERE: The home is between Thirteenth and Fourteenth avenues, just southeast of downtown. Tour tickets are sold in a gift shop behind the main house.

At this nicely restored mini-mansion, you'll learn much of the real truth about Denver's most misunderstood—and even mis-named—heroine. See page 34.

10 WINGS OVER THE ROCKIES AIR & SPACE MUSEUM • Academy Boulevard near Rampart Way.; (303) 360-5360. (www.dimension-al.com/~worm) Monday-Saturday 10 to 5 and Sunday noon to 5 mid-May through mid-September; closes at 4 the rest of *the year. GETTING THERE: Head east on Colfax Avenue about 2.5 miles, then go south on Monaco two miles and east (left) on Alameda. After half a mile, you'll pass through a traffic signal at Quebec Street; continue east briefly and you'll enter a roundabout. Spin off to the north onto Rampart Way and you'll see the museum's hangar ahead; turn right for the parking area.* ☺

It costs very little to see some of the U.S. Air Force's most unusual aircraft. The museum also has a rather uncommon exhibit—a replica of one of the rooms of President Dwight D. Eisenhower's summer White House; see page 29.

THE TEN BEST CHEAP EATS

We define "cheap eats" as places where you can get a filling entrée and at least one side dish—soup or salad—for less than $7.50. We're talking about dinner, not a light lunch. We don't include the popular franchise fast food joints, despite the fact that most of them can fill you up with greasy burgers and over-salted fries for well under our price ceiling. Eating at MacDonald's or Taco Bell isn't a dining experience; these places are more into marketing than providing healthy food for their customers. (I've never cared much for plastic dinosaurs or Beanie Babies with my meal.) Actually, three of our choices are fast-food places, although they're locally based and they're more concerned with good inexpensive food that promotional gimmickry.

Most of our Ten Best selections are ethnic—particularly Asian or Mexican. Denver doesn't have a large Oriental community, although there are several inexpensive Asian cafés—mostly Vietnamese—southwest of downtown on Federal Boulevard between Alameda and Mississippi. This isn't a concentrated Asian community, but a thin mix of Vietnamese and Mexican restaurants mingled with assorted other businesses. The largest concentration of Asian businesses—Vietnamese and Chinese—is in Far East Center at Federal and Alameda. Denver's busiest Mexican community is on Santa Fe Drive between Sixth and Fourteenth avenues. Santa Fe was Denver's original north-south highway.

1 RICHARD LEE NOODLE HOUSE • *472 S. Federal Blvd.; (303) 937-2946. Vietnamese, Thai and Chinese; no alcohol. Lunch and dinner daily except Tuesday; opens at mid-morning on weekends. MC/VISA. GETTING THERE: Go west on Colfax about 1.5 miles, then south on Federal just over two miles. Lees is just south of Alameda Avenue, on the left between Alaska Place and Virginia Avenue.*

Local food critics, "best of Denver" lists and the Zagat guide have all raved about the excellent food quality and low prices at Richard Lee. Yet this family restaurant takes its laurels modestly, remaining in a small, rather obscure building along Federal Boulevard's "Asian row."

The interior, done in green with a few Asian decorations, is more cheerful than most small family cafés, yet it remains rather austere. All the energy here apparently goes into the kitchen, from which numerous savory dishes emerge. When we last dined here, nearly every item on the large menu was $5. A few were a quarter less; some were fifty cents more. That left plenty of room in our $7.50 budget for drinks or a dessert—or both, if you just have tea. Lee specializes in huge bowls of noodle soup generously laced with fresh vegetables and meat, fowl or fish. They come in many nationalities, covering most of the Asian side of the globe. Some examples are roast duck with egg noodles, beef stew in tomato sauce with rice noodles, and five spice duck leg with thick noodles.

2 *CHINA JADE SEAFOOD RESTAURANT* • *375 S. Federal Blvd.; (303) 935-0033. Chinese. Lunch and dinner daily. MC/VISA, AMEX. GETTING THERE: It's in the Far East Center at Federal and Alameda. Go west on Colfax about 1.5 miles, then south on Federal for two miles. The shopping center is on the southwest corner.*

This small, simple family café specializes in seafood, which isn't particularly cheap. However, it does offer several filling one-dish meals within our price category. Try the roast duck, pork, soy sauce chicken or veggies, all served over steamed rice, and all for less than $6. Equally filling and even less expensive are several wonton and noodle soup bowls laden with various kinds of meat. China Jade also has several very inexpensive luncheon specials. And it does a brisk takeout business, in case you want to run and eat.

3 *CHIPOTLE MEXICAN GRILL* • *Several Denver area locations. Those closest to downtown are at 745 Colorado Boulevard near Eighth Avenue, (303) 333-2121; 333 E. Alameda Avenue between Logan and Grant Streets, (303) 733-1331; and 550 Broadway near Sixth Avenue, (303) 866-0725. Mexican; wine and margaritas. Lunch through dinner daily. MC/VISA; $.*

The Chipotle super burritos and special *baracoa* beef flour tortillas are large enough for a filling meal. They're so inexpensive that you can add a side such as chips and guacamole and still remain safely within our budget. Although they're takeouts, the Chipotles are rather attractive places with open kitchens, and most locations feature outdoor dining patios.

4 *CHUBBY'S* • *801 Santa Fe Drive at Eighth Avenue, (303) 755-1414; and 160 Federal Boulevard between First and Second avenues, (303) 935-2237. Mexican; no alcohol. Breakfast through early dinner Monday-Saturday; closed Sunday. MC/VISA, DISC.*

These basic walk-up diners are so inexpensive that you can order two entrées and get a very filling meal within our budget limit. They serve the usual burritos, tacos and enchiladas, plus *meneudo*. A nice feature here—both Chubby's are non-smoking.

5 *LIM'S MONGOLIAN BBQ* • *1530 Blake St.; (303) 893-1158. (www.limsbbq.com) Chinese; wine and beer. Lunch through dinner Monday-Saturday. MC/VISA. GETTING THERE: It's in LoDo between Fifteenth Street and the Sixteenth Street Mall.*

In the midst of LoDo's trendy and sometimes pricey restaurants, this combined Mongolian barbecue and Chinese café has an all-you-can-eat multi-item buffet for around $6. It also features several full meals well under our price limit, such as sesame chicken and shrimp, lemon chicken, and sweet and sour chicken, pork or shrimp. The regular Mongolian barbecue also is within our price range. For the uninitiated, diners at Mongolian Barbecues choose their ingredients, which are then stir-fried to order. The meal comes with fried or steamed rice, plus soup, egg rolls or wonton.

6 *PETE'S KITCHEN* • *1962 E. Colfax Ave.; (303) 321-3139. American; no alcohol. Breakfast through late evening daily. GETTING THERE: It's about a mile and a half east of downtown, on the corner of Colfax and Race Street. MC/VISA, AMEX.*

Housed in a small brick building, this old fashioned diner features several dinner entries within our price range, including hamburger steak, chicken fried steak and fried chicken. They're served with side dishes and a choice of soup or salad for a complete and very filling meal. A Denver fixture since 1942, it's an appealing old place with chrome-rimmed bar stools alongside a long counter with an open kitchen, plus a few booths and tables.

7 *SWIFT'S BREAKFAST HOUSE* • *932 Santa Fe Dr.; (303) 623-9743. American; no alcohol. Breakfast through late afternoon. No credit cards. GETTING THERE: Swift's occupies a small brick building between Ninth and Tenth avenues. Since Santa Fe is one-way north, take Klamath south from Colfax and shift over to Santa Fe.*

This old fashioned American diner, looking a bit out of place in the Santa Fe Hispanic district, serves some of the cheapest food in town. Although it's called a breakfast café, it also features inexpensive steaks, hamburger steaks, chili and other hefty meals through late afternoon. The best deal here is strip steak with potato, salad and toast for around $5. Swift's is a slightly weathered but well-kept café, decorated mostly with signs advertising its cheap food.

8 **QDOBA** • *Fifth and Grant, (303) 765-5878; Fifteenth and Market, (303) 629-1300; and Colorado Blvd. at Mississippi, (303) 756-3400. Mexican; beer and margaritas. Lunch and dinner daily. MC/VISA.*

Some of the local Mexican fast food franchises do a better job than many mom and pop restaurants in providing inexpensive, tasty food. Qdoba (pronounce it*cue-DOUGH-bah*) makes everything fresh daily, even its chips and guacamole. The list is short and simple—chicken burritos with pesto or molé; beef burritos; and chicken, beef or vegetarian tacos. You also can get taco salads, nachos or "naked burritos" with the ingredients in a bowl and the tortilla on the side. All entrées were less than $5 when we last noshed there, and they included cilantro rice and a choice of beans, salsa and cheese or sour cream.

9 **THÁI HIEP** • *333 S. Federal Blvd.; (303) 922-5774. Vietnamese; wine and beer. Lunch and dinner daily. Major credit cards. GETTING THERE: Go west on Colfax Avenue about two miles to Federal, turn left and go south to Alameda Avenue. The restaurant is in the Far East Center at Federal and Alameda.*

Like most Vietnamese restaurants, Thái Hiep offers several rice noodle "meals in a bowl" called *bún*, that provide a hearty and filling repast for well under our limit. A bonus here is that the servings are *huge* and this café has been named by some sources as the best Vietnamese restaurant in Denver. The owner's family operated a café in Saigon for forty years. It's an attractive place, prim and neat with a few Asian prints on the walls, plus hanging plants, burgundy Naugahyde booths and tables with rose nappery. Our favorite budget dinners here are spicy grilled chicken or beef *bún* with chiles, fresh sliced carrots, cucumbers, onions, lemon grass and rice noodles, dusted over with crushed peanuts. There are several milder versions of *bún* as well.

10 **WAHOO'S FISH TACO** • *1521 Blake St.; (303) 623-0263. Mexican; beer and margaritas. Lunch through dinner daily. MC/VISA. GETTING THERE: It's in LoDo between Fifteenth Street and the Sixteenth Street Mall.*

There's no shortage of inexpensive Mexican takeouts in Denver, although Wahoo's Fish Taco is definitely the most appealing. This Hispanic fast food outlet is housed in a fine old Lower Downtown brick building, and it's adorned inside with hundreds of decorative stickers. If this fun interior seems too distracting, you can adjourn to a sidewalk table. And this ain't no Taco Bell. It features huge "banzai" fish, chicken, beef or vegetarian burritos; or tacos with refried beans, rice, grilled fresh vegetables and nonfat sour cream for well under our price limit. That leaves plenty of room for a soft drink, beer or margarita.

THE TEN BEST CHEAP SLEEPS

As our criteria, we sought motels with high season rates of $55 or less per couple (although prices are subject to change). We chose only those that were well-maintained and clean, and reasonably close to downtown. Many of our selections are members of budget chains.

The main motel row is along Colfax Avenue east and west of Denver, since that was U.S. Highway 40 before the freeways came to town. Other motels are clustered around freeway offramps. Our selections are listed alphabetically.

1 AMERICAN MOTEL • *I-70 and Kipling Street, Wheat Ridge, CO 80033; (800) 90-LODGE or (303) 422-7200. Major credit cards. GETTING THERE: It's about ten miles west of Denver on the northwest side of the Kipling interchange; take exit 267 and follow the northside frontage road west.*

This fair-sized, well-kept motel has TV, room phones, a pool and guest laundry. A large marquee offering rates from $19.95 up is a bit misleading; a two-week reservation is required and that rate is for singles. However, normal rates for couples are well under our $55 limit.

2 BILTMORE MOTEL • *8900 E. Colfax Ave., Aurora, CO 80010; (303) 364-9286. Major credit cards. GETTING THERE: It's 5.5 miles east of downtown Denver at the junction of Highway 287.*

This older, nicely maintained motel has seventeen rooms with TV movies and refrigerators; there's a restaurant adjacent.

3 FAIRFIELD INN BY MARRIOTT • *1680 S. Colorado Blvd., Denver, CO 80222; (303) 691-2223. Major credit cards. GETTING THERE: Take I-25 exit 204 south of downtown and go east on Mexico Street to Colorado Boulevard.*

This attractive 170-unit inn has a few rooms under $55, although you should book early to get one. It has a small pool and some rooms have refrigerators.

4 HOMESTEAD MOTEL • *8837 W. Colfax Ave., Lakewood, CO 80215; (303) 232-8837. MC/VISA, DISC. GETTING THERE: It's about five miles west of downtown Denver. Take the Wadsworth Boulevard (Highway 121) exit from Freeway 6, go about a mile north, then go half a miles west on Colfax.*

This tidy 22-unit motel has TV movies, room refrigerators and a pool and spa. Several efficiency units are available.

5 *INTERSTATE I-70 MOTEL* • *4735 Kipling Street, Wheat Ridge, CO 80033; (800) 90-LODGE or (303) 423-0800. Major credit cards. GETTING THERE: It's about ten miles west of Denver on I-70 on the southwest side of the Kipling interchange (exit 267).*

This medium sized, well kept motel complex has TV movies, room phones and a swimming pool.

6 *MOTEL 6* • *Eight in the greater Denver area; call (800) 4-MO-TEL-6. (www.motel6.com)*

Motel 6's feature the usual spartan but clean rooms, with phones and cable TV.

7 *QUALITY INN DENVER WEST* • *12100 W. 44th Ave., Wheat Ridge, CO 80033; (303) 467-2400. Major credit cards. GETTING THERE: It's eight miles west of the I-70 and I-25 interchange. Take I-70 exit 266, go south on Ward Road to 44th, then southeast to the motel.*

This well-maintained 108-room motel has a few rooms within the $55 price range, although you should book early. Facilities include TV movies, refrigerators, dataports, a workout room, restaurant and cocktail lounge. It's near the Prospect Park recreation area.

8 *SLEEP INN DENVER TECH CENTER* • *9257 Costilla Ave., Englewood (Greenwood Village), CO 80112; (800) SLEEP-INN or (303) 662-9950. (www.sunbursthospitality.com) Major credit cards. GETTING THERE: Take exit 197 (Arapahoe) from I-25 south of Denver, go briefly east on Clinton Avenue to Costilla and then west.*

This attractive 119-room motel has extensive facilities for its modest room prices, including TV movies, speaker phones and voice mail, free continental breakfast, a sundeck and a small pool and spa.

9 *SUPER 8 MOTEL* • *Seven in the greater Denver area; call (800) 800-8000. (www.super8.com) Major credit cards.*

The local Super 8 motels are in the same price range as Motel 6 or a bit less, and they provide a free continental breakfast. Most have TV with HBO and free local calls.

10 *VALLI-HI MOTOR HOTEL* • *7320 Pecos St., Denver, CO 80221; (303) 429-3551. MC/VISA. GETTING THERE: It's about eight miles north of downtown. Take the Pecos exit from Highway 36.*

This tidy little motel has fifty neat-as-a-pin rooms with cable TV and phones, a lounge and a swimming pool.

A great hotel is like a duck swimming—composed and serene above the water, but paddling like hell underneath.

— Hotel executive Tim Carlson

Chapter five

PILLOW TALK
LISTS OF THE BEST LODGINGS

Like many major cities, Denver focuses most of its better hotels in the heart of downtown. These are handy locations, since they're near the Sixteenth Street Mall and within a short stroll of shops, the Colorado Convention Center, Denver Performing Arts Complex and some of the town's better restaurants. Slightly longer strolls will deliver you to the historic LoDo district and to the golden domed state capitol building and Civic Center Park.

Denver's primary motel row is along Colfax Avenue west of the city, since this was U.S. Highway 40 before the freeways came through town. The city also offers a few bed & breakfast inns, although not as many as most communities of this size.

This book isn't intended to be a detailed lodging guide. In keeping with our Ten Best theme, we have selected some of the city's finer hostelries—from it first class hotels to its coziest B&Bs. Since we've chosen only the best, this obviously isn't a budget directory. For that, you must retreat to the previous chapter.

There's an abundance of comprehensive Denver lodging guides available, including the *Denver & Colorado Official Visitors Guide* provided free by the Denver Metro Convention and Visitors Bureau. For room reservation aid or to obtain the visitors guide, contact the bureau at 1555 California St., Suite 300, Denver, CO 80202; (800) 645-3446 or (303) 892-1505. (www.denver.org; e-mail: info@denver.org)

PRICING: We use dollar sign codes to indicate room price ranges for two people, based on high season (summer) rates: *$* = a standard two-person room for $99 or less; *$$* = $100 to $149; *$$$* = $150 to $199; and *$$$$* = $200 or more.

THE TEN BEST HOTELS

Plan on spending $100 and well beyond per night at Denver's better hotels. Not everyone, including the authors of this book, can afford this sort of luxury. However, we're devoted lobby lizards who enjoy prowling about a city's fine hotels, sampling restaurants and lounges, window shopping the shops or just sitting in lobby chairs and watching people pass by. Each of our Ten Best selections features—in addition to luxurious rooms and full amenities—interesting lobbies and a good choice of cafés and lounges. Most of our choices are downtown; two are in the suburbs and one is in nearby Golden.

We have dual winners, and the rest follow in alphabetical order. The best hotel is the venerable Brown Palace and the best resort is the splendid Inverness Hotel & Golf Club, about fifteen miles south.

1 THE BEST HOTEL: *The Brown Palace* ● *321 Seventeenth St., Denver, CO 80202; (800) 321-2599 or (303) 297-3111. (www.brownpalace.com) Major credit cards; $$$$. GETTING THERE: It's downtown, cradled by Seventeenth, Broadway and Tremont.*

Step inside the "Brown" and you've stepped into another world and—indeed—another era. The noblest hotel in Denver and one of the most famous in the world, the wedge-shaped sandstone and granite Brown Palace is a required stop for city visitors. Not all can afford the rates, which start at more than $200 a night. However, the next-door Comfort Inn is quite affordable, and linked to the hotel by an elevated walkway. Inn guests have access to all hotel facilities. One also can experience this grand hotel by relaxing in the atrium lounge for an afternoon tea or evening drink, dining at one of its three restaurants or by taking an historic walking tour of the first two floors. Brochures are available at the desk and free tours are conducted periodically.

Built around an imposing six-story atrium, the Victorian-Italian Renaissance style hotel was completed in 1892, the handiwork of early Denverite Henry Cordes Brown (no relation to the more famous J.J. and Molly Brown). It has been in continuous operation since and recently underwent a complete renovation that modernized the hotel while preserving its original elegance. The 237 rooms and suites have amenities such as dataports and high speed modems and a mix of contemporary and classic European style furnishings.

Every U.S. President since Theodore Roosevelt has stayed here, and Dwight and Mamie Eisenhower often remained for weeks at a time. (Mrs. Eisenhower's mother was a Denver resident.) Other interesting guests have included the Beatles, American Football League founder Lamar Hunt who met with Bob Howsam in the lobby to hatch the Denver Broncos in 1959, and cowboy star Monte Montana, who used to ride his horse into the lobby. That would be frowned upon today, since the lofty lobby is a splendid study in Mexican onyx, European antiques and plush couches and chairs. Brown Palace diners have three good choices—the opulent **Palace Arms** (Chapter Three, page 59), the almost equally elegant **Ellyngton's** and the casual **Ship Tavern** with blue checkered tablecloths (Chapter Seven, page 114).

1 **THE BEST RESORT: *Inverness Hotel & Golf Club* •** *200 Inverness Drive West, Englewood, CO 80112; (800) 346-4891 or (303) 799-5800. (www.invernesshotel.com) Major credit cards; $ to $$$$. GETTING THERE: Head south about fifteen miles on I-25 and take exit 195 (County Line Road). Go left under the freeway to a traffic light, then turn left again onto Inverness Drive West.*

Sitting smartly on the edge of a lush green golf course, this low rise resort hotel has one of the most striking interiors in the Intermountain West. Living trees in giant planters reach toward the sunlight of a four-story glass A-frame roof. A large seating area in the main lobby with plush couches and chairs invite lingering. Overhead, several tiers of suspended bridges connect rooms of the hotel's two wings. Continue through the lobby toward the golf course side and you'll encounter the sunny Golden Terrace Garden Café and the Fireside Lounge. Both offer views of a fountain lake and the surrounding golf links. The Fireside is one of the Denver area's most appealing cocktail lounges; see Chapter Seven, page 113. Calling itself "Denver's only resort hotel," the Inverness is surprisingly affordable, with rooms for two starting at less than $100. Amenities in this 302-room AAA Four Diamond resort include golf, lighted tennis courts, bocci ball and volleyball courts, jogging paths and pools, spas and saunas. It has two restaurants, the elegant **Swan** (dinner only) and the breakfast-to-dinner **Golden Terrace.**

3 **ADAM'S MARK HOTEL** • *1550 N. Court Place, Denver, CO 80202; (800) 444-ADAM or (303) 893-3333. (www.adamsmark.com) Major credit cards; $$$. GETTING THERE: The hotel is downtown, rimmed by Court, Cleveland, Fifteenth and the Sixteenth Street Mall.*

A special appeal of this hotel is its location on the Sixteenth Street Mall, the pedestrian way that marches through the heart of downtown. *Bravo!*, its Italian restaurant, has outdoor tables on the mall, as does the Supreme Court café and bar. A circular settee is a comfortable focal point in the spacious hotel lobby. Note the life-sized sculpture of two prancing horses near the entrance to **Trattoria Colorado**, a lobby restaurant that serves breakfast through dinner. Adjacent is Tiffany Rose, a pretty bar with comfortable wicker-backed chairs.

Not counting the megaresorts of Las Vegas, Adam's Mark is one of America's largest hotels, with 1,200 rooms in two towers. Amenities include a luxury concierge level on the two top floors, a fitness center and steam room, pool and sun deck, shops, a beauty salon and barber shop. Rooms have work areas with speaker phones and dataports.

4 HOTEL MONACO • *1717 Champa St., Denver, CO 80202; (800) 397-5380. (www.monaco-denver.com) Major credit cards; $$$ to $$$$. GETTING THERE: The Monaco is downtown at the corner of Seventeenth and Champa.*

The various boutique hotels Monaco, created by the Kimpton Group of San Francisco, have a distinctive look that is at once elegant and campy; high style yet almost whimsical. Further, lonely guests can request that a gold fish be placed in their rooms to keep them company. We named ours "Finster." Denver's version has a vintage travel theme with a central chandelier styled after an early globe, with an old fashioned compass inlaid in the foyer. The colors are bold, with burgundy and hot orange wall coverings which supposedly suggest an explorer's tent.

The Monaco has one of the most comfortable lounges in town— again elegant yet cheerful with bright colors, plush chairs and couches, a gas fireplace and shelves lined with books. The 189 rooms feature— in addition to Finster—honor bars, armoires and dataports with FAX/copiers. Many have spa tubs. **Panzano Restaurant** served northern Italian fare with contemporary American accents.

5 HYATT REGENCY TECH CENTER • *7800 E. Tufts Ave., Denver, CO 80237; (800) 233-1234 or (303) 779-1234. (www.hyatt.com) Major credit cards; $$$$. GETTING THERE: Go south on Interstate 25 from Denver, or I-225 if you're approaching from the east. Ten miles south of town, at the junction of the two freeways, take exit 200 to the left if you're on I-25, or exit 2 from the right from I-225. Follow signs to DTC Boulevard, go south briefly and turn west (right) onto East Tufts. The hotel is about three blocks away.*

The sleek new Hyatt has some of the most appealing public areas of any hotel in the greater Denver area. Like the Brown Palace, it has an imposing multi-story atrium lobby—circular and ultra modern, in this case. A glass elevator encased in a dramatic iron framework reaches the upper floors. Off the main lobby are a gift shop, a coffee and snack café called Sarah's Pantry, a business center and a greenhouse-roofed pool, sauna and spa. A breakfast through dinner café and Garity's Sports Bar occupy a mezzanine deck accented with bold wrought iron frame canopies. The twelfth story **Centennial Restaurant** offers imposing views of Denver and the Rockies. This 450-room hotel has earned an AAA Four Diamond rating.

6 *LOEWS GIORGIO HOTEL* • *4150 E. Mississippi Ave., Denver, CO 80246; (800) 23-LOEWS or (303) 782-9300. Major credit cards; $$ to $$$$. GETTING THERE: The hotel is at Colorado Boulevard and Mississippi, about five miles from downtown. Go southeast on I-25, take exit 204 and follow Colorado Boulevard north for just under a mile. Look for the tall gray towers on your right.*

Although Loews Giorgio is rather opulent and only one of five Denver area hotels with an AAA Four Diamond award, its low end rates are rather moderate, starting around $100. The lobby is small yet elegant, done in marble and carved woods, with fine Italianate furnishings. A small library just off the lobby is particularly quiet and cozy. The 183 guest rooms and suites have modern furnishings with European touches, honor bars, FAX machines, three phones and data ports; many have TV\VCRs. Hotel amenities include free evening beverages, a fitness center and complimentary shuttle service. The elegant **Tuscany Restaurant** serves Italian fare and a dimly lit cocktail lounge is an inviting gathering spot. An attractive little park and fountain sits between the twelve-story hotel and adjacent Mountain Tower office complex.

7 *THE OXFORD HOTEL* • *1600 Seventeenth St., Denver, CO 80202; (800) 228-5838 or (303) 628-5400. (www.theoxfordhotel.com) Major credit cards; $$ to $$$. GETTING THERE: The Oxford is in the LoDo area, at the corner of Seventeenth and Wazee.*

A year older than the Brown Palace and designed by the same architect, the 1891 Oxford has been returned to its Victorian look. While not as opulent as the Palace, this five-story brick lodging is a pleasing study in early Denver finery; it's the city's oldest still-operating hotel. Burgundy columns hold up ornately painted coffered ceilings in the comfortable lobby. Romanticized paintings of the early West and antique furnishings give it a proper yesterday look. Its dining venues are **McCormick's Fish House** (Chapter Three, page 73), **Il Fornaio** Italian restaurant and the **Sage.**

A side corridor leading from the lobby to Wazee Street is lined with early day photos of the Mile High City. The Cruise Room lounge, modeled after a bar on the Queen Mary, is one of the town's sleekest watering holes; see Chapter Seven, page 116; and Chapter Eight, page 125. The hotel's eighty rooms are furnished with European antiques; amenities include honor bars and data ports. Complimentary evening beverages are served in the lobby. The Oxford is well located, within a short walk of Coors Field and LoDo's shops and restaurants.

8 *TABLE MOUNTAIN INN* • *1310 Washington Ave., Golden, CO 80401; (800) 762-9898 or (303) 277-9898. Major credit cards; $$. GETTING THERE: Golden is about fifteen miles north of Denver (I-70 exit 265 via State Highway 58). The inn is just west of downtown, between Thirteenth and Fourteenth streets.*

You'll think you're in Santa Fe instead of the Rocky Mountain foothills when you step into the lobby of the pueblo style Table Mountain Inn. This terraced, all suite hotel is within a brief stroll of Golden's museums and attractions, including the Coor's Brewery. The lobby and seventy-four rooms feature cheerful Southwest décor, and many rooms have balconies with views of the surrounding mountains. All have ceiling fans and several have spa tubs. The **Mesa Bar & Grill** continues the New Mexico theme, featuring Southwest fare.

9 *TEATRO HOTEL* • *1600 Seventeenth St., Denver, CO 80202; (800) WYNDHAM or (303) 228-1100. (www.wyndham.com) Major credit cards; $$$ to $$$$. GETTING THERE: El Teatro is on the edge of LoDo, at the corner of Fourteenth and Market.*

Although not originally a hotel, this attractive nine-story brick structure has the look of early Denver, with lots of marble and plush late nineteenth century furnishings in the lobby. It was fashioned from a 1911 office building by the Wyndham corporation. The 116 rooms have European style furnishings with Asian accents; all have CD players, three phones and computer ports with printer/copiers. The cozy lobby is accented by Shakespearean themes and framed costumes, since the Teatro is near the Denver Center for Performing Arts. Denver's celebrity chef operates both hotel restaurants—the elegant **Kevin Taylor** (Chapter Three, page 59) and less formal **Ju Ju.**

10 *WESTIN TABOR CENTER* • *1672 Lawrence St., Denver, CO 80202; (800) WESTIN-1 or (303) 572-9100. (www.westin.com) Major credit cards; $ to $$$. GETTING THERE: The Westin is downtown and near LoDo, on Seventeenth between Arapahoe and Lawrence.*

One of central Denver's most luxurious hotels, the Westin is only one of two with an AAA Four Diamond award. Yet the rooms are surprisingly inexpensive, starting at less than $100 for two. Further, it's in a great location between upper downtown and LoDo. The modern two-level lobby, rich in marble, is particularly impressive, with walls accented by huge multi-colored artworks that can best be described as "constructions." The Lobby Lounge and Bar is an inviting place, focused around a curiously modernistic fountain. A nice feature here—much of the lobby and other public areas of the Westin are non-smoking. Many of the 430 rooms have honor bars, safes, spa tubs and TV/VCRs. Dining happens at the **Palm Restaurant** and the breakfast-only **Augusta Restaurant.** The Westin sits on the spot where Leadville mining millionaire Horace A.W. Tabor ordered construction of one of Denver's first highrise buildings.

THE TEN BEST BED & BREAKFAST INNS

Although Denver has many fine Victorian-era homes—the kinds of structures often used in bed & breakfast conversions—the city doesn't have a lot of B&Bs. Smaller communities such as Colorado Springs and Estes Park have more. However, most of the few in Denver are quite nice, and we've reached into nearby communities to complete our list.

1 CAPITOL HILL MANSION BED & BREAKFAST • *1207 Pennsylvania St., Denver, CO 80203; (800) 839-9329 or (303) 839-5221. (www.capitolhillmansion.com) Eight units with private baths, TV and phones; full breakfast. Major credit cards; $ to $$$. GETTING THERE: From downtown, go east about half a mile on Colfax, then south three blocks on Pennsylvania to Twelfth Avenue.*

Denver's finest B&B is housed in a handsome turreted three-story ruby sandstone mansion in the historic capital hill area just southeast of downtown. Built in 1891, this Victorian mansion has earned a spot on national and state registers of historic places, and it has earned the highest award given by the American Bed & Breakfast Association. The elegantly decorated rooms—all with floral themes—have phone/modem outlets, cable TVs and refrigerators. Some have fireplaces, oversized spa tubs or balconies. Although the décor is primarily Victorian, it's light and cheerful, with lots of potted plants and cut flowers. A curving front porch, towering chimneys and an eight-foot beveled glass window create impressive architectural highlights.

2 ANTIQUE ROSE BED & BREAKFAST INN • *1422 Washington Ave., Golden, CO 80401; (303) 277-1893. (www.texas-guides.com; e-mail: antiquerose@worldnet.att.net.) Four rooms with phones and private baths; full breakfast. MC/VISA, AMEX; $ to $$. GETTING THERE: It's in the heart of historic downtown Golden, at the corner of Fifteenth Street.*

Uncluttered and elegant Victorian décor is the mark of this attractive inn, fashioned from an 1880s home built for a prominent senator from Golden. It's a classic Queen Anne style Victorian with dormers, gables and fishscale shingles. Each of the four individually decorated rooms is named for "Old Garden" roses that were introduced around the turn of the last century. Two have spa tubs and one has a TV set. Facilities include a sitting room with a fireplace and a spacious dining room. The inn is within a few blocks of downtown shopping and restaurants and the Coors Brewery tour.

3 **CASTLE MARNE** • *1572 Race St., Denver, CO 80206; (800) 92-MARNE or (303) 331-0621. (www.castlemarne.com; e-mail: diane@castlemarne.com) Nine rooms with phones and private baths; full breakfast. Major credit cards; $ to $$$$. GETTING THERE: Go east on Colfax about 1.5 miles, then turn north on Race and go one block; it's near the corner of Race and Sixteenth.*

This stone castle-like mansion in Denver's Thyman Historic District rivals Capitol Hill Mansion with its luxurious amenities and elegance. Rooms are furnished Victorian style with antiques and family heirlooms. Three have private balconies and two-person hot tubs and two have spa tubs. Completed in 1889, the three-story structure is on national and local historic lists and it was named one of the top twelve American inns by *Country Inns Magazine* in 1994. Amenities include a game room with a pool table, small business center with a computer and a meeting room.

4 **CLIFF HOUSE LODGE B&B INN & COTTAGES** • *121 Stone St., Morrison, CO 80465; (303) 697-9732. Ten rooms or cottages with private baths; continental breakfast. MC/VISA; $$ to $$$. GETTING THERE: Morrison is about twelve miles west of Denver, just beyond Red Rocks Park. Follow I-70 or Highway 6 freeway west, then take I-70 exit 259 southwest past Red Rocks Park to Morrison. The lodge is on the right as you enter the small town.*

The elongated title best describes this complex, which is a handy base for exploring Red Rocks Park, Dinosaur Ridge and nearby Golden. The 1873 sandstone Cliff House Lodge has two rooms, with another eight lodging units in country style cottages. Built among red rocks by town founder George Morrison, this romantic French country style inn is listed on the National Register of Historic Places.

All units are decorated with American and European antiques and many have TV/VCRs with free movies, plus stereos, fireplaces and hot tubs. Special "romance packages" feature units with hot tubs and wood burning fireplaces, with candlelit champagne breakfasts.

5 **HAUS BERLIN** • *1651 Emerson St., Denver, CO 80218; (800) 659-0253 or (303) 837-9527. (www.hausberlinbandb.com; e-mail: haus.berlin@worldnet.att.net) Four rooms with phones and private baths; full breakfast. Major credit cards; $$$. GETTING THERE: Go east about a mile on Colfax, turn left onto Emerson and follow it briefly north; the inn is between Sixteenth and Seventeenth avenues.*

Haus Berlin refers primarily to the heritage of co-innkeeper Christiana Brown and the inn's rich European décor. The building itself is a Victorian style townhouse built in 1892 and listed on the National

Register of Historic Places. Christiana and her husband Dennis have decorated it with a cheerful mix of modern European furnishings with Latin touches and international art. Three of the eclectically decorated rooms have TV sets; all have desks with modem hookups. The Browns are noted for their elaborate breakfasts.

6 HOLIDAY CHALET, A VICTORIAN BED & BREAKFAST

● *1820 E. Colfax Ave., Denver, CO 80218; (800) 626-4497 or (303) 321-9975. (www.bbonline.com/co/holiday) Ten suites and rooms with kitchens and private baths; extended continental breakfast. Major credit cards; $$ to $$$. GETTING THERE: This inn is eighteen blocks west of downtown, at the corner of High Street.*

Built in 1896, this large and handsomely elaborate three-story Victorian brownstone has been owned by the same family since 1912. Recently restored, it features all-kitchenette rooms and suites with comfortable "Victorian eclectic" décor, floral bedspreads and lace curtains. Other room amenities include TV/VCRs with free videos, phones with data ports and voice mail. Breakfast is self-serve, or guests can prepare fare in their rooms. The inn features a landscaped courtyard, barbecue area and comfortable sitting room with a TV, piano and guest phone. The inn is within walking distance of City Park, the Denver Zoo, Museum of Nature and Science and Denver Botanic Gardens.

7 MERRITT HOUSE BED & BREAKFAST INN

● *941 E. Seventeenth Ave., Denver, CO 80218; (877) 861-5230 or (303) 861-5230. (www.merritthouse.com; e-mail: info@merritthouse.com) Ten rooms with TV, phones and private baths; full or buffet breakfast. Major credit cards; $$ to $$$. GETTING THERE: Go less than a mile east from downtown on Seventeenth Avenue; the inn is at the northwest corner of Seventeenth and Ogden.*

Architect Frank Edbrooke, who designed the Brown Palace, also fashioned this three-story Queen Anne Victorian in 1889 for a Colorado senator. The structure is on the National Registry of Historic Places. Victorian furnishings blend easily with modern conveniences in the rooms, including old style cradle telephones with push-button dials and antique "electric filament lamps." Five rooms offer spa tubs; the others have showers. Amenities include a sun porch and garden patio. The inn contains a full-service restaurant open to guests and the general public. Guests have the option of full or buffet breakfasts; vegetarian dishes are a specialty.

8 ON GOLDEN POND BED & BREAKFAST

● *7831 Eldridge St., Arvada, CO 80005; (800) 682-0193 or (303) 424-2296. (www.-bbonline.com/co/ongoldenpond/) Five rooms with private baths; full breakfast. Major credit cards; $ to $$. GETTING THERE: Arvada is a* *residential community northwest of Denver. Take I-70 exit 266, follow Ward Road north to 72nd Street, turn left onto Alkire, right on 78th and then left onto Eldridge.*

This golden pond retreat is a contemporary farm home on ten acres at the end of a long gravel drive, well isolated from the growing bedroom community of Arvada. The pond from which it takes its name is occupied by friendly ducks, and surrounded by landscaped grounds. All rooms have balconies or private patios, and most overlook this pleasant farm setting. The hostess, a native of Germany, serves elaborate European style breakfasts in a comfortable dining room. The inn's amenities include a hot tub and pool; horses and bicycles are available for guests.

9 **QUEEN ANNE BED & BREAKFAST INN** • *2147-51 Tremont Place, Denver, CO 80205; (800) 432-4667 or (303) 296-6666. (www.queenannebnb.com; e-mail: travel@queenannebnb.com) Fourteen units with TV, phones and private baths; full breakfast. Major credit cards; $ to $$$. GETTING THERE: It's on the eastern edge of downtown near the corner of Twentieth Avenue, Grant Street and Tremont Place.*

Two late nineteenth century Victorians within blocks of downtown comprise Denver's first B&B, opened in 1987. Sitting beside a public park, yet within view of city highrises, they are linked by an elaborately landscaped garden patio. Victorian furnished rooms feature cut flowers and potted plants, piped-in chamber music and telephones with modem jacks. FAX and internet access are available. Five of the units are suites themed in honor of American artists. Some suites and rooms have oversized spa or soaking tubs; four have dramatic wall murals and two feature fireplaces.

10 **VICTORIA OAKS INN** • *1575 Race St., Denver, CO 80206; (800) 662-6257 or (303) 355-1818. Nine rooms; seven with private and two with share baths; expanded continental breakfast. Major credit cards; $ to $$. GETTING THERE: The inn is in the Capitol Hill Historic District, just off Colfax Avenue. Go east about a mile and a half on Colfax, then turn left (north) onto Race; the inn is near the corner of Sixteenth Avenue.*

Nicely refurbished yet rather moderately priced, Victoria Oaks is situated between Chessman Park and City Park. Amenities in this 1897 square-shouldered early American mansion include a kitchen, guest laundry and concierge services. All rooms have TV, radios and phones and two have fireplaces. It's furnished with antiques, accented by carved oak woodwork, leaded glass windows and tile fireplaces.

All the world's a stage,
And all the men and women merely players.
They have their exits and entrances,
And one man in his time plays many parts.
— **William Shakespeare**

Chapter six

NIGHTSIDE
DIVERSIONS AFTER DARK

It's called The Plex and it has made Denver one of the most culturally alive urban centers in America. William Shakespeare, who dabbled in drama, comedy and sonnets, would have loved this place.

The Denver Performing Arts Complex sprawls over four acres in the heart of downtown at Fourteenth and Curtis streets, with eight theaters capable of seating more than 10,000 people. It's the world's largest theater facility under one roof and it ranks second in America in seating capacity to New York's Lincoln Center. The Plex is home to the Colorado Symphony Orchestra, Colorado Ballet, Opera Colorado, Cleo Parker Robinson Dance Ensemble and the Tony Award winning Denver Center Theatre Company.

Construction of the complex began in the late 1970s as a monument to Helen Bonfils, daughter of *Denver Post* co-founder Frederic G. Bonfils. As the *Post's* chief stockholder after his death, she became one of Denver's leading philanthropists and a major supporter of the arts. She built a 550-seat theater on east Colfax in 1953 and starred in several plays there. After her death, her successor at the *Post*, Donald R. Seawell—a former Broadway producer—spearheaded the creation of the performing arts center in her honor. Started in 1978 and built in stages, it's linked by a dramatic barrel-arch glass canopy to the 1908

City Auditorium. The marriage of old and new architectures creates a pleasing effect. The older structure is now the Auditorium Theater.

The complex, built in an area that once housed the city jail, an empty sports arena and several parking lots, was established as the Denver Center for the Performing Arts. The overall facility is now called the Denver Performing Arts Complex, while the DCPA—with Seawell still at its helm—is a non-profit group within the facility.

Denver also boasts another noteworthy entertainment venue. Red Rocks Amphitheatre, fifteen miles to the west, was completed in 1941, constructed as a Depression-era Civilian Conservation Corps project. The 9,050-seat outdoor theater, set dramatically between 400-foot red rock spires, has hosted leading stars such as the Beatles, John Denver, U-2, Willie Nelson and Dan Fogelburg. Part of the 640-acre city-owned Red Rocks Park, it's also the scene of annual Easter sunrises services and Fourth of July fireworks.

To find out what's happening at the Plex, Red Rocks Amphitheatre and other entertainment venues, pick up a copy of the monthly *On-Stage* newspaper. It's available free at visitor centers, the Denver Center and some hotel lobbies, or call (303) 424-5426. If you live here or are a frequent visitor, you can get a subscription: *OnStage*, P.O. Box 1990, Arvada, CO 80001-1990.

CULTURE VULTURE SOURCES ● Both local newspapers print entertainment sections with their Friday editions. The *Denver Post's* version is "The Weekend Scene" and the *Denver Rocky Mountain News* prints "Weekend Spotlight." Both cover a wide range of leisure time activities, including theater, concerts, restaurants, popular music, TV and coming events in general. The *Post* also publishes the bi-monthly "Denver Venues," focusing primarily on performing arts and pop artists who are coming to town.

GETTING TICKETED ● The major local ticket company for performing arts and sports events is TicketMaster, (303) 830-TIXS. It has outlets at Foley's department stores, Budget Tapes and CD Stores and Blockbuster Music. The Denver Center ticket office at Fourteenth and Curtis streets is open Monday-Saturday 10 to 6. Call (800) 641-1222 or (303) 893-4100 or tickets or (303) 893-DCPA for recorded information. Red Rocks Amphitheatre tickets are sold through TicketMaster. Two firms specializing in hard-to-get ducats are Ticket Connection at (303) 758-1999, and Colorado Ticket Company at (303) 649-9999.

THE TEN BEST PERFORMING ARTS GROUPS

Obviously, much of what happens in town is happening at the Plex. Lively arts groups can be found elsewhere in this culturally focused city as well. Our selections are as varied as the Denver cultural scene. We have chosen for your convenience—and possible confusion—both performing arts groups and theaters that bring in outside artists. The peak theater and concert season is fall through early spring, while most of the action at Red Rocks Amphitheatre is from late spring through early fall, taking advantage of warmer weather.

1 DENVER CENTER THEATRE COMPANY • *Denver Performing Arts Complex, Fourteenth and Curtis streets; (303) 893-4100.*

The best professional drama group in the Intermountain West proved its mettle in 1998 by winning a coveted Tony Award for Outstanding Regional Theater. In a sense, the award came full circle, since it's named for legendary actress Antoinette Perry, who grew up in the Mile High City. The Denver Center Theatre Company was established in 1978 as part of the Denver Center for the Performing Arts. With a resident ensemble of more than forty performers, it presents a season of comedies, dramas and musicals from October to June. It's the largest professional theater company in the Intermountain West and has premiered several original plays.

2 CLEO PARKER ROBINSON DANCE ENSEMBLE • *119 Park Avenue West; (303) 295-1759.*

Established in 1970, this multi-ethnic group presents modern dance performances at the Denver Performing Arts Complex, at its dance school in the African Methodist Episcopal Church on Park Avenue and elsewhere in Denver. It also makes periodic national tours and appears annually in the American Dance Festival.

3 COLORADO BALLET COMPANY • *1278 Lincoln St.; (303) 837-8888.*

This small troupe performs traditional ballet at the Performing Arts Complex from fall through spring, and presents the classic *Nutcracker* during the holidays. It also takes annual national and international tours and has won critical praise for its "surprising maturity, presence and solid technique." Established in 1961 as the Colorado Concert Ballet, the Colorado Ballet Company is the only dance ensemble in the state that performs to live music.

4 COLORADO SYMPHONY ORCHESTRA • *1013 Thirteenth St.; (303) 986-8742 or (303) 98-MUSIC for tickets.*

The only major American symphony orchestra under a woman's baton, Marin Alsop's Colorado Symphony presents more than a 100 concerts a year. Most occur in Boettcher Concert Hall at the Performing Arts Complex. To lure a wide range of music lovers, it presents pops as well as classics, including low-price "Blue Jeans" and "Family Series" concerts. Its regular season is September to May, and it also presents free summer concerts at Red Rocks Amphitheatre and at several public parks in Denver.

5 DENVER CENTER FOR THE PERFORMING ARTS •
Fourteenth and Curtis streets; (303) 893-4100 for tickets and (303) 893-DCPA for a recorded performance schedule.

At the risk of redundancy, the DCPA should be listed as a sponsor of theater as well as the non-profit operator of the Plex. It books traveling Broadway shows, major performers and other groups to its eight theaters, as well as making them available to local groups. Its affiliate, Denver Center Attractions, books touring shows, cabaret theater and drama groups, offering more than 300 productions since the center's founding. It also produces its own plays and musicals and takes them on national tour. Its productions have earned two Tony nominations—for *Quilters* as best play and for actor Ian McKellen in *Richard III*.

6 DENVER CIVIC THEATRE • *721 Santa Fe Dr.; phone (303) 595-3800.*

After the theater built by Helen Bonfils was closed, some of its principles established this group in 1985 to produce classic and contemporary dramas. Within the group are two companies. Compass Theatre presents classics in Denver Civic's 250-seat main theater while the Industrial Arts Theatre offers contemporary and *avant garde* dramas in the smaller Dorie Theater.

7 OPERA COLORADO • *1315 Curtis St.; (303) 98-MUSIC.*

Founded in 1981 and based in the Performing Arts Complex, Opera Colorado is the only company in the nation performing grand opera in the round. During its four-month winter-spring season, it presents two "circular operas" in the Boettcher Concert Hall and a third opera on the Buell Theater's conventional stage. Its operas are staged in concert with the Colorado Symphony Orchestra and have attracted leading stars such as Placido Domingo. Operas are sung in their original languages, with supertitles for those who *really* want to know what the soprano is shrieking.

8 PARAMOUNT THEATRE • *1631 Glenarm Place, between Sixteenth Street Mall and Seventeenth Street; (303) 534-8336.*

This beautifully restored theater, built in 1930 for silent movies, imports an assortment of productions, ranging from comedies and pop stars to ballet. A typical season will lure the likes of the Natalie Cole and Ray Charles. It sometimes hosts local groups such as the Colorado

Symphony Orchestra. The theater is as interesting as its presentations, with its restored terra cotta *bas relief* trim, hand painted tapestries and plush main floor and balcony seating. It has one of only two working Wurlitzer twin console organs in the nation. The other is at New York City's Radio City Music Hall.

9 *RED ROCKS AMPHITHEATRE* • *2700 W. Alameda Parkway, Morrison; (303) 697-8801; tickets through TicketMaster at (303) 830-TIXS. GETTING THERE: Follow I-70 about eighteen miles west from Denver, take exit 256 and follow signs to Red Rocks Park.*

This has to be the most dramatic venue in the Intermountain West to see a concert, pop stars or even a fireworks show. Red Rocks Amphitheatre is cradled between towering seventy-million-year-old red rock sandstone spires and its dimensions are awesome. With a capacity of more than 9,000 people, it has sixty-nine seating rows ranging from 138 to 231 feet wide, with a 100-foot stage far below. More than twenty performances are presented here each summer, mostly pops stars past and present such as John Mellencamp, Willie Nelson, Motley Crue, Sting, Britney Spears and Ringo Starr. Which brings us full circle, since the Beatles performed here in 1963. People fussed about the outrageous $6.60 ticket prices.

10 *THE THEATRE GROUP* • *13 S. Broadway near Colfax;* (303) 860-9360.

Established in 1987 as the Lakewood Players, this group sponsors regional premieres of Broadway and off-Broadway plays. They're presented in the small 120-seat Theater on Broadway at 13 South Broadway and in the Phoenix Theatre at 1124 Santa Fe Drive.

THE TEN BEST NIGHTSPOTS

Nightlife is alive and thriving in downtown Denver. The creation of the Sixteenth Street Mall and the gentrification of LoDo have brought people back to the heart of the city. They crowd the sidewalk restaurants of the mall and LoDo for lunch, hit the hot bars for after work cocktails, stay for dinner and then party until the wee hours. Most of the late night action in Denver—as in most cities—is Friday and Saturday, when you'll be pressed to find a seat in a popular blues or jazz club. If you're visiting, hit these spots on other nights, unless you enjoy mob camaraderie.

Although the downtown nightlife scene is relatively new, Denver has been a lively city during much of its history. A traveler commented in 1860 that "every fifth house seems to be a bar." Market Street, in what is now LoDo, was busy with saloons, dance halls and brothels into the twentieth century. Then the early-century national reform movement, which led to the banning of prostitution and booze, shut down Denver's legitimate and illegitimate nightspots.

One of the first bars to open in LoDo after the 1933 Repeal was Tony's Restaurant, started by Tony Romano in a former brothel at 1962 Market Street. In the 1950s, it passed to his son Charlie, who was part Hispanic. He renamed it El Chapultepec and featured live mariachi music. His son-in-law took over in the 1960s and then in 1980, he converted it to LoDo's first jazz club. Other jazz and blues clubs were established shortly after World War II, mostly in an area just northeast of downtown called Five Points, where five streets converged. Other jazz, blues and dance joints were popular along Colfax Avenue until LoDo became the hotspot in recent years. Denver nightspots have drawn some of America's greats, including Nat King Cole, Duke Ellington, Charlie Parker and Tony Bennett. The Chapultepec has been featured on national TV as a hot jazz spot, and it's still active.

Two free newspapers are good information sources for the live entertainment scene in the greater Denver area, and both can be found on local newsracks. Despite its title, the monthly *Singles Entertainment* isn't a boy-seeks-girl newspaper. It provides comprehensive lists of live music venues in the area, with stories about artists and features such as "best happy hours" and karaoke places. For more information, write P.O. Box 440066, Aurora, CO 80014; (303) 744-0500. *Westword,* the popular alternative newspaper, published every other week, also covers the local entertainment scene. It reviews live shows and films, and it lists dozens of other events in the greater Denver area. Its offices are at 969 Broadway, near the corner of Tenth, or write: P.O. Box 5970, Denver, CO 80217; (303) 296-7744. Many lounges and clubs advertise in both newspapers, providing further clues to the mile high night scene.

Our Ten Best nightspot choices are varied, ranging from live music venues to dance clubs. We begin with the oldest and most famous:

1 EL CHAPULTEPEC • *1962 Market Street at the corner of 20th in LoDo; (303) 295-9126. Open nightly. Live jazz; one drink minimum.*

LoDo's oldest jazz club still packs 'em in, with live music every night of the week. It's rather smoky and dim, although it offers some of the best sounds in town. There's no cover; buy at least one drink and you can keep your seat.

2 BRENDAN'S MARKET STREET PUB • *1624 Market Street at Sixteenth in LoDo. Open nightly. Live blues and dancing; cover charge.*

This roomy cellar club beneath a restaurant is Denver's "House of the Blues," with local and national performers. When the music picks up a beat, couples can move to a dance floor. Monday is "jam night" when wanna-be blues stars are invited to the bandstand.

3 BLUEBIRD THEATER • *3317 Colfax Avenue; (303) 322-2308. Open most nights. A variety of jazz, blues, rock, country and pop concerts; admission charge. GETTING THERE: The theater is about two and a half miles east of downtown at Adams Street.*

Built in 1913 as a silent movie house, this venerable place has gone from talkies to porn house to an intimate cabaret theater. Completely renovated in 1994, it's an attractive showplace with tables on the main floor and theater seating in the balcony. Although the neighborhood is a bit scruffy, the theater is well-maintained. It has full bar service and a coffee bar, and it books both local and national groups.

4 COMEDY WORKS • *1226 Fifteenth Street near Larimer Square in LoDo; (303) 595-3637. Open Tuesday through Sunday nights. Stand-up comics; cover charge. Age twenty-one and over.*

Denver's most popular comedy club features local and occasional national performers Wednesday through Sunday. Tuesday is amateur night. Among comics who passed through this basement club on their way to stardom were Jay Leno, Jerry Seinfeld, Tim Allen and Roseanne Barr-Arnold.

5 COSMO LOUNGE • *1523 Market Street in Lodo, near Fifteenth. Open nightly. Dancing to recorded deejay music.*

Formerly the Velvet Lounge, the three-level Cosmo is one of Denver's cooler dance clubs, with a dress code and upbeat deejays spinning upbeat CD sounds. Dancing is on the third level, a restaurant occupies the second tier and deejay-directed jazz is played on the ground floor.

6 HERMAN'S HIDEAWAY • *1578 S. Broadway; (303) 777-5840 or TicketMaster at (303) 830-TIXS. Open Tuesday-Saturday. Live rock and pops bands with dancing; admission charge. Herman's is about four miles south of downtown, between Florida and Iowa avenues.*

A neighborhood roadhouse since the 1960s, Herman's now books local and occasional national groups. The music format ranges from soft to hard to acid rock to pops. The large club, which has retained its casual roadhouse look, has two bars and lots of room for dancing.

7 I-BEAM • *1427 Larimer Street between Fourteenth and Fifteenth in Larimer Square; (303) 534-2326. Open Wednesday through Sunday. Dancing to live or recorded music; cover charge some nights.*

Denver's most popular dance club swings to either deejay or live music. The sounds at this hip second story club ranges from hard to soft rock. There's a cover charge for occasional live groups, usually on Saturdays; it's free most other nights. The I-Beam has a pool room in addition to the large strobe-lighted dance floor. Big picture windows offer views of Larimer Square action below.

8 *JOSEPHINA'S* • *In Larimer Square at 1433 Larimer Street, between Fourteenth and Fifteenth; (303) 623-0166. Open nightly. Live rock, pops and rhythm and blues; no cover or minimum.*

Housed in one of LoDo's old brick buildings, Josephina's is a popular Italian restaurant and lively bar featuring nightly entertainment. Between sets, look about the place to enjoy the elaborate carved back-bar, high wheeler bicycle, antique signs and the photo mural behind the bandstand of giggling ladies in 1920s swimsuits.

9 *LOS CABOS II* • *1512 Curtis Street in LoDo between Fifteenth and the Sixteenth Street Mall; (303) 571-0007. Open daily for lunch and dinner. Latin dancing on Friday and Saturday; modest cover.*

This restaurant, which serves an interesting mix of Peruvian and Chinese food (Chapter Three, page 64), becomes salsa central on weekends, with either live or recorded Latin music. And if you don't know a rumba from a samba from a mambo, dance lessons are offered early Friday evenings.

10 *VARTAN'S JAZZ CLUB* • *1800 Glenarm Place at Eighteenth Street in LoDo; (303) 399-1111. Open Monday through Saturday. Live jazz; cover charge; reservations suggested.*

Both a restaurant and jazz club, this comfortable place features live music most nights. It draws national and international performers about once a week. The cover charge varies, according to the status of the performers. Vartan's opened in Cherry Creek in 1995, then moved to LoDo three years later.

There is more drinking and gambling here in one day than in Kansas City in six. In fact, about one-half of the population do nothing else but drink whiskey and play cards.

— G.N. Woodward, in a letter home from Denver in the 1860s

Chapter seven

PUB CRAWLING
THE BEST PLACES TO SIP SUDS

Colorado was more or less born in a Denver saloon, and its citizens haven't strayed too far from one since. In 1859, when a group of miners, entrepreneurs and drifters wanted to carve their own domain out of the vast Kansas Territory, they gathered at Uncle Dick Wootton's Saloon on the banks of Cherry Creek. Their proposed Jefferson Territory never took shape, although the federal government relented two years later and created Colorado Territory. Naturally everyone trouped back to Uncle Dick's—the town's first legitimate business—to celebrate. Although the territorial idea was born here, Denver didn't become the capitol until 1866.

"After its creation, a thirsty territorial legislature moved around to wherever they could find free drinks," writes Thomas J. Noel in *Colorado: A Liquid History & Tavern Guide to the Highest State*; © 1999. "They met in Golden from 1862 until 1864, where William A.H. Loveland offered them libations at his stone inn. Next, the legislature traveled to Colorado City, testing the hospitality there before returning to Denver, which had far more saloons than any town in the territory."

In fact, saloons outnumbered all other types of businesses. Denver boasted thirty-five drinking establishments when it became the territorial capital in 1866. By 1890, the number had grown to 319. The city also developed a reputation for beer brewing and drinking that continues to this day.

However, the national goody two-shoes movement early in the last century hit Denver and the state of Colorado particularly hard. Drinking was outlawed here in 1916, two years before federal Prohibition. Denver's saloon count shrunk from 400 to nearly none, and all of the state's breweries save one—Coors—eventually closed their doors. Denver's most famous libation station, the Buckhorn Exchange, survived as a soft drink parlor and was issued Colorado Liquor License Number 1 when Repeal came in 1933. Colorado still has a few hangovers from Prohibition, such as banning liquor sales on Sunday, and permitting supermarkets to sell only beer with 3.2 percent alcohol. All other libations are sold through liquor stores. They're privately owned and not state controlled, although these limited outlets tend to elevate liquor prices, compared with "free states" such as Nevada and California.

Drinking made a quick comeback after Repeal, with both saloons and retail liquor stores licensed to sell beer and spirits. Coors, the lone surviving beer maker, has become the world's largest single brewery. However, an old Prohibition law forbade making and selling beer at the same location, so Colorado's microbrew industry was slow in arriving. That changed in 1988 when John Wright Hickenlooper convinced Denver Senator Dennis Gallagher to spearhead the repeal of that law. Hickenlooper and some investors bought an old brick mercantile warehouse in LoDo and opened the state's first brewpub, Wynkoop Brewing Company. More than a hundred microbreweries now thrive in the state and a dozen of these are in Denver.

Incidentally, if you enjoy bar-hopping, head for Blake Street in north LoDo. The stretch between Nineteenth and Twenty-Third is a virtual saloon row, with nearly a dozen bars and a major brewpub. All are installed in Lower Downtown's old brick buildings.

THE TEN BEST WATERING HOLES

Saloons no longer outnumber all other businesses in Denver, although the Mile High City still has about five hundred places to get high. (That's just a play on words. Colorado has some of the Nation's toughest drinking and driving laws, so practice moderation as you follow this chapter.) The city's bars range from old brick-walled drinking establishments rich with the tapestry of history to sleek designer saloons sharing space with trendy restaurants or upscale hotel lobbies. Our favorite is of the latter type:

1 TIFFANY ROSE ● *In the Adam's Mark Hotel on Sixteenth Street Mall between Court and Tremont; (303) 893-3333.*

Tiffany is the most gorgeous cocktail lounge in the city—an elegant place for a quiet drink. Situated off the hotel's main lobby, it's done in dark greens, set off by mirrored columns, planters and impressionistic art. A dramatic multicolored canopy light fixture and icicle chandeliers draw the eyes upward. The serving bar has an *art moderne* look with a simple beveled glass backbar. Each table in Tiffany has a single red rose in a bud vase.

2 *BUCKHORN EXCHANGE • 1000 Osage St.; (303) 534-9505. Full bar service. Lunch weekdays; dinner nightly. GETTING THERE: Head west on Colfax Avenue for about a mile, turn left onto Osage just short of a viaduct and follow it south about half a mile to Tenth.*

Sitting all by itself in a redeveloping industrial and low-cost housing area, the old brick Buckhorn is primarily a restaurant and museum of the early West. It's popular with faithful locals and the darling of tourists. Filled with memorabilia and game trophies, it's Denver's oldest restaurant, dating from 1893. There's a fine old fashioned bar upstairs away from all those tourists, with a quiet seating area of comfortable couches and chairs. In fact, this building began life in 1886 as Denver's first brewery. Henry H. "Shorty Scout" Zietz opened a downtown saloon and restaurant in 1871 called the Rio Grande Exchange, then his son moved it to this spot in 1893. Look behind the handsome carved oak bar and you'll see that famous Colorado Liquor License Number 1, issued to the Exchange at the repeal of Prohibition in 1933. (For more on the Buckhorn, see Chapter Three, page 74.)

3 *DUFFY'S SHAMROCK RESTAURANT & BAR • 1635 Court St.; (303) 534-4935. GETTING THERE: It's uptown, at the corner of Broadway.*

Duffy's is an island of old brick in a forest of new highrise glass and steel office buildings. In fact, the owners were featured in a *Wall Street Journal* article in 1984 when they refused to sell the small two-story building to make room for a new office tower. It remains one of the few surviving old structures in the glossy downtown area. Although Duffy's is more of a restaurant than a saloon, it's worth a visit for its 72-foot-long bar with thirty-two old fashioned barstools. It's the longest plank in Denver and probably one of the longest west of the Mississippi. The place is popular with downtown workers and it's a serious gathering spot on St. Patrick's Day. Original owner Bernard Duffy is credited with starting Denver's modern St. Patrick's Day celebration with an impromptu parade by a group of regulars called the "Evil Companions." No surprise: Many among them were journalists.

4 *FADÓ IRISH PUB • 1735 Nineteenth St.; (303) 297-0066. (www.fadoirishpub.com) GETTING THERE: Fadó is in the old Union Pacific building between Nineteenth Street and Coors Field, just north of downtown.*

Denver is a long way from the *auld sod*, yet Fadó is about as Irish as a pub can get—at least in Colorado. *Fadó* means long ago and you'll think you're in old Dublin when you slip onto a stool at the long curved bar, order a pint 'o Guinness and admire the dark woods, stonework, Irish whiskey and beer signs, and cozy stone fireplaces. In fact, the interior was built in Ireland, shipped in pieces to Denver and installed in the old brick Union Pacific building. The exterior, which has an outdoor dining and drinking deck, doesn't suggest a Dublin street scene, although the interior will take you back to the old country. And so will the entertainment; the pub features Irish and Celtic music several nights a week and even sponsors rugby and soccer teams made up of faithful patrons. Fadó also serves proper Irish food and we selected it as Denver's best Irish restaurant in Chapter Three, page 67.

5 *FIRESIDE LOUNGE* • *At the Inverness Hotel & Golf Club, 200 Inverness Drive West, Englewood; (303) 799-5800. (www.invernesshotel.com) GETTING THERE: Go south about fifteen miles on I-25 and take exit 195 (County Line Road). Go left under the freeway to a traffic light, then turn left again onto Inverness Drive West.*

Fifteen miles may be a long way to drive for a martini. However, the Inverness is the most attractive resort hotel in the greater Denver area and its main bar is one of the region's most appealing cocktail lounges. Terraced down from the hotel's striking main lobby, the Fireside Lounge provides a splendid view of a fountain lake and surrounding golf course. It's a striking place with distinctive chevron ceiling beams, comfortable upholstered seating and a U-shaped black-topped bar. One seating area is open to the sunlight while another is built around that namesake fireplace. This is a particularly elegant spot, furnished with plush leather sofas and wicker chairs. A cute bit: The votive table candles have been formed in martini glasses.

6 *JOSEPHINA'S* • *1433 Larimer St.; (303) 623-0166. GETTING THERE: Josephina's is in Larimer Square, between Fourteenth and Fifteenth streets.*

Most people—particularly hungry ones—regard Josephina's as an Italian restaurant. However, it has one of the most interesting bar scenes in town. Housed in one of Larimer Square's fine old brick buildings, it has the look of an ancient bar, although it dates only from the 1970s. Slip your buns onto a stool and admire the gorgeous carved-wood backbar with its arched mirrors, and the great photo mural behind the bandstand of giggling ladies in 1920s swimsuits. A high-wheeler bicycle, antique signs and lazily turning ceiling fans complete the yesterday look. The bandstand offers live entertainment nearly every night of the week. The dining room is adjacent, featuring fare so classically Italian that you can smell the garlic from your barstool.

7 SHAKESPEARE'S • 2375 Fifteenth St.; (303) 433-6000.

GETTING THERE: From downtown, follow Fifteenth Street about a mile northwest and cross the South Platte River at Confluence Park; Shakespeare is on the right, at the corner of Fifteenth and Platte.

"Let us to billiards." That quote from Act II, Scene Five of *Anthony and Cleopatra* is the beginning and end of this large pub's relationship with the Bard. Using that cue (pun intended), Shakespeare's is Denver's largest—and certainly most attractive—pool and billiards hall. This cavernous space, clothed in old brick and dark woods, has twenty-five tables—nineteen for pool, four for billiards and two for snooker. If you regard pool as a spectator sport, the main bar and seating area are above all that green felt, so you can take a ringside table and watch the action below.

8 SHELBY'S BAR & GRILL • 519 Eighteenth St.; (303) 295-

9597. GETTING THERE: It's on the eastern edge of downtown, between Welton and Glenarm streets.

This friendly neighborhood bar has been sitting in its own little brick and masonry building since 1906. Now completely surrounded by highrise Denver, it looks both comfortable and defiant. Downtowners flock here for lunch and end-of-day cocktails, crowding into the darkwood interior or enjoying the sunshine of sidewalk tables. Shelby's centerpiece is a long U-shaped bar. To humor locals, trivia questions are written on chalkboard panels around its drop ceiling. Several cozy booths and tables line the walls and—in case the camaraderie becomes too intensive—one can adjourn to a quiet little room in the rear.

9 SHIP TAVERN • In the Brown Palace at 321 Seventeenth St.;

(www.brownpalace.com) GETTING THERE: The hotel is cradled by Seventeenth, Broadway and Tremont.

Claude Boettcher, whose father had purchased the Brown Palace from Henry C. Brown, couldn't bring the ocean to Denver, so he created an aquatic environment for this historic saloon in 1938. Using his collection of hundreds of nautical artifacts, he turned the tavern into a virtual seafaring museum, with an ornate mast and crow's nest as centerpiece. Exhibits include ships models tucked into niches on the surrounding walls, old maps and navigational charts and a ship's wheel clock. Note the Jamaican rum barrels on the backbar.

The Tavern also is the Brown Palace's most informal restaurant, with simple blue checkered tables sitting amidst the bar's dark carved wood elegance.

10 *WAZEE LOUNGE AND SUPPER CLUB* • *1600 Fifteenth St.; (303) 623-9518. Lunch through late evening daily. GETTING THERE: It's in LoDo at the corner of Fifteenth and Wazee.*

This lively hangout is a pub with many personalities. Dating from 1974, it was one of the first saloons to emerge during LoDo's gentrification. It's a serious drinking establishment, an occasional live entertainment venue, a gallery that displays works of local artists on bare brick walls—and it serves the best pizza in town (Chapter Three. page 72). The look is art deco funk, with dark wainscotting, black and white checkerboard tile floors, café curtains, converted gas lamps and lots of hanging plants. Leaded glass insets above the tall backbar give the place a splash of color. In addition to outstanding pizza, it serves assorted sandwiches, mixed drinks and nearly a score of draught beers.

THE TEN BEST "PERSONALITY BARS"

What are personality bars? They're watering holes with special character, such as a particular theme, style or attitude, and Denver has an abundance of them. Our favorites are listed in no particular order.

1 *THE COOLEST BAR:* **Sambuca Jazz Café** • *1318 Fifteenth St.; (303) 629-5299. GETTING THERE: It's in LoDo between Larimer and Market streets.*

This jazz club is one hip place, with *faux* leopard skin barstools and throw pillows, spearpoint wall sconces, and tiny tables set against a padded wall of orange, black and mauve. A "distressed" plaster and brick wall opposite the long main bar adds rustic contrast. A favorite perching place—for those wanting to see and be seen—is on a tiger-striped window seat in its storefront window. Of course cool jazz sounds—recorded or live—permeate the place.

2 *THE BEST IRISH PUB:* **Nallen's** • *1429 Market St.; 572-0667. GETTING THERE: It's between Fourteenth and Fifteenth street, a block below Larimer Square.*

Slightly scruffy Nallen's is Denver's best Irish pub for technical reasons. It's one of the few that's a serious drinking establishment, and not a restaurant thinly disguised as a tavern. This slender saloon is Denver's oldest Irish pub although that's not very old; it was opened by Irishman John Nallen in 1992. However, it *looks* like a properly aged watering hole, with wooden floors, ceiling fans and a brass rail at the foot of the bar. It's not cutely Irish but casually so, with framed scenes and posters of the *auld sod,* some soccer and hockey paraphernalia and a few farm implements to give it a rural Ireland look.

3 *THE BEST LOBBY BAR: Atrium Lounge • In the Brown Palace at 321 Seventeenth St.; (303) 297-3111. (www.brownpalace.com) GETTING THERE: The hotel is downtown, cradled by Seventeenth, Broadway and Tremont.*

Actually, the striking six-story Atrium Lounge *is* the lobby of the Brown Palace, and it's one of Denver's most popular gathering spots. It serves light lunch fare and afternoon tea, and then becomes a comfortable lobby bar in the evening. Settle back with a hand-crafted martini, listen to the pianist at the grand piano and admire the opulence of Mexican onyx, antique furnishings and that soaring balconied atrium with a stained glass skylight far above. Single malt Scotches and martinis are specialties here, and the lounge has a good selection of wines by the glass.

4 *THE BEST GLORIA STEINHAM MEMORIAL BARS: Hooters • 1920 Blake St., (303) 294-9299; and 1390 S. Colorado Blvd., (303) 782-0232. GETTING THERE: The downtown Hooters is near Nineteenth Street in LoDo, not far from Coors Field. The Colorado Boulevard version is at the corner of Arkansas Avenue in the Cherry Creek area. Take I-25 exit 204 and follow Colorado north about four blocks to Arkansas; Hooters is on the right.*

"Delightfully tacky, yet noncompliant," read signs at these harmlessly outrageous bars. Noncompliant, indeed. Hooters is noted for nubile young waitresses wearing orange hotpants and tight scoop-neck T-shirts. It has a long list of draft beers and a few wines by the glass, in addition to the usual cocktails. Those bosomy waitresses serve food as well as beer and pretty smiles. The fare is light, such as spicy chicken wings, shrimp platter, hamburgers and assorted other sandwiches. Downtown Hooters is dressed in knotty pine, neon beer signs and sports banners. The Colorado Boulevard edition has exposed heating ducts and strings of colored Christmas lights, with a porch open to the boulevard. And of course both are decorated by those pretty ladies.

5 *THE BEST MARTINI BAR: The Cruise Room • In the Oxford Hotel at 1600 Seventeenth St.; (303) 628-5400. GETTING THERE: The Oxford is LoDo, at the corner of Seventeenth and Wazee.*

To begin, what is a perfect martini? It is excellent gin or vodka with a whisper of vermouth and a dash of bitters, accompanied by a green pimento olive or pearl onion (which, for some silly reason, then makes it a Gibson). It should be shaken at your table and served straight up. The only variation that should be permitted—which is our preference—is a blend of two-thirds gin to one-third vodka. Anything beyond is not a martini; it is a gimmick.

All of that having been spelled out, the Oxford Hotel's gorgeous art deco Cruise Room serves the town's best martini. However, our barkeep commented with a proper grin: "Any good bartender can make a good martini. People say we make the best in town, when what we really make is the biggest."

That's not quite true, since excellent gin or vodka are required for martini perfection, and the Cruise Room features a choice of the very best of each. The generous martini is built before your eyes and poured into a relatively small glass with a cutely crooked stem. Small glass? Not to worry. You are then left with the shaker containing the rest of your drink, which is at least a double for the price of a single. The only problem with that crooked stemmed glass is that it's difficult to twirl it pensively between thumb and forefinger.

While attempting to do so, gaze around this cool, quiet and dimly lit place—certainly the most romantic bar in town. This art deco classic is called the Cruise Room because it was styled after a bar on the *Queen Mary*. It's a long, slender room with the bar on one side and cozy candle-lit booths on the other, all bathed in sexy indirect pink lighting. Shallow and slender *bas relief* panels on the walls represent drinking toasts from around the world.

6 *THE BEST TEQUILA BAR: Dixon's • 1610 Sixteenth St.; (303) 573-6100. GETTING THERE: Dixon's is in LoDo, on the corner of Wazee Street.*

We begin this listing with a disclaimer. Dixon's, which is primarily a restaurant, is not a great tequila bar. Apparently, Denver doesn't *have* a great tequila bar. However, Dixon's is as good as it gets, and it has won a couple of local awards for the best margaritas. To understand our attitude, you have to understand about tequila. This beverage is distilled in Mexico from the juice of the agave, and aficionados drink only 100 percent agave tequila. America's most popular import, José Cuervo Gold, is laced with sugar cane syrup to appeal to Americans' sweet teeth.

True tequila fans do not drink Cuervo Gold. And they don't necessarily drink margaritas; some prefer their tequila straight up at room temperature, or chilled—but not over ice. Dixon's best margaritas are over the rocks and hand shaken. They're made with Sauza Blue Agave tequila, or you can get a premium version with Sauza Hornitos tequila. You also can order one of several tequilas by the shot or by the glass. And if you must, you can order a those frothy crushed ice margarita, of the sort dispensed at Mexican-American tourist bars.

7 *THE QUIETEST BAR: Capitol Court • In the Adam's Mark Hotel, on the Sixteenth Street Mall between Court and Tremont streets; (303) 893-3333.*

You'll find no ranks of TV screens howling the latest ball games in this quiet bar. The video monitors in this businessmen's oriented lounge are tuned to CNN, so they're relatively quiet unless there's a war going on. A large multiple screen display on one wall is sometimes tuned to a ball game, although the volume is kept low.

The Capitol has a trendy, modern look with an interesting spiny fiber optic light fixture hanging above an attractive circular bar. It specializes in martinis and offers a good selection of wines by the glass. If you prefer to do your drinking outside, the Capitol has a large patio fronting the Sixteenth Street Mall. In addition to the usual liquor libations, it serves breakfast in the morning, plus designer coffees and snacks throughout the day and evening.

8 THE BEST SPORTS BAR: Chopper's Sports Grill ● *80 S. Madison; (303) 399-4448. GETTING THERE: It's in the Cherry Creek area southeast of downtown. The easiest approach is to follow Speer Boulevard, which blends onto eastbound First Avenue. Wrap around Cherry Creek Shopping Center on First and then Steele Street, then go left on Bayaud opposite Cherry Creek's east deck parking garage, and follow it three blocks to Madison.*

Look for the blue roof to find this lounge on the edge of a Cherry Creek residential area, and then look inside for the liveliest sports bar in town. A dozen or more oversized TV monitors hang from the ceiling, so you can catch all the games. However, during evening happy hours, you won't be able to hear them. Sports pennants and posters are strung wall to wall. Display cases house jerseys, footballs, basketballs, shoes and helmets, and walls are busy with posters and photos of Elway and others in action.

Since many sports fans are serious suds sippers, Chopper's has fifteen beers on tap and another thirty by the bottle. These can be accompanied by pizzas, fish and chips, burgers and such. It's a large complex, with two separate lounges and an outside patio area.

9 THE MOST ELEGANT BAR: Churchill Bar ● *In the Brown Palace at 321 Seventeenth St.; (303) 297-3111. GETTING THERE: The hotel is downtown, cradled by Seventeenth, Broadway and Tremont.*

Although it appears to be as old as this venerable 1892 hotel, the Churchill is relatively new. Sharing an entry foyer with the Palace Arms restaurant, it has the classy look of an elegant men's club, with overstuffed burgundy leather chairs, dark woods, subdued lighting and flocked wallpaper. The main bar and backbar are accented with elaborately carved woods. Unfortunately, since this is the Brown's cigar bar, the air quality is rather poor. The place could use a stronger ventilation system.

10 THE MOST HISTORIC BAR: My Brother's Bar •

2376 Fifteenth St.; (303) 455-9991. GETTING THERE: It's just across the South Platte River from downtown; take Fifteenth Street through LoDo to Platte Street and the bar is on the left hand corner.

Although this saloon's name is rather new, My Brother's Bar is the oldest Denver drinking establishment that's still on its original site. It is descended—if that's the proper word—from the Highland House, opened by Italian immigrant Maria Anna Capelli in 1873. (To avoid prejudices of that era, she used the name M.A. Capelli on her business records.) After going through several name changes, it became My Brother's Bar when Jim and Angelo Karagas from Detroit purchased it in 1970. Well-kept and just shy of scruffy, Highland House-cum-My Brothers Bar looks its age, with properly bare brick walls, ceiling fans, wainscotting and drop lamps. There's not much fancy here; the back-bar décor consists of towering rows of bottles. During quieter moments, the place is noted for its classical music collection and lack of TV. However, during the evening cocktail hour, the predominant sound is highly vocal camaraderie.

BEER HERE! THE TEN BEST BREW BARS

Forget the Colorado Kool-Aid, kids! Denver is beer country, and most serious suds sippers eschew Coors in favor of the many hearty Colorado microbrews. Step into any liquor store or Safeway beer department, and you'll find regional products by such firms as Boulder Beer, Breckenridge, Great Divide, Odell and Oasis. In addition to the usual pilsners, bocks and stouts, microbreweries feature curiosities such as blueberry ale, raspberry wheat and oatmeal beer. (Remember that beer sold in supermarkets is only 3.2 percent alcohol. You need to go to a liquor store or bar to get the full-strength stuff, which is 4.2 and beyond.)

If you want your beer fresh from the brew kettles or frothy from the tap, step into one of Denver's many brewpubs. Our list also includes establishments that don't brew their own but are noted for good beer selections. Incidentally, you'll find that virtually every Denver brewpub also is a restaurant.

1 WYNKOOP BREWING COMPANY • 1634 Eighteenth St.;

(303) 297-2700. Lunch through late evening daily. GETTING THERE: It's in LoDo at the corner of Wynkoop, near Union Station.

The best brewpub in Denver? It may be the best west of Chicago, and it's certainly the largest. Opened in 1988, this is Denver's first brewpub and owner-creator John Hickenlooper says it's the largest in

America. Occupying a huge former warehouse, the Wynkoop is a study in pressed tin ceilings, exposed heating ducts and raw brick walls, cascading over several levels. One of Denver's largest pool rooms occupies an upstairs loft, with twenty-eight tables.

Back down among the brew bottles, you can sip suds such as Railyard Ale, Sagebrush Stout and—if you like things spicy—Chili Beer. The kitchen is as creative as the brewery, issuing mango barbecued chicken with roasted potatoes, very good fish and chips with beer batter, and Denver elk medallions. For dessert, try the peach "Coopler" served hot with a scoop of melting vanilla ice cream.

2 *BRECKENRIDGE BREWERY & PUB • 2220 Blake St.; (303) 297-3644. GETTING THERE: It's between 22nd and 23rd in LoDo, just beyond Coors Field.*

One of Denver's largest microbreweries, the Breckenridge facility stretches nearly a full block, with a large, airy pub in the middle. It's an appealing place, occupying an old brick building with a distinctive curved ceiling. The large, open dining and drinking area shares the main floor with several stainless steel brewing vats. Their products include India Pale Ale, Avalanche Ale, Oatmeal Stout and Mountain Wheat. The beers have won several medals, which are immodestly displayed at the entrance. The kitchen issues hamburgers, chicken wings, steaks, fish and chips and several Ted-Mex dishes. Fresh air quaffers and nibblers can adjourn to the Tap Terrace above the sidewalk.

3 *DENVER CHOP HOUSE AND BREWERY • 1735 Nineteenth St.; (303) 296-0800. Lunch and dinner daily. GETTING THERE: It's in the old Union Pacific Building at the corner of Nineteenth and Wynkoop, immediately north of downtown.*

This large and handsome establishment is more restaurant than brewpub, although it does offer several micro-brews. Among them are Pilsner Lager, Singletrack Copper Ale, Nut Brown Ale and Oatmeal Stout. Honey Wheat is a curiously interesting beer, quite mellow and served with a lemon slice. On the food side, this is a serious chophouse, specializing in steaks, pork chops and other meaty American fare. Its entrées include several sorts of steaks, Iowa pork chops, veal chops with sun dried tomatoes and artichokes, plank salmon and a rather good hamburger. The look is chophouse as well, with high ceilings, dark woods, brick interior walls and polished wood floors. A few railroading posters and paintings remind diners that this once was a Union Pacific station.

4 *FALLING ROCK TAP HOUSE • 1919 Blake St.; (303) 293-8338. (www.thefallingrock.com) GETTING THERE: It's on LoDo's "saloon row" between Nineteenth and Twentieth streets.*

This midsize drinking establishment is Denver's penultimate tap house, with nearly fifty taps strung along the back of its lengthy bar. Thirsty patrons can get—by the pour—beers from America, Germany, Belgium, Great Britain, Ireland, the Netherlands and France. If you can't find your favorite along this great rank of spigots, the Tap House carries more than a hundred other American and international brands by the bottle. To help the undecided, its long beer list is broken down into pale, amber and dark. The primary décor here—other than that skirmisher line of taps—is hundreds of beer bottles lining narrow wall shelves. The menu is much smaller than the brew list, featuring pizzas, calzones and sandwiches. We like the fact that both the saloon and its large outdoor deck are back off the street, away from traffic's rumble.

5 PINTS PUB • *221 W. Thirteenth Ave.; (303) 534-7543. GET-TING THERE: It's between Bannock and Cherokee just southwest of the Civic Center. From downtown, go south on Broadway and then west (left) on Thirteenth for three blocks.*

Although not in Denver's saloon mainstream—neither downtown nor in LoDo—this English pub is easy to find. Head west on Thirteenth and look to your right for the red British style phone booth out front. There's another inside, with a working phone. Pints is casual British in look and attitude. It earns a spot on our beer pub list because it features a large assortment of hard-to-find brews of England, Ireland, Scotland and Wales. We counted two dozen taps when we last stopped by for a little Courage. If we had a category for the best Scotch pub, it would qualify as well, with a selection of more than a hundred single malts. Anglophiles will feel right at home in Pints, with its polished woods, dart boards, John Courage Ale signs and inviting fireplaces. However, the kitchen is more American than Brit, offering sandwiches, hamburgers, chicken and such. Read far enough down the menu, how-ever, and you'll find a plowman's platter of cheeses, sliced smoked tur-key, apple-smoked pork loin and pickled peppers. Pints is fashioned from a small brick apartment house and the front porch is a pleasant drinking deck.

6 ROCK BOTTOM BREWERY • *1001 Sixteenth Street Mall; (303) 534-7616. (www.rockbottom.com) Lunch through late evening Monday-Saturday. GETTING THERE: Rock Bottom is in LoDo at the cor-ner of Curtis Street.*

If you like hearty beers and noisy ambiance, wedge yourself into this popular place on the Sixteenth Street Mall. Happy sippers and din-ers jam its large interior and spill out onto a patio dining area at lunch time, and from the cocktail hour through late evening. It has the stereotypical brewpub look—high ceilings, exposed heating ducts, brick walls, stainless steel brewing kettles and hanging TV monitors whose programs no one can hear. Our favorite beer here is a copper colored and mildly hearty Single Track Copper Ale. Other choices include Rockies Premium Ale, Falcon Tail Ale, Red Rocks Red and Molly's Titanic Brown Ale. From the kitchen comes requisite brewpub fare such as pizzas, hamburgers, several pastas, meatloaf, chicken fried steak and fried chicken.

7 *ROCK BOTTOM BREWERY II • 9627 E. County Line Rd., Englewood; (303) 792-9090. GETTING THERE: Go south about fifteen miles on I-25 and take exit 195 (County Line Road). Turn right at the County Line Road traffic light and then go right again into a shopping complex called Centennial Promenade, across from Park Meadows. The brewpub is toward the rear of the mall, back near the freeway.*

A second edition of Rock Bottom, the former Walnut Brewery Restaurant, is a fair distance south of Denver. We don't suggest driving all that way just for a glass of Single Track Copper Ale. However, there are a couple of other attractions in this area—Park Meadows Mall and the striking Inverness Hotel and Golf Club, featured respectively in Chapter Nine, page 140 and Chapter Five, page 94. So if you happen to be in the neighborhood— This is yet another contemporary brewpub with high ceilings, naked heating ducts and stainless steel brewing vats. Rock Bottom produces a variety of micro-brews and you can order a "tasting menu" if you're undecided. The menu offers fish and chips, chicken fried steak, barbecued ribs, several pastas and brick oven pizzas. If the weather temps, you can have your beer and victuals in the Beer Garden out front.

8 *ROUNDERS AT THE SANDLOT • 2151 Blake St.; (303) 312-2553. Lunch Monday-Saturday, until late afternoon prior to night games. GETTING THERE: The pub is wedged into the northeast corner of Coors field at Blake and 23rd Street.*

This unique brewpub—the only one in America built into a ball park—leads a double life. When the Rockies aren't playing at home, it's open to the public via its street entrance. During game time, those doors are closed and it's accessible only to ticket-toting baseball fans, who can enter from the stadium. Anyone from anywhere in the stadium can use the pub. Of course its brews and food have cute baseball names. You can sip a little Power Alley Ale, Right Field Red Ale, Slugger Stout or Squeeze Play Wheat, and nosh on Base Hit Burgers, Mile-High Dagwood sandwiches and such. Housed in an old brick building that's fused into a corner of the stadium, Rounders has a few copper kettles to prove it's a functioning micro-brewery and window walls onto Coors Field.

9 *SPORTS COLUMN* • *1930 Blake St.; (303) 296-1930. GET-TING THERE: It's in LoDo between Nineteenth and Twentieth streets.*

Living up to its name, the Sports Column is one of Denver's best sports bars, and it's particularly popular because it's within a block of Coors Field. It's also a serious beer pub, with several by the tap and many more by the bottle. And of course, beer goes with baseball. Expect the place to be jumping with pre- and post-game revelry. In fact, patrons can see the brick façade of the ballyard from a rooftop deck; an alert eye might even be able to spot a high pop fly. That deck, obviously a popular sunny day spot, has its own bar. The large, open downstairs area features the requisite raw brick walls, exposed heating ducts, sports memorabilia and—of course—an abundance of TV monitors, along with three large pull-down projection screens. If you miss the game action here, you just aren't paying attention. Like most local drinking establishments, it serves the usual pub fare.

10 *ZANG BREWING COMPANY* • *2301 Seventh St.; (303) 455-2500. GETTING THERE: From downtown, take Fifteenth Street through LoDo and cross the river to Platte Street. Turn left and follow it past REI, where it curves to the right to become Water Street. Zang's is opposite Ocean Journey, on the corner of Water and Seventh.*

Zang's makes our beer pub list on a technicality. This bold brick structure and the original brewmaster's house half a block away are all that remain of Zang Brewing Company, once the largest brewery in the Intermountain West. The handsome brick bar building, dating from 1871, formerly housed a tavern with small upstairs sleeping rooms for teamsters that hauled Zang's beer kegs to their markets. Today's Zang has a history of sorts; it was reopened in 1975 as Denver's first sports bar, with the obligatory satellite systems to pull in all the ball games.

The saloon retains its late nineteenth century look with bare brick walls, a leaded glass backbar, pressed tin ceilings and tulip chandeliers. To barely qualify as one of our Ten Best beer pubs, it has ten beers on tap, including a couple brewed specifically for the pub—Zang's Amber Ale and Zang's Columbine Ale. And of course it's also a restaurant serving light fare. It also has a family section, plus a patio out back.

The most romantic thing a woman ever said to me in bed was: "Are you sure you're not a cop?"
                                                                      — Larry Brown

Chapter eight

ROMANCE
...AND OTHER PRIMAL URGES

Early Denver wasn't short on romance or primal urges, and the distinctions between the two often were blurred. There is romance in its history, for it was founded as a lively mining camp. It was settled predominately by men, which is typical of frontier towns established by adventurers and not by migrating families.

Its first businesses were bars and bawdy houses and many of its first women were prostitutes. Ladies of the night remained active well into the last century, although Denver today is regarded as a rather conservative and culturally oriented city. It is not a city of high emotion or much controversy. Both its gay and straight sexual appetites keep rather low profiles. Further, we wouldn't regard it as a romantic city in the sense of San Francisco or Paris.

However, recent developments have made the city more appealing for romantic souls—the creation of the Sixteenth Street Mall with its sidewalk cafés, a shift from steak and potatoes diners to candle-lit *nouveau* restaurants, the conversion of old brick buildings into intimate boutique hotels, and its embracing of the performing arts. It's not the sort of place one would target for a honeymoon. However, should circumstance bring the two of you here, Denver has many intimate corners, romantic restaurants and miles of sheltered walking trails where assorted lovers can stroll hand-in-hand. And of course, the nearby mountain resorts, covered later in this book, offer an abundance of romantic getaways.

THE TEN BEST PLACES TO SNUGGLE WITH YOUR SWEETIE

Can you really find privacy in a city as large and busy as Denver? Certainly, since this urban community also is a city of more than 250 parks and public gardens. With so many parklands and so many walkways offering so many places to be alone, it's never difficult to shed the madding crowds. However, our favorite snuggle corner is a very public yet cozy cocktail lounge:

1 THE CRUISE ROOM • *In the Oxford Hotel at 1600 Seventeenth St.; (303) 628-5400. GETTING THERE: The Oxford is in the LoDo area, at the corner of Seventeenth and Wazee.*

This art deco classic is the most romantic bar in town, and its comfortable high-backed booths provide intimate places for private conversations. The sexy hot pink indirect lighting is dim, votive candles flicker on the tables, the music is soft and there are no TV monitors. Should you be able to take your eyes off one another, peer through the dim light at the wall panels; they represent drinking toasts from around the world. And so here's to romance... (For more on the Cruise Room, see Chapter Seven, page 116.)

2 CHERRY CREEK SHOPPING CENTER • *3000 E. First Ave.; (303) 388-3900. GETTING THERE: The center is rimmed by First, University Boulevard, Steele Street and Cherry Creek. From downtown, follow Speer Boulevard southeast about three miles along Cherry Creek; it blends into First Avenue, which crosses the front of the center.*

A large shopping mall is a rather public place for snuggling. However, if you're content just to hold a quiet conversation, this upscale shopping complex has very comfortable couches-for-two in its seating sections. The largest take-a-break area is just past the First Avenue entrance. Immediately beyond are sleek glass elevators that can take you to the second-level shops. And why should you want to go up there? Because there's a Victoria's Secret perfume and bath boutique nearby. Surely, you didn't just bring her here just for quiet conversation...

3 CHERRY CREEK TRAIL • *Between Champa and Arapahoe streets, just southeast of downtown. GETTING THERE: You can reach this section of the walkway via the Colfax Street access at Speer Boulevard,* *then stroll a couple of blocks northwest on the creekside walk. Approaching from the other direction, the trail is accessible from Larimer Street, beside the University of Colorado at Denver campus.*

Although the Cherry Creek Trail has few benches where a couple might pause to snuggle, there are four along a two-block section between Champa and Arapahoe. And they're widely spaced—suitable for private conversations. Further, the walkway is several feet below street level, so couples suffer neither the noise nor intrusion of traffic. Only an occasional passing stroller or runner will intrude on your privacy. (Cyclists and skaters are restricted to the opposite bank on this section of the Cherry Creek Trail.)

4 **DENVER BOTANIC GARDENS** ● *909 York St.; (303) 331-4000. Wednesday-Friday 9 to 5 and Saturday-Tuesday 9 to 8, May through September; then daily 9 to 5 October through April. Moderate admission fees. GETTING THERE: Go east from downtown about a mile and a half on Colfax Avenue, then south half a mile on York Street.*

Despite their appeal, botanical gardens are rarely crowded, particularly on weekdays. With their landscaped grounds and cheerful blooms, they're nice places to be alone with someone special. Denver Botanic Gardens is one of the largest and finest in America, and our favorite sweetie snuggle place is in its Shofu-en Japanese Garden. The specific spot is beneath a giant weeping willow beside a lily pond near the teahouse. A couple of rough stone benches just large enough for two make ideal perches beneath the willow's shade. Sit and gaze through the sheltering bowers, admiring the lily pads and the simple geometric grace of the garden. Don't forget to say hello to the *koi*, the huge brightly colored goldfish in the pond. They represent good luck in Japan—something any loving couple needs.

5 **FERRIL LAKE SHORELINE AT CITY PARK** ● *South shore of the lake. GETTING THERE: To reach the park, go east on Colfax Avenue about two and a half miles to Colorado Boulevard. Turn north (left) for half a mile, then go left again into the park on 22nd Avenue and drive southwest to Ferril Lake (formerly City Park Lake).*

Park your car near the Spanish style Pavilion at the west end of City Park and walk—hand-in-hand, of course—a couple of hundred yards along Ferril Lake's southern shoreline. You'll soon encounter a really cute sculpture of three kids staring down into a fountain while three frogs stare up at them. A pair of benches face the sculpture and a more secluded bench is between the sculpture and the lakeshore, facing out on the water. Expect this area to be relatively deserted on a weekday, although you won't get much privacy in this popular park on a sunny weekend.

6 *HUDSON GARDENS* • *6115 S. Santa Fe Dr., Littleton; (303) 797-8565. (www.hudsongarden.org) Daily 9 to 5 May-September and 10 to 2 October-April; modest admission fee. GETTING THERE: Head south on I-25, take the Santa Fe Drive exit and continue south for about eight miles to Littleton. The gardens are on the right, half a mile south of the major intersection of Littleton/Bowles in downtown Littleton.*

This is a complex of sixteen gardens near the South Platte River. Its best sweetie snuggle place is in the Secret Garden, with an oversized swing big enough for two. Nearly surrounded by protective foliage, you can swing together in relative privacy, like a couple of little kids. The higher you swing, the more you can see from this hidden garden; or just sit quietly and listen to the birds—and the rumble of distant traffic. The landscape architect who created this cozy enclave obviously wasn't superstitious; this is Garden Number Thirteen.

7 *LOEWS GIORGIO HOTEL PLAZA* • *Colorado Boulevard at Mississippi Street. GETTING THERE: The hotel is about five miles from downtown. Go southeast on I-25, then take Colorado Boulevard (exit 204) just under a mile north. Look for the tall gray towers on your right.*

Unknown to most residents and to virtually all visitors except hotel guests, a small plaza is tucked between the hotel and the adjacent Mountain Tower office complex. It's an exceptionally cozy little enclave with a striking black and red spillover fountain and a small swatch of rolling green lawn. A few benches invite lingering.

8 *LOOKOUT MOUNTAIN PRESERVE* • *On Colorow Road, near the Buffalo Bill Grave and Museum above Golden. GETTING THERE: Head west from Denver on I-70 for about eighteen miles and begin climbing into the Rockies; take exit 256 onto Lookout Mountain Road (marked "Buffalo Bill Grave"). After about a mile and a half, before you reach the Buffalo Bill memorial, turn left onto Colorow Road and follow it a short distance to the nature preserve.*

An attractive nature center occupies this 110-acre wooded preserve, although that's not where we suggest seeking natural solitude. If you cross the road from the preserve parking lot, you'll see a trailhead, a single picnic table and a one bench, sitting among the pines. What a cozy coincidence! If you come up here on a weekday, you'll probably have the place to yourselves, with a choice between snuggling on the bench or having a romantic picnic. You can enjoy fine tree-filtered views across the Front Range to the rooftops of Golden, the Coors Brewery and the faraway highrises of Denver. If you failed to bring a picnic lunch, you can drive a mile to the Buffalo Bill Grave and Museum and pick up fare from the snack bar.

9 *RED ROCKS PARK & AMPHITHEATRE • 12700 W. Alameda Parkway, Morrison. GETTING THERE: Go west on I-70 to exit 259 (Morrison/Red Rocks), then drive about a mile south. The entrance is on your right.*

This dramatic amphitheatre can seat more than 9,000 people, but if you go up there on a weekday—particularly in the off-season—you just might have the place to yourselves. Our favorite Red Rocks snuggle perch is on the very top row, on seats 48 and 49, which are sheltered by an overhanging juniper. Enjoy the awesome view across the Denver Basin, framed by dramatically tilted strata of red sandstone. For more on Red Rocks, see Chapter Two, page 51.

10 *SHOEMAKER PLAZA • On the west bank of the Platte River opposite Confluence Park, just below the REI store. GETTING THERE: Follow Fifteenth Street about a mile northwest from downtown and cross the South Platte River at Confluence Park. Turn left onto Platte Street beside REI, park and walk down to the river. You'll find a small enclave just to the left of a series of concrete viewing platforms.*

Shoemaker Plaza is a tiny park right at water's edge, slightly removed from the more popular river-viewing platforms to the right. You and your sweetie can sit on one of its risers, retreat to a park bench on a strip of lawn just above or—really cool—perch on the plaza's edge and dangle your tootsies in the cool stream. Don't come here on a sunny weekend because you won't enjoy much privacy. Should you wonder—and we did—this little enclave was named for Joe Shoemaker, Platte River Development Committee chairman.

THE TEN MOST ROMANTIC RESTAURANTS

As we noted above, Denver is making an appealing transition from steak and potatoes cafés to more trendy and intimately styled restaurants. There are thus many cozy cafés for dining with your sweetie. One of them, in fact, is Morton's, a steak and potatoes place.

PRICING: We use simple strings of dollar signs to indicate the price of a typical dinner with entrée, soup or salad, not including drinks, appetizers or dessert: **$** = less than $10 per entrée; **$$** = $10 to $19; **$$$** = $20 to $29; **$$$$** = "Did you say you were buying?"

1 *THE BROKER • Seventeenth and Champa; (303) 292-5065. Eclectic menu; full bar service. Lunch weekdays, dinner nightly. Major credit cards; $$$ to $$$$. GETTING THERE: It's downtown, in the cellar of the Colorado Business Bank building between Champa and Stout.*

The name sounds rather businesslike, yet this is the most romantic restaurant in Denver. The look is clubby and dim, with an elegant Victorian décor. The large restaurant is divided into smaller dining areas, each with intimate banquettes or booths for two. Its coziest corner is in the original bank vault, isolated from the main restaurant and with the massive vault door still in place. Several paneled booths in here are virtual hideaways. However, the staff won't close the vault door on request. Soft music, dark wood paneling and tables with tiny lamps and bud vases complete the setting for the city's most sensual restaurant. The menu is eclectic, rather straightforward and expensive, without a lot of *nouveau* gadgetry. Offerings when we last visited included trout amandine, duckling with cherry Schambord sauce, roasted pork tenderloin with apple and walnut stuffing and porterhouse steak.

2 AUBERGINE CAFÉ • *225 E. Seventh Ave.; (303) 832-4778. Mediterranean-Italian; wine and beer. Dinner Tuesday-Sunday. Major credit cards; $$$. GETTING THERE: Head south from downtown on Broadway, then go left (east) four blocks; the café is between Grand and Sherman streets.*

A Zagat dining guide contributor says Aubergine features "the most romantic setting in the city." It is indeed an intimate little place. It's romantic in a rustic kind of way, with a French seaport bistro look with mustard colored walls, works of art, brown paper table coverings and dried herbs hanging in the windows. There is intimacy in this simplicity, and its eclectic menu with creative American *nouveau* touches will kindle culinary appetites if not romantic ones. To generate a properly amorous mood, peruse the excellent wine list. For more on this creative little café and its versatile menu, see Chapter Three, page 57.

3 BRIARWOOD INN • *1630 Eighth St., Golden; (303) 279-3121. American and continental; full bar service. Lunch weekdays and Sunday brunch; dinner nightly. Major credit cards; $$$ to $$$$. GETTING THERE: It's just beyond Golden near the junction of highways 6 and 58. From downtown, take Highway 6 to the western edge of Golden, or follow I-70 and then Highway 58 (exit 265) to and through the town.*

Is it a prime place for romance, or is it past its prime? Although this tucked-away café in a country mansion gets mixed reviews, it has been a special occasion place for decades. And since your significant other is special, why not take this occasion to drive out to Golden? Make reservations first and get specific directions, since Briarwood is rather tucked away—as a romantic country restaurant should be. Everything about this place exudes romance—the carefully tended landscaping, the little bridge leading to the mansion, the crisp white nappery and flawless crystal. The dining area is divided into several intimate rooms. The menu, more traditional than *nouveau,* is *prix fixe* and pricy. Multicourse dinners are huge, so plan on arriving hungry for food as well as for romance. The changing and rather small menu offers steaks and chops, some interesting game dishes and several traditional European entrées. The wine list is large and quite international.

4 THE FORT • *19192 Highway 8, Morrison; (303) 697-4771. American; full bar service. Dinner nightly. Major credit cards; $$$ to $$$$. GETTING THERE: The Fort is about twelve miles southwest of Denver. The fastest all-freeway approach is to go west on U.S. 6, which blends into I-70 after about eight miles. Continue west briefly, then go south at exit 260 on Highway 470 for five miles. At the interchange with U.S. 285, go southwest (toward Fairplay) about a mile, take the Highway 8 exit (Morrison) and the restaurant is immediately on your right.*

Can the area's most contrived tourist restaurant also be one of its most romantic? This reconstruction of an adobe fort built around a quadrangle can provide an amorous evening if approached properly. And the food is excellent. Call ahead for reservations and ask for a table in one of the more intimate dining rooms, away from the tourist crowd. Arrive after dark—romantic dining should be late anyway— and linger before a courtyard campfire, then step into the trading post and buy your mate something in Navajo silver. At some point in the evening, you must adjourn to the large deck outside the main dining room—drink in hand—to drink in the glittering stars and the lights of Denver. This will not be an inexpensive evening, although it can be a memorable one. For more on the Fort, its history and its food, see Chapter Three, page 57.

5 HIGHLANDS GARDEN CAFÉ • *3927 W. 32nd Ave.; (303) 458-5920. Contemporary American; wine and beer. Lunch Tuesday-Friday and dinner nightly. MC/VISA; $$ to $$$. GETTING THERE: It's in Denver's Highland Park area northwest of downtown, between Osceola and Perry streets. Follow Speer Boulevard about two miles, then fork to the left on 32nd Avenue and go six blocks west.*

What could be more romantic than an intimate, dimly lit dining room in an old Victorian home? How about two cozy dining rooms in paired Victorian homes? Owners of the Highlands Garden Café met with such initial success that they bought the adjoining home, built a connecting hallway and opened a second dining room. Both are similar, with brick walls, wooden floors and white nappery. Some walls are graced with framed watercolors; others have pretty murals painted directly onto the surface. Hungry lovers also can opt for a romantic dinner under the stars, and again they can choose between two patio dining areas—one brick and the other a wooden deck. For more on this restaurant and its fine, constantly changing fare, see Chapter Three, page 58.

6 *LITTLE RUSSIAN CAFÉ* • *1424 Larimer St.; (303) 595-8600. Russian-Hungarian; wine, beer and vodka. Dinner nightly. Major credit cards; $$$. GETTING THERE: The restaurant is in a small enclave called Kettle Arcade, off Larimer Square between Fourteenth and Fifteenth streets.*

Russian food may not be very sensuous (goulash for two?), although this restaurant is one of the most intimate in Denver. It features several cozy little tables for two, including a couple tucked into alcoves. Silver chandeliers shed soft light on white table linens accented by saucy red napkins. One is expected to begin dinner by slamming back an icy cold shot of vodka, which certainly should put you in an amorous mood. Follow this with entrées such as *golubsti* (stuffed cabbage with ground beef), *zharke* (oven-roasted sliced beef, mushrooms and carrot and onion casserole), beef stroganoff, chicken Kiev or Hungarian goulash. No, those dishes don't sound very romantic. Just reach for the vodka bottle and keep eating.

7 *MORTON'S OF CHICAGO* • *1710 Wynkoop St.; (303) 825-3353. American; full bar service. Dinner nightly; bar opens at 5. Major credit cards; $$$ to $$$$. GETTING THERE: Morton's is in LoDo, opposite Union Station.*

If you think of Morton's as a clubby men's hangout, bring your significant other to the Denver version. The dining room is rather light and almost cheerful, with votive candles on white nappery for a properly romantic aura. Since two cigarettes silhouetted in candlelight are no longer socially correct, Morton's has a non-smoking area and the most of the puffers are relegated to a mahogany bar that *does* have a men's club feel. Morton's is primarily a steak house, although you can really impress your date by ordering whole baked Maine lobster at "market price" and isn't she or he worth it? For more on Morton's menu, see Chapter Three, page 73.

8 *PALACE ARMS* • *In the Brown Palace at 321 Seventeenth St.; (303) 297-3111. (www.brownpalace.com) Continental; full bar service. Lunch weekdays and dinner nightly. Major credit cards; $$$$. GETTING THERE: The legendary downtown hotel is cradled by Seventeenth, Broadway and Tremont.*

The two of you will want to dress the part for Denver's most elegant special occasion restaurant. In fact, jacket and tie are required, to help guests fit into the Palace's gilt-edge opulence. The restaurant is lushly sensuous with its ostentatious old European décor, intimate booths, white nappery on tables charmed with tiny European lamps, and tuxedo-clad waitstaff. Zagat calls the service both "impeccable" and "snooty," although we sensed none of the latter. However, we're not intimidated by excessively formal waiters, particularly when we're in a romantic mood and for the most part ignoring the staff. For more on this "superelegant" restaurant (another Zagat adjective), see Chapter Three, page 59.

9 *TANTE LOUISE* • *4900 E. Colfax Ave.; (303) 355-4488. French, wine and beer. Dinner Monday-Saturday; closed Sunday. Major credit cards; $$$ to $$$$. GETTING THERE: It's about three miles east on Colfax, on the corner of Eudora Street.*

Pretend the traffic isn't buzzing past on adjacent Colfax Avenue—which you can't hear from inside—and this becomes one of Denver's most romantic restaurants. A culinary landmark for nearly three decades, it occupies a fine old house perched in a transition zone between Colfax commercialism and a quiet, well-tended old neighborhood. The intimate café is fashioned as a charming French inn, with polished wood floors, dark wainscotting, floral wallpaper, lace curtains and fireplaces. Ask for a quiet table in one of the cozier corners. Although the sense of this place is rural France, the menu is rather contemporary, with light sauces and some American *nouveau* accents. If you want to prime one another with wine, the list is extensive and expensive. A sheltered, lushly landscaped garden is a nice romantic spot for an evening aperitif or after dinner cognac. For more on Tante Louise and its creative cookery, see Chapter Three, page 60.

10 *TUSCANY* • *In Loews Giorgio Hotel at 4150 E. Mississippi Ave.; (303) 782-9300. Italian and American; full bar service. Breakfast through dinner daily, with Sunday brunch. Major credit cards; $$ to $$$. GETTING THERE: The hotel is at Colorado Boulevard and Mississippi, about five miles from downtown. Go southeast on I-25, take exit 204 and follow Colorado Boulevard north for just under a mile. Look for the tall gray towers on your right.*

Although sensuous restaurants are plentiful in Italy, most of Denver's pasta parlors are more bistro-like, with red checkered table cloths, raffia-wrapped bottles dangling from the ceilings and lots of spaghetti. A gorgeous exception is Tuscany, the lone dining salon in the highrise Giorgio Hotel. We like the hotel's small patio for a snuggle place (above, page 127) and we like its restaurant for romantic dining. Although it serves from breakfast on, save it for dinner, since it's difficult to get romantic over waffles, and lunches are nearly as expensive as dinners. In the evening, you can revel in Tuscany's northern Italian opulence of frescoed walls, classic paintings and marble topped dining tables, with old style high backed chairs that almost embrace you. Since this is Denver's best bit of Italian elegance, relax and enjoy a slow-paced evening of creatively spiced chicken, veal, seafood and beef entrées or freshly prepared pastas. Clink your glasses over a predominately Italian wine list and savor this moment of *la dolce vita*. You'll find it hard to imagine as you toy with your cacciatore that you're in a city known mostly for buffalo steak and beer.

DENVER'S TEN FRISKIEST DIVERSIONS

Denver is a lot tamer than it was during its rowdy frontier days, when saloons and brothels outnumbered churches. Most were centered in what is now the gentrified LoDo district, and particularly along Market Street. From the late nineteenth to the early twentieth century, more than a thousand prostitutes plied their trade along Market, in bordellos and tiny one-bed shacks called cribs. Most were closed down during Prohibition, which carried with it a strong antiprostitution movement.

Fallen angels returned in the 1930s, primarily in the guise of rooming house "maids." These "rooming houses" were closed during World War II under federal government pressure as servicemen were drawn to nearby military bases. Prostitutes then went underground and stayed there through the fifties, reemerging as "masseuses" in the sixties and seventies, then as "escorts" in the eighties. Local newspapers started refusing to run escort service adds, so the prostitutes went even further underground, where they pretty much remain today, keeping a very low profile. As well they should. Anyone who solicits sex in this age of AIDS is being recklessly foolish.

With the fear of Aids and the pressures to ban prostitution in recent decades, most lonely johns have been getting their jollies through porn shops. Colfax Avenue was the city's porn promenade during the latter part of the last century, busy with sex shops and adult movie houses. They've thinned out in recent years, although a fair number are still scattered along Denver's main east-west boulevard, including the largest in town, which is at the beginning of our list. However, these frisky diversions are listed in no particular order, since one person's turn-on is another person's sexual shut-down.

1 BROWSE THROUGH A VERY ADULT BOOK AND VIDEO STORE • *Kitty's Adult Entertainment Centers, 735 E. Colfax, (303) 832-5155; 119 S. Broadway, (303) 733-2411; and 3333 W. Alameda, (303) 936-6314.*

Miss Kitty hasn't completely cornered the market on sex shops, although she apparently has the largest number of outlets. Some never close and the Broadway and Alameda locations have theaters showing naughty films. Kitty's sells the usual X-rated books, movies, playthings made of latex and "marital aids," which does not refer to marriage manuals and counseling. However, even voyeurism isn't free; Kitty charges a one dollar "browse fee."

2 *LET THEM ENTERTAIN YOU* • In the Yellow Pages, under *"Entertainment-adult."*

If you flip through the Denver Yellow Pages, you'll find listings for "exotic dancers", "room service stripteasers" and "hot bodies strip-o-grams." Again, with the dual threat of AIDS and possibly being busted by the Denver vice squad, don't go beyond being a voyeur. Incidentally, since this is a liberated society, ladies, we noted an ad for "Hard-bodies Striptease, Inc."

3 *READ ALL ABOUT IT IN A NAUGHTY NEWSPAPER* • *The Rocky Mountain Oyster, P.O. Box 27467, Denver, CO 80227-0467. (www.oyster.com)*

This weekly newspaper is a favorite of swingers and voyeurs and us farm kids know that the term "Rocky mountain oysters" has a double entendre. The *Oysters* pages are busy with ads for bosomy girls offering escort and outcall service, graphic advice to the lovelorn and personal ads for swingers. Of course, to understand the ads, you must understand the code: "Dominant M wants to meet submissive OR for B&D and a little SSD; LTR possible." You won't find this lively little newspaper on streetside newsracks, since it's busy with nudes and naughty words. However, your local friendly porn shop should have a stack of copies.

4 *CHECK OUT THE SINGLES SCENE* • *Westword newspaper; office at 969 Broadway near the corner of Tenth; mailing address P.O. Box 5970, Denver, CO 80217. For "romance information," call (303) 293-6417. (www.westword.com)*

This popular alternative newspaper, published every other week and available free on news racks, has a large classified section called "Romance: The Dating Connection." It features scores of ads for boy-seeks-girl, girl-seeks-boy and some interesting combinations thereof. While not as raunchy as the *Rocky Mountain Oyster,* it at also carries a few ads for phone sex and Denver area topless clubs.

5 *GET YOUR SEX BY WIRE* • Phone sex has been around for years, and so has call-blocking to keep it from tender ears. However, if you're a broad-minded adult visiting Denver and you want a little frisky conversation, who ya gonna call? Flip through the pages of the good old *Rocky Mountain Oyster* and you'll find several ads for "naughty local girls who want to talk dirty." *Westword* also carries a few frisky phone sex ads.

6 *GET YOUR SEX ON THE INTERNET* • Sex on the internet has taken over where phone sex left off. A recent U.S. Supreme Court ruling called it freedom of expression, stating that it couldn't be limited to late hours, after the kiddies have gone to bed. So where do you find freedom of expression in Denver? Log on to *www.oyster.com* for lots of "Colorado naked babes" and "XXX true stories from readers!" And if you need a date, boot up *www.denverwebgirls.com*.

7 *WATCH THOSE LADIES PEEL* • *Centerfold Show Club, 3480 Galena St., (303) 755-2575; The Bare Essence, 8485 Umatilla, (303) 426-5454; Saturday Night Live, 7950 Federal Blvd., (303) 428-7042; and Cheer Leaders Gentlemen's Club, 6710 N. Federal Blvd., (303) 426-6996.*

Denver doesn't have a lot of topless clubs, although there are a few scattered about. Those listed above are the most popular and *Westword* carries ads for these and a few more.

8 *DRINK AND DINE AMONG LADIES DIVINE* • *Hooters, 1920 Blake St., (303) 294-9299; and 1390 S. Colorado Blvd., (303) 782-0232. GETTING THERE: The downtown Hooters is near Nineteenth Street in LoDo, not far from Coors Field. The Colorado Boulevard version is at the corner of Arkansas Avenue in the Cherry Creek area. Take I-25 exit 204 and follow Colorado north about four blocks to Arkansas; Hooters is on the right.*

Sexuality and sexism are alive and well at the two Denver Hooters restaurant-bars. Here, bosomy ladies in scoop-neck T-shirts and orange hotpants serve simple fare, good drinks and sweet smiles to a mostly male clientele. And that's all they serve; this national bar-and-restaurant chain offers only charm with its hamburgers, chicken wings, salads and pastas. These places are harmlessly outrageous, boasting that they're "delightfully tacky yet unrefined." The fare is typical sports bar grub, supported by a long list of beers and wines by the glass. The décor consists mostly of the girls and their pin-ups, calendars and logo items, plus TV sets that are usually tuned to the Broncos, Rockies, Nuggets or AVs.

9 *SURPRISE SOMEONE WITH A NAUGHTY PASTRY* • *Lé Bakery Sensual and Lé Bakery Artiste, 300 E. Sixth Ave.; (303) 777-5151. Weekdays 9:30 to 6 and weekends 10 to 4. GETTING THERE: The bakery is about a mile south of downtown in a crescent-shaped mall on the southeast corner of Sixth and Grant. From Colfax, turn south on Grant and follow it to Sixth.*

Calling itself "the sexiest bakery in town," *Lé Bakery Sensual* specializes in naughty pastries and cakes—the ideal stop if you're planning a bachelor party or want to titillate your lover. The rather graphic shapes are all hand-crafted and the bakery even has a photo catalog of suggested—and suggestive—designs. It also sells sex toys and naughty gifts and cards. However, the place has a dual personality: Its adjacent alter ego, *Lé Bakery Artiste,* can create pastries and cakes suitable for a formal wedding or church social.

10 *BUY HER A SEXY NIGGLE-JIGGLE:* **Victoria's Se-cret** • *Aurora Mall at 14200 E. Alameda Ave., (303) 344-8977; Cherry Creek Shopping Center, 3000 E. First Ave., (303) 399-9121; Denver Pavilions downtown, Sixteenth Avenue Mall between Tremont and Welton, (303) 825-2505; Park Meadows Mall, I-25 at County Line Road in Englewood, (303) 792-5737; and Southglenn Mall at University Boulevard and Arapahoe, (303) 798-9440.*

Unmentionables are quite mentionable these days, and Victoria's Secret has brought new levels of exotic dignity to scanty and sexy underthings. The firm even advertised during the Superbowl a few years ago, using sexy yet angel-winged models. The Cherry Creek outlet is a perfume and bath boutique, so she'll smell as sweet as she looks, while the others are full-scale lingerie stores. Always with class and never in poor taste, Victoria's Secrets are the best places to buy something nice for your lady. The naughty comes later.

Live within your income, even if you have to borrow money to do so.
— Josh Billings

Chapter nine

CREDIT CARD CORRUPTION

SHOPPING UNTIL YOU'RE DROPPING

Since it serves a trading area the size of Europe, Denver has an excellent selection of shopping malls, scores of smaller strip malls and hundreds of individual stores and boutiques. If you can't find it in Denver or its sprawling suburbs, it probably hasn't been manufactured yet.

THE TEN BEST MALLS & SHOPPING AREAS

Malls and shopping areas are focused in downtown Denver and in the upscale Cherry Creek area, which happens to be our favorite. Others are scattered widely about the city's great suburban sprawl, particularly—although not always—near freeway interchanges.

1 CHERRY CREEK SHOPPING CENTER • *3000 E. First Ave.; (303) 388-3900. Most stores open weekdays 10 to 9, Saturdays 10 to 7:30 and Sundays 11 to 6. GETTING THERE: The center is rimmed by First Avenue, University Boulevard, Steele Street and Cherry Creek. From downtown, follow Speer Boulevard southeast about three miles along the creek; Speer blends into First Avenue, which crosses in front of the center.*

Cherry Creek is a modern, thriving commercial area cradled between its namesake creek and Colorado Boulevard, with Cherry Creek Shopping Center as its centerpiece. There are larger shopping malls in the West, although we've found none finer. It's a remarkably comfortable mall; seating areas offer soft chairs and couches, not hard benches. Most of the shops are high end and the marble-trimmed bathrooms are so posh that they were written up in *Time Magazine*. Cherry Creek is fully enclosed and thus a great place to spend nasty-weather days. We even recommend it as one of our Ten Best walking routes; see Chapter Ten, page 150. The mall is arrayed on two levels and accented with potted plants, with skylights to let in all that Denver sun. Among its high end amenities are concierge service and valet parking. You can even have your car washed while you shop. Although there are larger malls in America, Cherry Creek isn't small. It has nearly 200 shops, stores and cafés under its roof, anchored by Neiman Marcus, Saks Fifth Avenue, Foleys and Lord & Taylor.

2 *AURORA MALL • Alameda Avenue at I-225, Aurora; (303) 344-4120. Monday-Saturday 10 to 9 and Sunday 11 to 6. GETTING THERE: The mall is about thirteen miles east of Denver off I-225. An interchange under construction at the freeway and Alameda may be ready by the time you arrive. Otherwise, the fastest approach is to go east two and a half miles on Colfax, south two miles to Alameda Parkway, then head east. It'll take you across I-225 and straight to the mall.*

Although it's a bit far from downtown Denver, Aurora Mall is worth the trip if you like a lot of shopping in one place. JCPenney, Sears and Foley's are the anchors, which suggests a medium-priced shopping area. However, it has a good selection of higher end stores, including several specialty gift shops. The store count is about 120, plus twelve food venues. Most are in a combined restaurant and fast food court on the second level. This is a very attractive shopping place—a two-level atrium with skylights, fountains and lots of seating areas. An old fashioned carousel appeals to kiddies and wanna-be-kid parents.

3 *BUCKINGHAM SQUARE MALL • 1306 S. Havana St., Aurora; (303) 755-3232. Most stores open 10 to 9 Monday-Saturday and 11 to 6 Sunday. GETTING THERE: Go east on Colfax for about six and a half miles, turn south (left) onto Havana Street and follow it about three miles to Mississippi Avenue.*

This attractive midsize mall is anchored by Dillard's, Montgomery Ward and Mervyn's, with about ninety smaller stores, boutiques and food outlets. It's on one level and the main promenade is rather appealing, with several planters, fountains every few dozen yards and plenty of seating for weary shoppers. Buckingham has a four-screen movie theater and four fast food outlets, although it doesn't have a central food court.

4 DENVER PAVILIONS • *Sixteenth Street Mall between Tremont and Welton streets downtown; (303) 260-6000. (www.denverpavilions.com) Various hours for shops and restaurants.*

This unusual center is a triple-terraced complex running parallel to Sixteenth Street Mall for three blocks, anchored not by department stores but by large specialty stores and a multi-screen movie complex. It also contains the largest restaurant concentration downtown—Maggiano's Little Italy (Chapter Three, page 67), Hard Rock Café (Chapter Three, page 74), Wolfgang Puck's, the wildly decorated Café Odyssey and the large Corner Bakery for quick bites. Its anchors are a huge Virgin Megastore and NikeTown (both detailed below), Banana Republic and Barnes & Noble. Filling in the gaps are nearly fifty specialty shops.

5 FLATIRON CROSSING • *One West Flatiron Circle, Broomfield; (720) 887-7467 or (720) 887-0600 for recorded information. (www.flatironcrossing.com) Most stores open Monday-Saturday 10 to 9 and Sunday 11 to 6. GETTING THERE: The complex is about seventeen miles northwest of Denver on the west side of the Boulder Turnpike. Take I-25 north about seven miles, then go northwest on the turnpike (U.S. 36) about ten and a half miles and take the Interlocken Loop exit.*

Opened in late 2000, Flatiron Crossing rivals Cherry Creek as one of the greater Denver area's most appealing shopping complexes. It's a distinctive indoor-outdoor facility with 170 stores and restaurants in a two-story covered mall and another forty-three along landscaped walkways of adjacent Flatiron Crossing Village. Primary mall anchors are Foley's, Nordstrom, Dillard's and Lord & Taylor; among its large specialty stores are Crate & Barrel, Old Navy, Galyan's Trading Company and Eddie Bauer. The complex also has a multi-screen theater, a large food court and thirty acres of parklands, patios, terraces and fountains. Wood trusses, stone walkways and limestone columns give it a properly rustic Colorado look and large skylights admit sunshine into the two-deck mall. Flatiron is one of the area's largest shopping centers with 1.5 million share feet of retail space.

6 LARIMER SQUARE AND LODO • *Larimer Square is a one-block section of Larimer Street between Fourteenth and Fifteenth streets on the northwest edge of downtown. The rest of LoDo reaches several blocks northwest to Wynkoop Street and northeast to Twentieth Street.*

Larimer Square marks the start of the LoDo district, where Denver began in 1858. The city's original wooden buildings—on the site of present-day Writer Square—burned to the ground in 1863 and re-emerged in brick and stone. Later, the area fell to neglect as the business district shifted southeast toward the capitol and civic center.

Those fine old buildings with Victorian trim became flophouses, cathouses and tough bars where—to quote the old frontier gag—"the sawdust on the floor is yesterday's furniture." Now, through a redevelopment program that began in the 1970s, Larimer Square is one of the trendiest areas of the city, trimmed with gaslamps and busy with boutiques, upscale clothing shops, galleries and restaurants. It's supposedly the second most visited site in Colorado, after the Air Force Academy in nearby Colorado Springs. (However we suspect that statisticians count every business person who stops by for a power lunch.)

Writer Square, adjacent to Larimer Square, also has several shops, galleries and boutiques, although they're housed in more contemporary quarters. It thus provides an architectural transition zone between the modern downtown area and Victorian LoDo.

LoDo spreads north and east from Larimer Square toward an area of grand old brick warehouses along Wynkoop Street. The Tattered Cover, one of America's largest book stores, is at Wynkoop and Sixteenth Street and Wynkoop Brewery, Denver's first microbrewery, occupies a warehouse at Seventeenth and Wynkoop. The imposing Union Station is across the way and the huge Icehouse warehouse is kitty corner from Wynkoop's, sheltering several restaurants, with residential lofts above. Other galleries, boutiques, specialty stores, restaurants and nightclubs are scattered throughout the area.

7 *PARK MEADOWS* ● *8401 Park Meadows Center Dr., Littleton; (888) 333-PARK or (303) 792-2999. (www.parkmeadows.com) Most stores open Monday-Saturday 10 to 9:30 and Sunday 11 to 6. GETTING THERE: Go south about fifteen miles on I-25 and take exit 195 (County Line Road). Turn right at the County Line Road traffic light, go west briefly and turn left into the mall.*

This area of Littleton rivals Cherry Creek for its choice of shops, with Park Meadows mall on one side of County Line Road and Centennial Promenade on the other. The Park Meadows complex has about 200 stores, and scores more are across the street. Like Cherry Creek, this is an attractive, rather upscale covered mall, although it spans the full budget spectrum from moderate to high end. This is reflected in its five major stores—Nordstrom, Dillard's, JCPenny, Lord & Taylor and Foley's. The two-level mall's interior is light and attractive, beneath glass-paneled pitched roofs. Curiously, there is very little seating here. Are folks really expected to shop until they drop? However, there's plenty of seating in the huge food court, called the Dining Hall. It has a dozen international and domestic takeouts.

8 *THE SHOPS AT TABOR CENTER* ● *Sixteenth Street Mall, between Larimer and Arapahoe streets; (303) 572-6868. Most shops open Monday-Saturday 10 to 7 and Sunday noon to 5.*

The most appealing aspect of this mall is its glassed-in galleria design, which lends itself to the sunny disposition of the Sixteenth Street Mall. Renovated during the fall of 2000, this two-block-long complex has more than sixty shops and restaurants on two levels. There are no major anchor stores here; Tabor Center specializes in specialty shops and boutiques. The upper level spans Lawrence Street, with several small shops, kiosks and carts on the glassed-roofed pedestrian bridge. A fast food court on the upper level features more than a dozen takeouts. The food court's attractive seating area, like most of the rest of Tabor Center, resides under glass.

9 **SOUTHGLENN MALL** • *6911 S. University Blvd., Littleton; (303) 795-0834. (www.southglenn.com) Most stores open Monday-Saturday 10 to 9 and Sunday 11 to 6. GETTING THERE: The most direct route—on a relatively fast surface street—is to take Broadway ten miles south, then go east a mile and a half on Arapahoe Road to University. If you prefer a freeway approach, head south about ten miles on I-25 to exit 197, then go west on Arapahoe about four miles.*

Southglenn is an older midsize mall that's been refurbished and expanded, now offering nearly a hundred shops. Its anchors are Dillard's, JCPenny, Foley's and Sears. Most of the mall is single level, with a small second level suspended between the two-story Penney and Dillard's stores. The mall covers a shopper's full economic range, from Walgreen's to Abercrombie & Fitch. A combined food court and restaurant row provides fast food, plus sit-down Chinese and Mexican cafés.

10 **WESTMINSTER MALL** • *5433 88th Avenue at Sheridan Boulevard, Westminster; (303) 428-5634. Most stores open Monday-Saturday 10 to 9 and Sunday 11 to 7. GETTING THERE: This large mall is about twelve miles northwest of Denver. Take I-25 north, cross I-70 and I-76, then go northwest on Highway 36 (Boulder Turnpike) at exit 217. After five miles, take the Sheridan Boulevard exit and go west under the freeway to the center.*

With six anchors and 180 smaller stores, Westminster is right up there with Cherry Creek and Park Meadows as one of the largest covered malls in the Intermountain West. It was undergoing a complete renovation as we went to press, so it also should be one of the most attractive. Its anchors are Dillard's, Mervyn's, Sears, Montgomery Ward, Foley's and JCPenney. The huge mall is on one level, built in the shape of a "T" with a crooked leg. It's possible to get lost among its scores of stores, although directory kiosks are numerous. It has a large food court with ten takeouts and a central seating area beneath a skylight, plus a few other takeouts and cafés scattered about. A six-screen movie complex is part of this large facility.

THE TEN BEST SPECIALTY STORES

What's your shopping specialty? As we noted above, since Denver serves an area larger than Europe, it has hundreds of specialty shops and stores, including some of the largest in the Intermountain West. Several of these outlets, such as the Tattered Cover, REI, Virgin Megastore and NikeTown, are so elaborate in design and selection that they're tourist attractions as well as shops.

1 *THE BEST BOOK STORE: The Tattered Cover* • 1628 *Sixteenth Street, corner of Wazee in LoDo, just below Larimer Square; (303) 777-6060. Also at 2955 E. First Avenue at Milwaukee Street, opposite the Cherry Creek Shopping Center; (303) 322-7727. Fourth Story café at Cherry Creek store; lunch and dinner Monday-Saturday and Sunday brunch; (303) 322-1824. (www.tatteredcover.com)*

Every great city should have a great book store, and the Tattered Cover performs that role admirably in Denver. The main store was established in an old warehouse in 1974 by Joyce Meskis; she took a gamble since this section of LoDo was still in a state of urban decay. By offering an extensive stock, employing book-knowledgeable clerks and providing a comfortable environment for sitting, reading and sipping coffee, she succeeded beyond expectations. And of course, LoDo has since become gentrified, drawing even more people to the store. The Tattered Cover is one of America's largest book stores, with more than half a million titles spread over four floors.

A branch been opened on First Avenue adjacent to the upscale Cherry Creek Shopping Center. Although it occupies a modern building, it has the same rustic warm wood look and feel of the original. Both have coffee cafés and plenty of places to sit and thumb through their storehouses of reading material. The Fourth Story, a locally popular restaurant, sits atop the Cherry Creek store, serving tasty American regional cuisine.

2 *THE BEST CD & TAPE STORE: Virgin Megastore* • 500 *Sixteenth Street Mall; (303) 534-1199. (www.virginmega.com) GETTING THERE: This mega mecca of recorded music is in the Denver Pavilions section of the Sixteenth Street Mall, near Welton.*

Denver's largest recorded music store has tens of thousands of CDs and cassettes, plus large video cassette and videogame departments. Every kind of recorded sound is here—pops, jazz, new age, rhythm and blues, gospel, country, classic, international folk, American folk, reggae and bluegrass. This is where you come for your *Denver Broncos Greatest Hits,* obscure bluegrass sounds and recordings by local performers whose music never quite made it across the state line. MTV videos wail from more than a dozen TV monitors suspended from the ceiling. Want to listen before you commit? Virgin has dozens of listening stations for a variety of music types, including a station for each of the current Top Forty hits. If you can't find the sound you like in this place, you're beyond tone deaf.

3 THE BEST HEALTHY FOOD STORE: Alfalfa's Market •
870 Colorado Blvd.; (303) 691-0101. GETTING THERE: It's about five miles from downtown. Go southeast on I-25, then take Colorado Boulevard (exit 204) north about a mile. The store in a shopping center on your right, between Kentucky and Ohio streets.

We call this a "healthy food store" instead of a health food store because it's a rather broad-based grocery store with a typical supermarket selection, and yet with a focus on proper nutrition. It goes beyond a preoccupation with MSM and organically correct pep pills to feature a complete range of foodstuffs. Most are organic and pesticide free. It has a large natural foods section, a vitamin and health supplement department, books on health and nutrition, a large cheese department, deli with very creative vegetarian salads and a "Juice and Java Bar." And it doesn't sell cigarettes.

4 BEST PLACE FOR COLORADO SOUVENIRS: Only in Colorado • *601 Sixteenth Street Mall at Walton; (303) 623-0193. (www.madeincolorado.com)*

Despite the store's name, selections in this large souvenir store aren't limited to Colorado. You can buy curios and stuffed animals that hail from just about anywhere. However, it does have the largest selection of Colorado souvenirs in town—more than two thousand items. This is where you go for your Colorado Rockies, Colorado Avalanche, Denver Nuggets and Denver Broncos T-shirts, sweatshirts and caps. Don't fail to miss the extensive selection of Denver and Colorado refrigerator magnets, books and videos, key chains and coffee mugs, plus a few localized specialty foods. And if you really want to play tourist, you can even pan for Colorado gold here.

5 THE BEST SNACK ATTACK STORE: Harry and David •
Cherry Creek Shopping Center, 3000 E. First Ave.; (303) 399-5777. (www.harryanddavid.com) GETTING THERE: See directions above, under "Cherry Creek Shopping Center" on page 137. Harry and David is on the lower floor.

Harry and David started decades ago as a fruit and vegetable stand in Medford, Oregon. It has grown into one of the nation's largest specialty food shops, and it's *the* place to go for creative snacks. Some examples—many of which are available for sampling—include cinnamon raisin mix, assorted flavored pretzels, double-dip macadamia nuts, Cajun pea trail mix and peanut butter pretzel party mix. It also features dozens of specialty jams, pasta mixes, pastas, salsas, relishes, designer candies and other specialty foods.

6 *THE BEST ATHLETIC WEAR SHOP: NikeTown* • *Denver Pavilions at 500 Sixteenth Street Mall; (303) 260-6000.*

Looking a bit like a space station with its modern, curving design, the double-decked NikeTown doesn't just sell running shoes, although it has those a-plenty. It covers the entire gamut of sports clothing and gear for games people play—men's and women's golf, tennis, soccer, organized team sports, basketball and more. An atrium-style main floor is linked to second floor shops by a staircase wrapped around a dramatically curving rough-tiled wall.

7 *THE BEST KIDS' STORE: FAO Schwarz* • *Cherry Creek Shopping Center; (303) 333-5100. GETTING THERE: Cherry Creek center is rimmed by First Avenue, University Boulevard, Steele Street and Cherry Creek. From downtown, follow Speer Boulevard southeast about three miles along Cherry Creek; it blends into First Avenue, which crosses in front of the center. FAO Schwarz is on the ground floor.*

Kids will be kids—no matter what their age—in these wonderful stores full of toys, games, stuffed animals, electronic kids' gadgets and beyond. Although not as large as many FAO Schwarz outlets, the Cherry Creek edition still has the same whimsy, with talking trees, windup toys scooting constantly about and oversized cuddly stuffed creatures bigger than most kids.

8 *THE BEST STORE FOR OUTDOOR TYPES: REI* • *Platte Street near Fifteenth Street; (303) 756-0272. GETTING THERE: Take Fifteenth Street about a mile northwest from downtown and cross the South Platte River at Confluence Park. Turn left on Platte Street and you're at the store.*

This is the ultimate outlet for the outdoor fanatic. It's all under one massive, lofty roof in one of the riverfront's grand old brick buildings. It was built in 1901 to house the Denver Tramway Power Company. It now houses everything we outdoor types could ever want—camping and backpacking gear, tents, kayaks and canoes, winter sports stuff, street and mountain bikes, outdoor and travel books and maps, all sorts of outdoor wear and even a gallery devoted to outdoor art. The huge complex also has a 45-foot climbing wall, a short test track for mountain bikes, pack-fitting and camp stove testing stations, a print-your-own-map station, a gear repair center and kids play area.

And when you've shopped until you're ready to drop your pack, fetch a cup of caffé latte at the store's Starbucks Café and retire to an outdoor deck, where you can enjoy a view of Confluence Park and the city skyline. This is the second largest of the REI stores, after the flagship in Seattle.

9 **THE BEST SCIENCE STORE: Store of Knowledge** • *Second level of Cherry Creek Shopping Center, 3000 E. First Ave.; (303) 388-3900. GETTING THERE: The center is rimmed by First Avenue, University Boulevard, Steele Street and Cherry Creek.*

This is your place if you want to show off or shore up your knowledge. The science-and-information-based store features learning games, fascinating almost-perpetual motion mobiles, tabletop kinetic sculptures, serious telescopes, science kits, globes, educational toys, build-your-own dinosaurs, science books and more.

10 **THE BEST WINE AND LIQUOR SHOP: Argonaut Wine & Liquor** • *700 E. Colfax Ave.; (303) 831-7788. GETTING THERE: It's just east of the Civic Center, at the corner of Washington Street.*

This barn full of booze is Denver's largest liquor store (although Applejack near Golden is even larger). Like Applejack, Argonaut is as big as a supermarket, offering just about every sort of libation currently available. It has an extensive wine selection, particularly from California, with a good assortment of imports as well. We're partial to Zinfandel and it's the only place we've found in Colorado with a wide selection. And we *don't* mean white Zinfandel, which is a wimpy abomination and a terrible thing to do to an honest red grape. Those partial to beer will find virtually every Colorado micro-brew, plus most major American brands and many imports. The hard liquor selection is extensive as well; this is where you go for Cabo Wabo tequila and rare sour mash whiskeys.

The only way to keep your health is to eat what you don't want, drink what you don't like and do what you'd rather not. — **Mark Twain**

Chapter ten

GETTING PHYSICAL
BEST PLACES TO WORK OFF MICRO-BREWS

Denver is one of the nation's greatest biking and walking cities. Since most of the town is flatter than thin pancake batter, strolling and cycling are easy. Further, it has several large city parks with miles of marked walking and cycling trails, and a citywide system of designated bike routes. The most popular recreational trails are shoreside paths along Denver's two downtown streams—the South Platte River and Cherry Creek. They are so popular, in fact, that you might want to avoid them on weekends, particularly sunny summer ones.

Since greater Denver is a serious walking and cycling area, two local agencies have produced route maps. The first is essentially a bike map, although many of the suggest routes will interest walkers as well. The second is a trails guide, aimed at both cyclists and walkers.

The Denver Parks and Recreation Department has developed and signed several bike routes, which are shown on the ***Denver Bike Map***, available for a modest fee at most bike shops, or at Denver Central Services at 671 S. Jason Street; (303) 698-4940; open weekdays 7 to 5. GETTING THERE: Take I-25 south, go west on Alameda (exit 208), cross the South Platte River and take an immediate left onto Platte River Street, which becomes Jason Street. Follow it about half a mile; Central Services is in a low brick building opposite the Denver Municipal Animal Shelter. To order a map in advance, call for the current price and then send a check payable to *Manager of Revenue* to: Denver Central Services, 671 S. Jason St., Denver, CO 80223-2305.

The Colorado Lottery funds a **Denver Metro Trails Guide** that's available free at visitor centers and most bike shops. Or you can pick up a copy at the Denver Parks and Recreation Department's administrative office in the Riverfront building on Fifteenth Street on the north side of the Platte River.

If you like routes that are a bit more challenging, the next-door Rockies are laced with hiking and mountain biking trails. Local book stores carry several mountain trail guides.

THE TEN BEST WALKS AND HIKES

Most of our walks are easy strolls. However, we'd added a couple of hikes in the nearby foothills, in case you *really* need to work off those micro-brews and buffalo burgers. For considerably more walking guidance than we offer here, pick up a copy of **Walking Denver** by Stewart M. Green. It's available at local book stores, or Falcon Guides, 1718, Helena, MT 59624; (800) 582-2665. (*www.falconguide.com*)

Note: Bold face items marked with ❖ are described in more detail elsewhere in this book; check the index for page numbers.

1 **DENVER DOWNTOWN** ● *From the state capitol along Sixteenth Street Mall, through Larimer Square to Union Station. Easy stroll, about three miles round trip. A fold-out map on the back page of the* Downtown Denver Map and Directory, *available at visitor centers, clearly shows the area covered by this route. GETTING THERE: The state capitol complex is just southeast of downtown, off Colfax between Lincoln and Grant streets. You'll find a couple of pay parking lots just off Broadway, at Cleveland Place and Fifteenth Street.*

Put this walk high on your things-to-do list shortly after you arrive, since it will provide a fine preview of downtown Denver. It will take you past many of the city's shopping areas, restaurants and major hotels. It's an historic walk as well, meandering from the stately statehouse through the newest parts of Denver to the oldest.

Just for the fun of it, begin your walk on the western steps of the ❖ **Colorado State Capitol** at the spot marking Denver's mile-high elevation. Actually, there are two markers—an original engraved in the concrete face of one of the steps, and newer and more accurate brass survey marker three steps higher.

Walk down the steps and go east through **Civic Center Park,** where you'll encounter the ❖ **Denver Art Museum, Colorado History Museum, Byers-Evans House** and **Denver Mint.**

From the Mint, stroll northeast on Court Place, crossing Fourteenth and Fifteenth streets and then pass between the bisected towers of the ❖ **Adam's Mark Hotel**. It fronts on the ❖ **Sixteenth Street Mall**, with the highrises of Republic Plaza opposite. Cross the mall and continue another block on Court to Broadway and turn left to visit the splendid ❖ **Brown Palace Hotel**. Return on Court or Tremont and head northwest along the west side of the Sixteenth Street Mall.

As you stroll, you'll pass half a dozen sidewalk restaurants and assorted shops in the shadow of the city's highrises. If you're in a window-shopping mood, check out the two-level ❖ **Denver Pavilions** between Tremont and Welton. Six blocks beyond, hang a half left through ❖ **Writer Square**, another planned shopping complex. A special attraction here is a collection of realistic bronze statues, some whimsical and some historic. Our favorite is a bronze of two kids riding on the back of an alligator.

Writer Square provides a transition between very new and very old Denver. As you emerge from the complex onto Larimer Street, you'll enter the ❖ **Larimer Square** area, a gathering of shops, boutiques and restaurants housed in some of Denver's oldest brick and masonry buildings. This is the beginning of ❖ **LoDo**, that silly local acronym for lower downtown. Walk the one-block length of Larimer Square, turn right onto Fourteenth Street beside a small park, then right again onto Market Street. This will take you past several other handsome brickfronts with shops, galleries and cafés. You'll also encounter ❖ **Blazing Saddles**, where you can take a load off by renting a bike.

Continue zigging and zagging through LoDo by turning left from Market onto Fifteenth and then right onto Blake. Follow it to Sixteenth Street which at this point is no longer a mall. Go left a block on Sixteenth to Wazee Street, where you'll encounter the ❖ **Tattered Cover**, Denver's legendary book store. Stroll another block on Sixteenth to Wynkoop, turn right and stroll a block to the grand old stone **Union Station**, one of Denver's most imposing structures. Completed in 1914, it still serves as a railway passenger depot, with Amtrak's *California Zephyr* offering service east and west from here. Cavernous is the only adjective to properly describe the interior, with its sixty-foot ceilings, Spanish arch windows and classic high-backed wooden pews.

Since it borders the railyard, Wynkoop is lined with huge red brick warehouses. They're no longer used for cargo, having been gentrified into professional offices and loft apartments, with shops and restaurants on their ground floors. Continuing another block past Union Station, you'll encounter ❖ **Wynkoop Brewing Company** in one of those venerable warehouses at the corner of Eighteenth. Kitty-corner is the Ice House, another brick stronghold, with several restaurants in its base, including ❖ **Rodizio Grill**.

From the Ice House, continue northeast on Wynkoop past the old Union Pacific warehouse building, which houses two popular restaurants, the ❖ **Denver Chophouse** and ❖ **Fadó,** a great 0Irish pub.

Press on through the traffic-free Wynkoop Plaza to ❖ **Coors Field,** Denver's downtown baseball park. This is your turnaround point; double back on Wynkoop to Seventeenth, turn left and start up toward the city center. Swing right onto Market Street, which marks the transition zone between brick and masonry LoDo and glass and steel uptown. Turn right onto the Sixteenth Street Mall and follow it back to your starting point.

If you aren't all shopped out, pause at the ❖ **Shops at Tabor Center,** paralleling Sixteenth between Larimer and Arapahoe. On the other hand, if you're weary of shopping and walking, catch one of the free mall trams. It will deliver you to **Civic Center Station** at Sixteenth and Broadway, not far from your starting point.

2 CHEESMAN PARK ● *Easy stroll of varying lengths; each loop around this large park is about a mile and a half. GETTING THERE: From the Civic Center area, go south on Broadway for a mile, turn east (left) onto one-way Sixth Avenue and take it just over a mile to Williams Street Parkway. Turn left and follow this landscaped boulevard north for about a quarter of a mile into the park.*

Named for one of Denver's founding fathers, Cheesman Park is a large, gently sloping swatch of green rimmed by mature trees, overlooking downtown Denver. A trail loops the park's perimeter, traveling across open parklands and then ducking through trees that rim its outer edge. It's open to both walking and biking, and some sections have separate asphalt paths for cyclists and dirt ones for walkers and joggers. You'll get fine views of downtown highrises and occasional slices of the Rockies from here. A few decades ago, Cheesman Park provided grand panoramas of the mountains, although downtown highrises and the park's own trees are obscuring the view.

This walk doesn't require much direction; just keep to the outer perimeter and turn inward at the edges to avoid strolling out onto adjacent streets. We found this park to be relatively uncrowded, even on a sunny May Saturday. We encountered mostly overly friendly red squirrels who sat boldly on their haunches within feet of the path, glaring at us for failing to bring peanuts. Incidentally, Cheesman Park also is a starting point for one of the bike routes below.

3 CHERRY CREEK TRAIL ● *Hungarian Freedom Park to Confluence Park. All level asphalt path beside the creek; seven-mile round trip. GETTING THERE: From downtown, follow Speer Boulevard southeast about three miles along Cherry Creek. Just before Speer merges onto First, turn right onto Corona Street and cross the creek to small Hungarian Freedom Park. There's meterless street parking here, but check signs for street sweeping days. From here, you can drop down to the Cherry Creek Trail and start your stroll.*

Seven miles may seem like a long haul for you and your Nikes, although this trail is virtually level as Cherry Creek drifts lazily toward its marriage with the South Platte River. And of course, you don't have to walk the full round trip; you can cut it in half by walking one way and taking a bus the other. (Call 299-6000 for transit information.) The path is sunk several feet below street level, so you're sheltered from the rumble of traffic. The full length of Cherry Creek Trail is about fifteen miles one way, from Confluence Park to Cherry Creek Reservoir, which we suggest below as a bike route.

This is both a walking and biking trail, so remember to stay to the right. There's no posted speed limit for cyclists and some of them really blast through here. Although you'll be below street level during your stroll, you won't get lost, since most of the street crossings over Cherry Creek are labeled. Once you reach ❖ **Confluence Park**, an appealing area of lawns and observation decks on the South Platte, you can head back or take a pedestrian bridge across the Platte and follow its walkway for a bit.

If you want to visit downtown during your stroll, bail out at a small creekside plaza marked by several Southwest native graphics on its retaining wall. Follow steps upward—or a bike ramp if you're cycling—and you'll emerge onto Larimer Street, beside the urban campus of the University of Colorado at Denver. The popular shopping and dining areas of ❖ **Larimer Square** and the ❖ **Sixteenth Street Mall** are just beyond.

4 *CHERRY CREEK SHOPPING CENTER* ● *3000 E. First Ave.; (303) 388-3900. Doors open weekdays 10 to 9, Saturdays 10 to 7:30 and Sundays 11 to 6. GETTING THERE: From downtown, follow Speer Boulevard southeast about three miles along Cherry Creek; it blends into First Avenue, which crosses in front of the center.*

Whazzis? Hiking through a shopping center? We like to do a brisk five-mile walk every day and we're frustrated when the weather outside is frightful. Weather's not a problem if you head for Cherry Creek Shopping Center. It's completely covered and *huge* and the shops are on two levels, forming a long, irregular oval. A complete turn around each level is about two-thirds of a mile. By hitting both levels, you can crank off nearly a mile and a half without seeing the same shop twice. Eight laps—four on each floor with brisk runs up the stairways between the two levels—and you'll have covered five miles. Then head for the Peabody coffee bar on the first floor for a well earned caffé latte and a soft seat.

5 *SLOAN LAKE PARK* ● *Walking/cycling path circling Sloan and Cooper lakes. About two and a half miles; easy stroll. GETTING THERE: Drive about three miles west on Colfax Boulevard, turn north* *(right) onto Sheridan Boulevard and follow it a mile to the northwestern edge of Sloan Lake Park.*

Sloan Lake Park's large blue centerpiece is a double lake—Sloan and Cooper, and a recreational trail loops their combined shorelines. It's partly concrete, partly asphalt and partly a park road that's usually free of vehicular traffic. The trail follows the lakeshore most of the way, then occasionally veers away to wrap around a playfield or tennis court. It's a fun stroll, particularly on a weekend when this popular park is busy with activity. (The path is more popular with strollers than cyclists and skaters, so you won't be dodging a lot of wheeled traffic.) Strolling along, you can watch boaters and water skiers out on the lake, admire the distant Denver skyline and watch tennis matches, volleyball games and impromptu soccer games.

At the beginning, walking south from the parking area, you'll have to contend with the rumble of traffic as you parallel busy Sheridan Boulevard. However, the route soon swings inward and away from the noise. The rest of your walk will be near quiet neighborhoods; the noisiest things you'll encounter is occasional ghetto blasters playing rap or *Latino* music. If you prefer a more peaceful stroll, come on a weekday.

6 *HIGHLINE CANAL TRAIL* • *Round trip from Magna Carta Park to Monaco Street in southeast Denver; easy stroll, about seven miles. GETTING THERE: Go south on I-25 about six miles from downtown, take Colorado Boulevard exit 204 and continue south another two miles to Magna Carta Park at East Hampden Avenue. The park is on your left, opposite Wellshire Golf Course. Turn left onto Hampden, go a block to Ash and go left again and you'll find shaded street parking. Or, drive through the First Universalist Church grounds and you'll encounter a parking area for Magna Carta Park. The trail begins here.*

This pleasant path along one of Denver's oldest canals is rarely crowded and it's nearly all traffic free, with only occasional street crossings. We encountered very few people even on a recent Memorial Day Weekend. The canal was built between 1880 and 1883 to bring water to growing Denver and its surrounding farmlands. This was quite an engineering accomplishment more than a century ago, since the canal drops only two feet per mile. It extends seventy-one miles from Platte Canyon to the Rocky Mountain Arsenal.

The trail follows the canal for fifty-eight miles, although we certainly don't recommend walking its full length. However, we also suggest it as a cycling trail below on page 157. The path follows an elevated berm, so you often can see over rooftops and canal-side foliage to the distant Rockies. Through the decades, the canal has become a skinny riparian woodland, thickly vegetated and shaded occasionally with large cottonwoods.

Begin your walk by strolling through Magna Carta Park, and then follow an asphalt path northward along Colorado Boulevard for less than half a mile. You'll see a Highland Canal Trail sign at the corner of Colorado and Girard, which directs you eastward along the edge of large **Mamie Dowd Eisenhower Park**. You've only just begun, although this is one of the more pleasant sections of the trail, with the lush green park on one side and the slow-flowing canal on the other.

You'll be far from the rumble of traffic for most of the route, except when you follow a pedestrian tunnel beneath I-25 and then parallel that busy freeway for about half a mile. Then you'll return to quiet neighborhoods along the canal bank. Our recommended turnaround point is Monaco Street, although the path continues far beyond here. Actually, the best turn-around point is half a block to your right, at the intersection of Monaco and Yale Avenue. You'll find a small shopping complex and you can take a refreshment break at a Safeway with a deli and bakery, or at several fast food places.

7 *AURARIA CAMPUS* ● *Just west of downtown, alongside Speer Boulevard. All level; various lengths. GETTING THERE: Most roads into the campus have been converted into pedestrian paths, and parking is limited, particularly during the school year. We suggest parking nearby and walking into the campus on Lawrence Street.*

This huge campus is home to three separate institutions of higher learning—Community College of Denver, Metropolitan State College of Denver and the University of Colorado at Denver. The area was settled in 1858 as one of three pioneer towns that later merged to become the city of Denver. Through the years, periodic floods and then redevelopment removed most of the town of Auraria. The odd name, incidentally, comes from *aura*, the Greek word for gold.

With wide green promenades, traffic-free streets and an interesting mix of architecture, it's a fine place for a leisurely stroll. We'll suggest a walking route, or you can just wander around at will. If you grow weary, there are plenty of places to sit on this park-like campus.

To begin, stroll into the campus from downtown on Lawrence Street, which crosses Speer Boulevard. It then becomes a wide, landscaped pedestrian promenade between the modern brick buildings of the University of Colorado and Metropolitan State College. If you need a refreshment pause, duck into the North Classroom Building of UCD, under a large clock. Turn left down the hallway and you'll shortly encounter Rockies Deli. You can dine inside or take your fare to an outside patio and watch others stroll the promenade.

Back on your feet, continue along this wide green swatch until you come to the twin-towered **St. Cajetans Church**. Then retrace your route back up the mall. At the rather unattractive steel gray Auraria Library and Media Center, go right for about a block alongside the brick West Classroom building, then go left to the distinctive rough-cut stone 1896 **St. Elizabeth of Hungary Catholic Church**, with its towering steeple. Retrace your steps and take an outdoor passageway through the West Classroom building. Continue for another block, passing some nineteenth century homes that have been restored and converted into campus offices and activity centers. They're left over from a time when this was a smart residential area.

Turn left at a corner occupied by the Mercantile Restaurant and stroll into the most appealing section of the campus, called **Ninth Street Park**. This former street is lined with more late nineteenth century homes, with a landscaped park strip between them. Bronze plaques provide brief backgrounds on each of these fine old houses. If you continue through this park strip, you'll pass the Child Care Center and exit the campus onto Colfax Avenue.

8 **WASHINGTON PARK** • *This route circles two lakes in the park, Smith and Grasmere. The paths are asphalt and level; combined distances around both lakes, including the path that links them, is about three miles. GETTING THERE: Follow I-25 about two and a half miles south of downtown, then go east onto Alameda Avenue (exit 208) a mile and a half to Marion Parkway. Turn right (south) and follow Marion about two blocks into the park.*

It's amazing what people can do with a buffalo wallow. In 1889, city officials created 160-acre Washington Park, then they dredged an old buffalo watering hole and brought sand from Cherry Creek to create Smith Lake, the city's first swimming area. (Ironically, it's now closed to swimmers because of pollution concerns.) A larger lake, Grasmere, was dredged about half a mile south. Both have shoreline paths and are perfectly pleasant places for strolling. And they've been stocked with fish, in case you brought hook, line and sinker. Smith Lake's perimeter is about two-thirds of a mile. After circling it a time or two, you can follow a path to Grasmere Lake and stroll around its shoreline, which is just under a mile.

Two early structures, built as bath and boat houses and winter warming huts for ice skaters, stand on opposite shores of Smith Lake. The renovated 1912 Dos Chappell Bath House on the north shore is being operated as an outdoor information center by a nonprofit group called Volunteers for Outdoor Colorado; (303) 715-1010. The Pavilion on the south shore was being redone when we last visited.

9 **DINOSAUR RIDGE** • *Dinosaur Ridge Visitor Center at 16831 W. Alameda Parkway (Highway 26), Morrison; (303) 697-3466. It's open Monday-Saturday 9 to 4 and Sunday noon to 4, although you can take this hike if it's closed. This is a two-mile round trip on the shoulder of a highway, with upslopes at each end. GETTING THERE: The easiest approach—if not the most direct—is to head west from Denver either on*

I-70, or Highway 6 which blends into I-70. Take exit 159 south toward Red Rocks Amphitheatre and Park, then fork to the left opposite the park entrance. This route—Highway 26 and Alameda Parkway—curves around a brushy mound called Dinosaur Ridge and takes you a mile to the visitor center. This is the starting point for your hike. A simpler, slower approach is to pick up Alameda Avenue (I-25 exit 208) and follow it west to the visitor center.

NOTE: The parking lot gate is locked after the visitor center closes, so park your car outside if you begin this hike near closing time.

This short but moderately steep hike will be appealing if you're a dinosaur fan. Dinosaur Ridge is the site of the world's first major dinosaur find. This trail, essentially the shoulder of the highway, leads about a mile from the visitor center to the discovery site. You'll encounter several informational signs as you walk. You'll initially climb upward, breach a highway crest and then stroll downhill to the final marker, where local school teacher Arthur Lake made his find in 1877. From there, simply reverse your route and head back. This hike isn't only about dinosaurs, however. You'll enjoy some nice views of the Denver Basin as you stroll. See Chapter Two, page 51, for more on Dinosaur Ridge and the visitor center.

10 *LOOKOUT MOUNTAIN* • *Hiking trail system through the Lookout Mountain Nature Preserve, plus a trail to the nearby Buffalo Bill Memorial. Varying lengths and degrees of difficulty. Most trails are moderate with a steep finish for the Buffalo Bill round trip. GETTING THERE: Head west from Denver on I-70 for about eighteen miles and begin climbing into the Rockies; take exit 256 onto Lookout Mountain Road (marked "Buffalo Bill Grave"). After about a mile and a half, before you reach the Buffalo Bill memorial, turn left onto Colorow Road and follow it a short distance to the nature preserve.*

This 110-acre preserve is an appealing swatch of thin eastern slope pine, high on the flanks of Lookout Mountain. This is one of the area's most popular vista points and it's also home to most of Denver's TV and radio antennae—although they're a discreet distance from the preserve. Two "hikers only" trails wind in and out among the pines, providing occasional vistas of the Denver Basin below; they cover about a mile and a half. This area also is a launching point for an extensive system of hiking trails through the Front Range foothills. Most are open to hikers, mountain bikers and equestrians. Trail maps are available at the handsome ❖ **Lookout Mountain Nature Center**, which also has some wildlife exhibits.

After you've done the hikes around the nature center, follow a moderately difficult one-mile trail to the ❖ **Buffalo Bill Museum and Grave**, one of the Denver area's most popular attractions. Of course you can drive there, and most people do. However, the walk is much more interesting. It's pine-shaded, accented by occasional rocky outcroppings and flower-lined in spring. It offers frequent vistas of the Denver Basin and high snowcaps of the Continental Divide. The return to the center is a little tough unless you're in good shape, since it has a half-mile uphill climb.

THE TEN BEST BIKE ROUTES

As we noted above, Denver is a great city for bicyclists. It recently was selected as one of North America's "Top Ten Cycling Cities" by *Bicycling Magazine*. The city even has a cyclist's hotline: **(303) 640-BIKE.** June is "Denver Bike Month" with several cycling oriented activities are scheduled. Call the above number for details.

Regional Transit District buses are equipped with bike racks and they'll tote your cycle at no extra charge. Also, bikes can be taken on light rail during off-peak hours, although a free permit must first be obtained. Call (303) 299-6000 or (800) 366-7433 for information on RTD's Bike-n-Ride program.

Two maps, *Denver Metro Trail Guide* and the *Denver Bike Map* show many of the city's cycling routes. To obtain them, see pages 146 and 147 above.

If you didn't bring a bike, you can rent one from **Blazing Saddles** at 1432 Market Street, between Fifteenth and Sixteenth streets in LoDo; (303) 534-5255. These cycles come with mileage computers and detailed directions for five suggested bike routes. Four of them can be reached from the shop and a fifth is a challenging mountain bike run in the adjacent Rockies. (*www.blazingsaddles.com*)

1 *CHERRY CREEK TRAIL • Confluence Park to Cherry Creek Reservoir along the Cherry Creek Greenway. Thirty-mile round trip; all level and mostly traffic-free. GETTING THERE: Take Fifteenth Street about a mile northwest from downtown and cross the South Platte River at Confluence Park. Most of the parking in the area is metered, although you'll find inexpensive all-day parking by turning left onto Platte Street and following it around to the right—it becomes Water Street—past Ocean Journey. Pass the aquarium and turn left onto Seventh Street, headed for the Denver Children's Museum and you'll see a large fee parking area before you reach the museum's lot.*

Thirty miles is a long pull for most of us but of course, you don't have to pedal the full distance. This is a great route for cyclists, virtually traffic free as it follows Cherry Creek along a landscaped greenbelt. After the first mile, you'll be parallel to downtown and you can peel off on Stout Street or Colfax to explore the Sixteenth Street Mall, although these are not marked biked routes.

Pressing southeasterly, you'll emerge from the sunken greenway at the junction of Speer Boulevard and First avenue. You must leave the creek here and follow the First Avenue sidewalk to skirt around the Denver Country Club, whose members don't want mere mortals intruding into their creekside retreat. You'll then skirt the edge of ❖ **Cherry Creek Shopping Center**, which provides plenty of excuses to take a break. The trail rejoins Cherry Creek on the far side of the shopping complex.

Cycling southeasterly, you'll pass through spreading Denver residential and commercial areas and then hit some nice greenery as you pedal past Los Verdes Golf Club. It blends into **Hentzell** and **Havana/Cornell** parks, which then blend into J.F. Kennedy Municipal Golf Course. The creek ends—or begins, depending on your perspective—at Cherry Creek Dam. Skirt around the dam and you're in **Cherry Creek Reservoir State Park**, which has the usual water sports, a sandy beach and more bike trails.

2 CHEESMAN PARK TO WASHINGTON PARK ● *Southeast of downtown. About six miles round trip, plus additional mileage within the two parks; level and easy. There are no separate bike lanes in some sections, although traffic is light on most of the route. GETTING THERE: From the Civic Center area, go south on Broadway for a mile, turn east (left) onto one-way Sixth Avenue and follow it just over a mile to Williams Street Parkway. Turn left and follow this landscaped boulevard north for about a quarter of a mile into the park.*

This route connects two of Denver's most attractive parks while passing through some of its grandest old tree-lined neighborhoods. Many wealthy early Denverites built their homes in this area southeast of downtown and most of these mansions survive. Equally appealing is the fact that several streets through this area are landscaped boulevards. The homes—virtually all unfenced and sharing common lawns—sit well back from the streets, providing broad park strips shaded by century-old trees.

Unload your bikes in Cheesman Park and, before you start pedaling the boulevards, cycle around the park itself. Its roads are lightly traveled and a walking-biking path rims this grand swatch of tree-lined green. You'll catch frequent views of downtown high rises and swatches of the Rockies as you ride.

When you've finished looping the park a time or few, pedal south onto Williams Street Parkway, crossing Eighth Avenue. You'll be following the city's D-11 bike route most of the way from this point. Four blocks after you've departed the park on Williams, swerve briefly right and then go left, following those D-11 signs and continuing south on Gilpin Street. Three parallel streets in this area—Franklin, Gilpin and High—are landscaped boulevards, and you might want to cruise up and down them, admiring all those handsome homes.

Next, follow Third Avenue four blocks west to Downing Street, turn left and cross a bridge over Cherry Creek. Although the Downing Street bridge is one-way the wrong way, bike route signs directs you to a sidewalk that avoids oncoming traffic. After a long block, veer to the left and blend onto Marion Street Parkway, another landscaped boulevard. Follow it south about half a mile to large, long and skinny **Washington Park**. This is one of the best cycling and walking parks in the city. A two and a half mile road loops through the park and most of it is closed to vehicular traffic, so you can pedal about to your heart's content. The park contains two large, shallow lakes and both are rimmed by walking trails that we recommended above.

NAVIGATIONAL NOTE: Avoid this route during the rush hour since streets in the area become quite busy. As you pedal on Marion toward Washington Park, you must cross Alameda Avenue, a major thoroughfare with no stop sign or traffic light to help you across.

3 *HIGHLINE CANAL TRAIL* • *East from Magna Carta Park in southeast Denver. Mostly level; varying distances. GETTING THERE: See directions for the Highline Canal Trail walk above, on page 151.*

This is the same starting point we recommended for a walking route above. Of course, you can cycle much further than you can walk, and the trail extends for fifty-eight miles. After reaching Monaco Street—where we suggested ending the walk—the route continues on a lazily curving course through Aurora, a large community immediately southeast of Denver.

The trail curves around the southern tip of **James Bible Park**, crosses south Quebec Street and then crosses the **Cherry Creek Trail**. It snakes northward through the outer edges of Denver, then it lurches eastward and crosses under I-225, where it eventually sheds housing tracts for pasturelands. This is marked Route 6 on the *Denver Metro Trail Guide*, although more of the route is shown on the *Denver Bike Map*, which follows it until it disappears under I-225. We turned back there, so you're on your own.

4 *MONACO PARKWAY* • *East side of Denver from Martin Luther King Jr. Parkway to Cherry Creek. All level, about ten miles round trip. GETTING THERE: Go east on Colfax about four miles to Monaco Parkway and turn left. Drive north about a mile and a half to MLK Parkway, find a place to park and start pedaling south.*

This route isn't on either of the bike/walking maps listed above. However, we like it because it passes through some of Denver's most opulent neighborhoods and nearly all of the route is along a landscaped greenway. It also takes you past several city parks. However, there is traffic exposure in some areas, so stay alert. We suggest Martin Luther King Jr. Parkway as a starting point because Monaco narrows north of there and the parkway soon ends. The homes through here—many of them gorgeous brick creations—are set back off the street and their immaculately-tended unfenced front lawns form a continuous park strip. Monaco has a landscaped center median, although there's no path along it. Most of your riding will be on sidewalks which are often set well back from the street, or on the street itself. It's usually not heavily traveled and there are few parked cars.

Many of the side streets also are lushly landscaped and lined with elegant homes, so explore at will. You'll find some particularly imposing mansions west along Montview Boulevard and Seventeenth Avenue and their cross streets.

Traffic on Monaco becomes busier after you cross Colfax, although it retains its nice park strip. It becomes an ordinary four-lane street after passing Sixth Avenue, then it regains the park strip as it passes **Crestmoor Park**. This midsize park has its own walking/biking paths, so you may want to turn left on Cedar and left again on Locust to explore it. Monaco narrows again below Crestmoor, then it passes the David C. Garland Park, which borders on Cherry Creek. You can pick up the **Cherry Creek Trail** here. Or cross the Monaco Street bridge and pedal through **Judge Joseph E. Cook Park**. It has a concrete path and a pretty little creek running through its two-block length. The park ends at Mexico Avenue, which this is our suggested turnaround point.

5 CITY PARK ● *Just east of downtown. Cycling on park roads plus a loop path around Ferril Lake. All level; various lengths. GETTING THERE: Go east on Colfax Avenue about two and a half miles to Colorado Boulevard, turn north (left) for half a mile then turn left again into the park on Montview Boulevard or 22nd Avenue.*

Nearly a mile square, Denver City Park is laced with roads and trails and it contains two of the city's major attractions, the ❖ **Denver Zoo** and ❖ **Museum of Nature & Science**. The surface streets get busy on weekends, although they're lightly used on weekdays, so you should have little traffic interference.

After entering the park on Montview or 22nd, you can park your car near the zoo or nature museum and start pedaling westward. If you shift northward, you'll parallel the City Park Golf Course. Then you can head south briefly along the park's eastern edge. (If you miss the turn and accidentally exit the park, go south on York Street and turn back into the green at 21st Avenue.)

As you pedal about the park, you'll encounter large **Ferril Lake** (formerly City Park Lake) with a Spanish style Pavilion as a focal point. The lake was named in honor of Thomas Hornsby Ferril, who was Colorado's poet laureate until he died in 1996 at the age of 100. An asphalt walking/cycling path circles the pond's one-mile perimeter and it's generally not too busy on weekdays. If you'd like to take a break from cycling, you can rent paddleboats and other water-play craft at a boat house in front of the Pavilion. Beyond the lake, several paths and closed-off roads are open to cyclists and walkers.

6 *SIXTH AVENUE PARKWAY* • *Colorado Boulevard to Uinta Street. Level and easy ride; about six miles round trip. GETTING THERE: Go east from downtown on Colfax Avenue for two and a half miles, turn right (south) onto Colorado Boulevard and follow it about nine blocks to Sixth Avenue.*

Like the Monaco Parkway above, Sixth Avenue cuts a wide swath of landscaped green as it travels east from Colorado Boulevard and skims across the top of the former Lawry Air Force Base. This also is a good walking route. It travels past a mix of fancy and ordinary homes, although nearly all are well-kept and nicely landscaped. A rather casual dirt path meanders along the avenue's broad green center median strip, which is shaded by ancient trees. This is a busy boulevard, although you can avoid traffic by using that dirt path. However, not all cross streets have curb cuts, so you may have to dismount occasionally, or test your shocks over the curbs.

When you cross Quebec, you'll encounter a newly planted median strip with young trees, part of a residential development on the former air force base. There's no center path here, although there are sidewalks on either side of the parkway. This cycling route ends at a traffic circle at Uinta. Just spin around and head on back.

7 *PLATTE RIVER TRAIL* • *Confluence Park to Chatfield Reservoir. Level and easy traffic-free ride; about fifteen miles one way. GETTING THERE: See "Cherry Creek Trail" bike route above on page 155.*

Also known as the Platte River Greenway, this is one of Denver's most popular cycling, walking and skating routes, so expect it to be busy on sunny weekends. Pick your choice of directions; it follows the South Platte River north to Adams County Regional Park and south to Chatfield Reservoir. It's about fifteen miles each way from Confluence Park, for a total of thirty, making the this one of the longest recreational trails in Denver.

We like the southern route, which offers views of Elitch Gardens and the Denver skyline before it clears the heart of Denver and heads into the city's great suburban sprawl. Although you'll see little open space, virtually all of the route is traffic-free. Just south of Colfax, a spur leads west to a pair of parks, **Sanchez** and **Lakewood Gulch**. Continuing southward, you'll pass between **Ruby Hill Park** and Overland Hill Golf Club, and then skim the edge of Englewood Hill Golf Course in the community of Englewood. Several more miles of pedaling will deliver you to the long and large **South Platte Park** and finally to **Chatfield Reservoir State Recreation Area**. A biking/walking trail loops through this large parkland for several miles, providing nice views of the distant Rockies.

8 CENTENNIAL TRAIL • *Either direction from Chatfield State Recreation Area. Moderate with some hills; various distances. For information: Colorado Department of Transportation Bicycle Program, 4201 E. Arkansas Ave., Denver, CO 80222; (303) 757-9982. GETTING THERE: From downtown Denver, head south on I-25 about three miles, take the Santa Fe Drive exit (U.S. 85) and continue south another ten miles. Go west briefly on the Centennial Freeway (Highway 470) and follow signs to the recreation area.*

If you want to crank off a lot of miles, with some low hills and turns thrown in for variety, follow this lengthy path alongside the Centennial Freeway. The multi-purpose recreation trail is popular with skaters as well as cyclists. It's not *on* the freeway; it's a separate path paralleling it, built by the Department of Transportation.

You can reach the Centennial Trail by heading briefly northwest from Chatfield State Recreation Area, peddling under the Centennial Freeway. The trail extends both directions from here, although the westbound route is more interesting, taking you toward the Front Range foothills. The path follows the freeway in a wide, gentle turn, heading west and then north, traveling across the prairie and out of reach of the greater Denver suburbs. It cuts through **Bear Lake Park** and ends at I-70 about thirteen miles from your starting point, between Morrison and Golden. You might want to pause and explore Bear Lake Park, which has five miles of paved and ten miles of dirt bike trails. Or press northward and bail out at Alameda Parkway. Go west briefly for the ❖ **Dinosaur Ridge Visitor Center,** and then continue around Dinosaur Ridge into ❖ **Red Rocks Park.** This section has some challenging hills. However, Alameda Parkway does not have marked bike lanes.

9 BEAR CREEK TRAIL • *From the Platte River Trail near Hampden Avenue in Englewood, west to Bear Creek Lake Park. Level and traffic-free; about six miles one way. GETTING THERE: Start following directions toward the Centennial Trail above, but turn west from Santa Fe Avenue onto Hampden Avenue. Cross the South Platte River and park in one of the nearby residential areas.*

This very appealing tree-lined route goes through a chain of parks, so it's virtually all remote from traffic. A westward spur from the Platte River Greenway, it follows Bear Creek and then reaches **Bear Creek Park** within a couple of miles. Shortly beyond, it enters the long and slender **Bear Creek Greenbelt,** goes through a few suburbs and then reaches **Bear Creek Lake Park.** This large recreation area has three lakes, a marina with water sports rentals and—as noted above— several miles of paved and dirt trails.

10 *WESTMINSTER CITY TRAILS* • *Starting at Northglenn Mall. All level and mostly traffic free; various distances. For information: Westminster Parks, Recreation and Libraries, 4800 W. 92nd Ave., Westminster, CO 80030; (303) 430-2400, ext. 2192. GETTING THERE: Follow I-25 about eleven miles north from downtown Denver to Westminster. Take exit 221 briefly west to Northglenn Mall.*

A fast-growing northern suburb of Denver, Westminster has built an extensive network of cycling and walking trails. Most are parallel to—but free from—street traffic. Many were created as this booming community expanded. You can get a *Westminster Parks, Open Space & Trails* map from the city rec department.

We suggest starting at Northglenn Mall because of its easy freeway access and ample parking space. (So be good guys and buy something while you're there.) From the mall, you can pedal westward on the **Church Ranch-104th Avenue Trail** about two and a half miles to **Westminster City Park,** with a good assortment of recreational facilities. Then continue another couple of miles to **Standley Lake County Park.** This large reservoir offers windsurfing, boating and fishing. There are no rentals available, so you'll just have to watch the others have fun on the water.

Another pleasant ride is northeast from Standley Lake on **Big Dry Creek Trail** through some still undeveloped areas of Westminster. The path ends at 128th Avenue. A highlight of this route is the ❖ **Butterfly Pavilion and Insect Center,** which you'll encounter shortly after pedaling under I-25.

A variety of mere nothings gives more pleasure than the uniformity of something.
— Jean Paul Richter

Chapter eleven

ODD ENDS

LISTS THAT DON'T FIT INTO OTHER LISTS

Denver offers such an interesting mix of attractions, flavors, viewpoints and sounds that it's difficult to categorize them. This chapter is intended to gather up some loose ends that just don't seem to fit anywhere else.

THE TEN BEST PLACES TO PEOPLE-WATCH

In a city brimming with things to do and places to go, sometimes it's nice just to sit and watch humanity's passing parade. Here's where:

1 *SIXTEENTH STREET MALL* • *Downtown, between Cleveland and Blake streets. GETTING THERE: The mall begins just northwest of Civic Center Park and the state capitol building. Several all-day parking lots are in this area, mostly along Fifteenth near Cleveland.*

If you enjoy sitting and watching the rest of the world stroll past, there's no better place than the Sixteenth Street Mall. It's busy with benches, chairs and even a few tables, and it's nicely landscaped so you always can find tree shade on warm days. Should you require food or drink, the mall has more outdoor restaurants and takeouts than any other place between Chicago and San Francisco. If you're on a budget, you can grab a 75-cent hot dog from one of several venders along the mall and retire to one of those many benches or chairs. If you prefer an aerial view of the mall with your lunch or snack, ride an escalator to **Eat Up** near the corner of California Street. It's a collection of a dozen fast food places, with a two-level seating area that features a balcony hanging right over the mall. For more on the mall, see Chapter Two, page 28.

2 CHERRY CREEK SHOPPING CENTER ● *3000 E. First Ave.; (303) 388-3900. Most stores open weekdays 10 to 9, Saturdays 10 to 7:30 and Sundays 11 to 6. GETTING THERE: The center is rimmed by First Avenue, University Boulevard, Steele Street and Cherry Creek. From downtown, follow Speer Boulevard southeast three miles along Cherry Creek. It blends into First Avenue, which crosses the front of the center.*

Most shopping malls have seating areas where people can stop before they drop from shopping. However, Cherry Creek is one of the few with plushly upholstered chairs and sofas at its rest stops. The largest of these R&R areas is just inside the First Street entrance to the mall. It's a fine place to sit and relax while watching others abuse their credit cards.

3 DENVER BOTANIC GARDENS ● *909 York St.; (303) 331-4000. Wednesday-Friday 9 to 5 and Saturday-Tuesday 9 to 8, May through September; then daily 9 to 5 the rest of the year. Modest admission fees. GETTING THERE: Go east from downtown about a mile and a half on Colfax Avenue, then south half a mile on York Street.*

Botanical gardens typically are attractive, quiet and peaceful—nice places to sit and relax. Denver's horticultural retreat is particularly suitable for people-watching. Regarded as one of the five finest botanical gardens in America, it's busy with fountains, patios and shaded benches where one can sit and watch others prowl and sniff the posies. One of our favorite places is Waterfall Court, a quiet courtyard where water spills over a stucco wall and gathers in a reflection pool. And on a cold winter day, what better place to relax than the tropical Boettcher Memorial Conservatory? For more, see Chapter Two, page 25.

4 WATER JET FOUNTAIN IN CITY PARK ● *At the rear of the Denver Museum of Nature & Science. GETTING THERE: Go east on Colfax Avenue about two and a half miles to Colorado Boulevard, turn north (left) for half a mile, then turn left again into the park on Montview Boulevard. This puts you in the museum's parking lot. Walk around to the rear of the museum to the fountain.*

This is the best kid-watching place in Denver. A large circular "jet fountain" squirts little geyser blasts of water at irregular intervals. Kids love to dash about its flat surface, trying to guess where the next jets are coming from. They either want to get hit or missed, depending on the day's temperature. Another pastime is to place an aluminum can on one of the jet holes and watch the water pop it into the air.

If you're as easily entertained as we are, you'll enjoy sitting on the rear steps of the museum and watching the kids play. If it's a *really* hot day, you just might be tempted to join them.

5 DENVER PAVILIONS • *Downtown, along Sixteenth Street Mall between Tremont and Welton.*

If your favorite people-watching place—Sixteenth Street Mall—becomes too busy with people, buses and cross-traffic, retreat to the more sheltered plazas and patios of Denver Pavilions. It's removed from the main mall, with benches on all three levels. Or you can dine as you people-watch. **Maggiano's Little Italy** has an outdoor patio (Chapter Three, page 67), or you can grab a quick bite from the **Corner Bakery** and adjourn to one of its outdoor tables.

6 OUTSIDE COORS FIELD ON GAME DAY • *The 20th and Blake entrance. GETTING THERE: Coors Field is an easy walk from downtown or LoDo. If you're driving, go northwest on 20th or 21st streets or northeast on Wazee Street and you'll see several parking lots around the stadium.*

Since Coors Field is on the northern edge of downtown Denver, many of the Colorado Rockies fans walk the games. A patio area opposite the 20th and Blake entrance is a fun place to watch a game-day parade of happy fans, ticket hawkers, peanut vendors and program sellers. You can even listen to the game since it's broadcast outside the stadium. And if you suddenly have the urge to catch the inside action, you'll find plenty of hawkers lowering their ticket prices by the top of the third.

7 SKYLINE PARK • *Downtown, running along Arapahoe Street between Fifteenth and Eighteenth streets.*

This narrow tree-shaded greenway extends three blocks through the heart of downtown. Despite its "Skyline" name, most of it is below street level, offering shelter from the sights and sounds of traffic. The most appealing section is opposite the **Westin Tabor Center** near Seventeenth Street, where water splashes over a modernistic cut-stone block fountain. If it's a not day, you can walk through the fountain's stone corridors and enjoy the spray, or just sit on a nearby riser and watch playful kids get deliberately wet.

8 **STARBUCKS DECK AT REI** • *REI Denver Flagship Store, Platte at Fifteenth streets; (303) 756-0272. GETTING THERE: Take Fifteenth Street about a mile northwest from downtown and cross the South Platte River at Confluence Park, then turn left on Platte Street.*

The southeast corner of REI's huge warehouse store is occupied by a Starbucks café. An outside deck overlooks Confluence Park, where the Platte River and Cherry Creek merge. It's a fine place to take a shopping break and watch walkers, joggers and cyclists on the Platte River Greenway just below. If you don't feel the need for a caffé latte and/or you want to get closer to the river, walk down to a series of viewing platforms at river's edge, where you can watch the stream spill over a low diversion dam. A nice place to sit and relax is **Shoemaker Plaza**, a little terraced enclave right at water's edge. You can perch on one of the risers here, or on park benches just above the plaza.

9 **SUPREME COURT CAFÉ** • *1550 Court Place on the Sixteenth Street Mall; (303) 892-6878.*

If you prefer people-watching with a glass in your hand, adjourn to the patio of the Supreme Court café and bar alongside the Sixteenth Street Mall. It's part of Adam's Mark Hotel and it serves lunch and dinner and the usual libations. Umbrella tables shade you from the sun in summer and heat lamps shelter you from the cold in winter.

10 **WRITER SQUARE** • *1512 Larimer Street at Sixteenth Street Mall, opposite Tabor Center.*

Writer Square forms a shopping transition zone between the Sixteenth Street Mall and Larimer Square. A small wedge of a park here is a particularly pleasant spot, and shaded benches invite one to take a break. Strolling or sitting, you can admire the square's fine collection of life-sized contemporary bronze works. Our favorite, called "Crocodile Dandy," features a pair of kids riding the back of a friendly crock. Across the small park is another bronze of kids teetering on high stilts. If you stroll further into Writer Square, you'll encounter several other bronze works. This small shopping complex specializes in art galleries, and it has several boutiques featuring clothing, giftwares and jewelry.

THE TEN BEST SPECIALTY GUIDES TO THE DENVER AREA

We assume that you've purchased this guidebook and aren't still standing in the book store, catching a free read. Having sold you on this one, we can recommend several others that may prove useful.

These are specialty guides, generally available only in the greater Denver area. We've listed address of the publishers, so you can order copies before you start out. However, don't just send them a check; there'll be shipping charges and prices may have changed, so inquire first.

We have no favorite guidebooks other than our own, so these are listed in alphabetical order.

1 **CRABBY GOURMET** • *By Pat Hiller. TDF Publishing, Ltd., 10,000 E. Yale Ave., Suite 38, Denver, CO 80231-5959; $12.95 (www.gabbygourmet.com)*

Although unnecessarily hoakey with its pig symbols, including jet-propelled ones for the best restaurants, this is the most comprehensive guide to local dining. Written by the host of "The Gabby Gourmet" radio show, it covers more than 400 restaurants in greater Denver.

2 **THE DENVER CHRONICLE** • *By David Kent Ballast. Gulf Publishing Co., P.O. Box 2608, Houston, TX 77252-2608; $18.95*

In this interesting guide, a Denver native and architectural consultant traces the city's history through its architecture. It's illustrated with black and white historical and contemporary photos.

3 **DENVER HIKING GUIDE** • *By David Rich. Books West, 5757 Arapahoe Rd., D-2, Boulder, CO 80303; $12.95.*

This book features "forty-five hikes within forty-five minutes of Denver," with directions and trail maps.

4 **DENVER'S FAVORITE PLACES** • *Photos by Jack Shumaker and text by Wayne Sirmons. Westcliffe Publishers, 2650 S. Zuni St., Englewood, CO 80110.*

This small picture book has fifty-two full-color photos of Denver, with brief descriptions. Think of it as a coffee table book in miniature. If you want to shoot Denver, you can pick up some photo angle ideas.

5 **KIDS DISCOVER DENVER AND BOULDER** • *By Sarah Goodman Zimet. Discovery Press Publications, P.O. Box 201502, Denver, CO 80022-7502; $12.95.*

The title says it—this is a comprehensive guidebook to kids' lures in the Denver and Boulder.

6 **MOUNTAIN BIKING BOULDER AND DENVER** • *Falcon Guides, P.O. Box 1718, Helena, MT 59624; (800) 582-2665; $10.95 (www.falconguide.com)*

Mountain biking is popular in the adjacent Rockies and an alarming number of guidebooks have been written about this rather specialized subject. This is the most comprehensive guide to the area.

7 *QUICK ESCAPES FROM DENVER* • *By Sherry Spitsnaugle. Globe Piquot Press, P.O. Box 833, Old Saybrook, CN 06475; $14.95. (www.globe-piquot.com)*

Ready to get out of town? This book features twenty-five weekend getaways. Most are driving guides, with attendant maps and suggested places to dine and reclines.

8 *ROCKY MOUNTAIN TOP RESTAURANTS* • *Zagat Guides, 4 Columbus Circle, New York, NY 10019; (212) 977-6000; $9.95. (www.zagat.com)*

Although the Zagats don't consider Denver to be enough of a dining mecca to warrant an individual guide, this Rocky Mountain edition lists more than 150 restaurants in the greater city area, plus another 100 in the adjacent Rockies. And should you be headed for Mormon country, it also covers the greater Salt Lake City area.

9 *THE SEAMY SIDE OF DENVER* • *By Phil Goodstein. New Social Publications, P.O. Box 18026, Denver, CO 80218; (303) 333-1095; $18.95.*

Denver may have appeared innocent in the idealized Hollywood version of *The Unsinkable Molly Brown,* although it was hardly so. Like most boomtowns, it has a wild and lusty history and Goodstein's book covers it in a humorous, highly readable fashion.

10 *WALKING DENVER* • *By Stewart M. Green. Falcon Guides, P.O. Box 1718, Helena, MT 59624; (800) 582-2665; $10.95 (www.falconguide.com)*

Small enough to fit in your fanny pack, this guide describes nineteen walks in Denver and surrounding areas.

EASY LISTENING: THE TEN BEST RADIO STATIONS

What turns you on when you turn on your radio? Mellow sounds, light rock, jazz, classics or Garth Brooks? Our choices, while quite varied, reveal that we don't like hard rock or rap and that we tilt toward more mellow sounds.

1 *KHIH—FM 95.7* • *Calling itself "K-high," it plays cool jazz and light pops. It's all easy listening and our favorite Denver station.*

2 *KQKS—FM 107.5* • *Contemporary rock and pops sounds issue from this broadcast band.*

3 *KCKK—FM 104.3* • *Wanna call in your favorite cowboy song on your cell phone? This station plays new and old country, and it likes requests.*

4 *KXKL—FM 105.2* • *This station plays oldies light rock and pops.*

5 *KBCO—FM 97.3* • *Soft, pleasant alternative rock, folk and blues issue from this station.*

6 *KOSI—FM 101.1* • *This is your basic top forties rock and pops venue.*

7 *KCFR—FM 90.1* • *This Colorado Public Radio station offers soothing sounds, news and features.*

8 *KLZ—AM 560* • *This station plays pops oldies from the 1950s onward.*

9 *KOA—AM 850* • *It's one of Denver's stronger news, sports, traffic and talk stations.*

10 *KKFN—AM 950* • *What's happening with the Broncos, Rockies, Nuggets and Avalanche? This all-sports station will keep you posted.*

Part II

THE ROCKY MOUNTAINS

It has been estimated that from seventy to eighty percent of the people who vacation in Denver also venture into the adjacent Rocky Mountains.

Assuming that our readers aren't a minority, we've fashioned side trips into three areas of those grand hills—north to Boulder and Rocky Mountain National Park, west for a summer visit to the famous ski country of the Vail Valley, and south to the many tourist attractions of Colorado Springs and Manitou Springs.

We've interconnected them so folks with lots of time on their hands can explore the Rockies in one grand sweep, traveling from one area to the next without having to pass back through Denver. For those who haven't time to explore all three, access from Denver is rather obvious. U.S. Highway 36 heads directly to Boulder, Interstate 70 hurries through the Eisenhower Tunnel and into the Vail Valley, and busy I-25 whisks travelers quickly south to the Colorado Springs area.

While all three regions are in an area of the Rockies known locally as the Front Range, each has a distinct personality. In the Rockies North, we discover an outdoor-oriented college town and a fine slice of those mountains preserved in a national park. The Rockies West offers contrasts within itself—funky old mining towns and some of America's most upscale winter-summer alpine playgrounds. The Rockies South is so busy with family tourist attractions that some unkind souls call it "the Orlando of Colorado." However, the scenery is a lot prettier than in the land of Mickey Mouse.

If heaven has a college town, it's probably as beautiful as Boulder.
— **Sunset Magazine**

Chapter twelve

ROCKIES NORTH
THE BEST OF BOULDER AND
ROCKY MOUNTAIN NATIONAL PARK

Boulder is what you do after you've had enough of Denver and its suburban sprawl. Or perhaps it's what you do *instead,* since it's one of the most appealing towns in Colorado. *The Denver Post* once described it as "The little town nestled between the mountains and reality."

Boulder also is useful as a staging area to explore nearby Rocky Mountain National Park and wilderness regions of the Front Range.

As we drove northwest from Denver on Highway 36, the Boulder Turnpike, we passed through the monotonous flatlands of Colorado's high plains. We wondered if Boulder—twenty-five miles from the Mile High City—might just be another flat place on the map. Then the highway topped a rise and we peered down into a green basin rimmed with blue lakes—mostly reservoirs—to the east and the wooded escarpments of the Rockies to the west. The foothills were marked with dramatically tilted sandstone slabs which—we learned later—were the Flatirons, the area's most acclaimed geological landmarks.

If you approach Boulder by this route, pull into a scenic turnout to admire that view, and you can load up on visitor brochures from an unmanned kiosk.

As we drove into the town's southern edge, Boulder looked like most other midsize cities, with ordinary suburbs, strip malls and service stations. Its secret self lies just to the west, huddled contentedly against the steep downslope of the Rocky Mountain foothills. It is a secret easily discovered. We walked the Pearl Street Mall, strolled Boulder Creek Path, explored the red sandstone campus of the University of Colorado and followed Canyon Drive up into the mountains. We soon discovered why several publications have called Boulder one of the most livable cities in America. Within twenty-four hours, it became our favorite city in Colorado.

Home to the main campus of the University of Colorado, this community of about 100,000 is caught in a pleasant time warp, somewhere between the 1960s and the high-tech new Millennium. Walking the streets of its low-rise downtown area, one gets the sense of a liberal college town. There's a suggestion of Berkeley's Telegraph Avenue here, particularly along Pearl Street Mall, with its book stores, sidewalk cafés, art shops, guys with long hair and gals with longer dresses. Yet, Boulder is becoming a high tech hub, with several firms working in conjunction with the computer and science nerds on the university campus.

This city also is a major outdoor center. When its youthful residents aren't taking classes, voting against Republicans or working in computer labs, they're hiking and mountain biking and kayaking in the adjacent mountains. *Outside* magazine rated it as the leading outdoor city in America. Boulder has more than a hundred miles of bicycle paths and marked bike lanes, and it's one of the few cities that you can kayak through.

Shortly after arriving, we caught a classic glimpse of Boulder's pleasant multiple personality—a long-haired youth wearing Nikes, strumming a guitar and sipping caffé latte in a trendy Starbucks café.

FINDING YOUR WAY

Boulder is rather easy to navigate. As you approach the outskirts, Boulder Turnpike blends into 28th Street. If you turn left onto Arapahoe Avenue, Canyon Boulevard or Pearl Street, you'll soon be in the downtown area. Canyon is State Highway 119, which takes you west and uphill into the Rockies. Broadway is the main north-south corridor. Head north and it's State Route 7, which blends into Highway 36, bound for Rocky Mountain National Park. Southbound, it skirts the edge of the University of Colorado campus and becomes State Highway 93, headed for Golden and a junction with Interstate 70.

Most shops and services are along Arapahoe, Canyon, Broadway, and Pearl Street. The large Crossroads Mall shopping center is just east of downtown at 28th Street and Arapahoe.

Boulder has no motel row. Its mix of hotels, motels and bed breakfast inns are randomly spaced around the city. This is a town that invites walking, so find close-in lodging. We chose Quality Inn & Suites Boulder Creek because of its proximity to the Boulder Creek Path, downtown and University of Colorado campus.

The organic thing

A good way to sample Boulder—literally—is to stroll through its Farmers Market, held along Thirteenth Street between Canyon Boulevard and Arapahoe every Wednesday from 10 to 2 and Saturday from 8 to 2. Citizens of this health-conscious community set up several dozen organic produce stands, herb and flower stalls and specialty health food outlets. One wing of the market is an outdoor food court where you can buy everything from organic breads and fruit smoothies to Russian *borscht,* sinful baked goods and huge breakfast burritos. (*www.boulderfarmers.org*)

TO LEARN MORE: Contact the Boulder Convention & Visitors Bureau, 2440 Pearl St., Boulder, CO 80302; (800) 444-0447 or (303) 442-2911. (*www.bouldercoloradousa.com; e-mail: visitor@boulder-cvb.com*) The office is at Pearl and Folsom, and it operates an information kiosk in the Pearl Street Mall between Thirteenth and Fourteenth.

Boulder Magazine, available at visitor centers, shops and brochure racks, contains long lists of events, activities, hiking trails, attractions, lodgings and restaurants.

The ten best attractions

Our ten favorite things in Boulder are presented in a vaguely logical order of appearance. A good place to begin is the Pearl Street Mall, a landscaped pedestrian promenade and a national historic district. It's both an attraction and an activity, and our favorite place in Boulder.

1 PEARL STREET MALL • *Downtown, between Eleventh and Fifteenth streets. GETTING THERE: If you're coming into town from Denver, stay on Highway 36, which becomes 28th Street. Turn left onto Pearl Street and follow it several blocks to the beginning of the mall.*

This four-block mall is a key to Boulder's distinctive personality. Traffic-free except for cross streets, it's the town's gathering spot, social and counter-cultural center and human circus. It draws a polyglot of university students, tourists, wanna-be hippies, street musicians, clowns, fortune tellers, pushcart vendors and a few of the homeless. Tree-shaded and busy with plazas and benches, it even has a couple of kids' play areas. And the mall isn't just coffee cafés, book stores and funky shops. It's home to several restaurants—virtually all with outside tables—art galleries and trendy retail outlets such as Banana Republic and Abercrombie & Fitch. Most of the shops and cafés occupy handsome old brick and masonry buildings that give the area a look of both age and vitality.

The best time to hang out is on a warm evening or any Friday or Saturday night when the weather is rational. Pearl Street Mall becomes Boulder's happening place—its hot summer night front porch. Folks crowd into restaurants and coffee houses and spill onto the outside tables. You're likely to encounter a magician working a crowd, guitar players and banjo pickers, a percussion group on the courthouse lawn or a hammered dulcimer player (a description of his instrument, not his condition). The last time we strolled Pearl Street, we encountered two young blonde belly dancers, a tap dancer with her own little wooden portable stage and a guy wearing a white satin wedding gown with a six-foot train, swaying to the beat of a friend's bongo drum.

Although Pearl Street Mall is technically between Fifteenth and Eleventh street, it stretches—in vitality and temperament—another two blocks to Ninth. Several popular restaurants and the hip-funky **Trident Bookstore and Café** are in this section. The Trident, at 939-940 Pearl, serves espresso coffees, assorted teas and pastries. A similar haven, on the main mall, is **Bookend Café** linked to **Boulder Bookstore** at 1115 Pearl Street.

2 UNIVERSITY OF COLORADO CAMPUS ● 1050 Regent Dr.; (303) 492-1411. GETTING THERE: Turn into the campus from Broadway onto Euclid Avenue, opposite Sixteenth Street.

The handsome 600-acre campus of the University of Colorado is the city's scholastic and cultural core—the seat of much of Boulder's liberal/environmental identity. It can't avoid influencing the town; during the school term, every fourth resident is a university student.

With its dramatic rough-cut pink sandstone, tile-roofed buildings, the university definitely is worth a visit. Turn into the campus on Euclid Avenue and you'll pass in front of the **University Memorial Center**, which houses the student union. Euclid Avenue Autopark is just beyond—a handy place to stash your car. You can pick up a campus map at an information desk in the union's main foyer. Nearby is the Glenn Miller Lounge, honoring the famous bandleader, a CU alumnus. Several photos and gold records are on display. Downstairs, you'll find the main cafeteria with several fast-food takeouts and—on the next floor down—the student book store, which also sells CU logo apparel and student supplies.

Two blocks northwest along Broadway, you'll encounter the **University of Colorado Museum of Natural History** in the Henderson Building. It's open weekdays 9 to 5, Saturday 9 to 4 and Sunday 10 to 4; (303) 492-6892. This fine museum has three major exhibit rooms focusing on the anthropology, biology and geology of the American Southwest, plus another room with changing exhibits.

If you walk eastward from the backside of the Henderson Building, you'll encounter the great grassy swatch of Norlin Quadrangle, rimmed by several of the university's older buildings. Cross the lawn to **Old Main,** CU's oldest surviving structure, dating from 1874. Walk around to the east side, enter through a pair of massive cathedral style doors and climb polished wooden stairways to the **Heritage Center** on the third floor. It's open weekdays 10 to 4 and Saturday 10 to 2; (303) 492-6329. Exhibits focus on the history of the university and some of its distinguished students, such as Glenn Miller, golfer Hale Erwin, skier Billy Kidd and actor-director Robert Redford.

As you leave the campus, cross Broadway onto Sixteenth and turn right onto Euclid and you'll encounter the **Boulder Museum of History** at Euclid and Twelfth Street. It's open Tuesday-Friday 10 to 4 and weekends noon to 4; (303) 449-3464; (*www.bcn.boulder.-co.us/arts/bmh*) Occupying the 1899 Harbeck-Bergheim House, it contains a rather undisciplined clutter of early-day artifacts tracing Boulder's history. The house itself is quite impressive, with floral wallpaper, leaded glass windows and carved moldings and columns.

3 *BOULDER DUSHANBE TEAHOUSE* ● *1770 Thirteenth St.; (303) 442-4993. Lunch through dinner daily with weekend brunch from 8 to 3. (www.boulderteahouse.com) GETTING THERE: The teahouse is on the banks of Boulder Creek, opposite Civic Park on Thirteenth between Arapahoe and Canyon.*

Leave it to Boulder to adopt as its sister city a place that most people never heard of—Dushanbe, Tajikistan. Actually, it was a rather noble gesture. A former Soviet satellite, Tajikistan has fallen on hard times since the breakup the USSR, and Boulder has sponsored several programs to help this small nation. In appreciation for its adoption as a sister city, the mayor of Dushanbe—the country's capital—presented Boulder with a handcrafted *tajik* teahouse, a traditional Tajikistan gathering spot. Its decorative elements were produced there, shipped here in 200 crates, reassembled on the banks of Boulder Creek and now functions as a restaurant and community gathering place. Stop by to admire the fantastic detail of its Islamic design in ceramic tile and carved woods. The best way to appreciate the teahouse—and support its activities—is to have a meal or at least a cup of tea, so you can take time to admire the intricate handiwork. The kitchen serves a variety of international dishes, or you can order interesting teas and very tasty pastries. If the weather's nice—and it usually is—ask to be seated in the patio alongside Boulder Creek. You can study the elaborate detail of the *frieze* while enjoying the relaxing song of the stream.

The **Boulder Museum of Contemporary Art** occupies a building adjacent to the tea house, at 1750 Thirteenth Street. It's open Tuesday-Saturday 10 to 6; closed on Sundays; (303) 443-2122. (*www.bmoca.com*)

4 **BOULDER CREEK PATH** • *Sixteen-mile walking and cycling path from the base of Boulder Canyon through downtown Boulder Creek to Valmont Lake. GETTING THERE: There are multiple accesses to the path downtown; ask at your lodging desk or just about anyone on the street.* A Boulder Greenways Self-guided Tour Map *is available at visitor centers and local bike shops.*

Like Pearl Street Mall, this paved path along the riparian woodland of Boulder Creek makes this town special. The creek flows through the heart of town, splashing cold and clear down from the Rockies. This cycling and walking path follows its course through Boulder and beyond, occasionally switching from one bank to another on gently arched bridges. Benches along its route invite one to linger and listen to the rustling water. Signs and exhibits discuss the creek's flora and fauna.

For residents, the path is as much a thoroughfare as city streets. Many walk or peddle to work or to downtown shops. Students use it to reach the University of Colorado, which lies alongside its banks. Visitors who choose lodging near the creek, such as **Quality Inn & Suites** or **Millennium at Boulder** can stroll downtown on the path, or use it for their morning wake-up walks. Several local bike shops rent cycles, including the **Boulder Bikesmith** in Arapahoe Village Shopping Center at 2432 Arapahoe Ave.; (303) 443-1132.

Incidentally, many riders whizz rapidly along the path. If you're a timid rider, you might want to avoid the busiest section, between Thirteenth and 28th avenues. And always stay to your right, whether cycling or walking.

This is one of a series of greenways along the creek and its tributaries. More than twenty miles of these riparian corridors have been developed as linear multiple use parks. Complete details and routes are on the *Boulder Greenways* map.

5 **BOULDER CANYON & FALLS** • *West of Boulder, up Canyon Boulevard.*

Boulder Canyon is the source of the creek that gives the city much of its character. Drive west from town on Canyon and you'll be in this rock-ribbed, tree-shrouded chasm within a mile. Its lower section is part of Boulder Mountain Park (see below) that rims the city's western flank, with a network of hiking trails, climbing areas and picnic stops. Cascading Boulder Creek is rarely out of sight as you drive the gently twisting highway. Frequent pullouts invite you to pause and admire the views of canyon and creek. Six miles from town, pull over to the left, then walk across the highway and follow a short, rocky trail up to **Boulder Falls**. This short but violent cascade gushes down a sheer rock face, then tumbles into a series of cataracts alongside the trail.

The canyon route ends ten miles later at **Nederland**, a scruffy former silver mining town sitting near the shore of a reservoir that could pass for a pretty mountain lake. The small town sits at 8,236 feet, nearly 2,000 feet higher than Boulder. At this point, you've intersected the **Peak to Peak Highway** that travels along the high shoulders of the Rockies from Estes Park at Rocky Mountain National Park's entrance to Idaho Springs near I-70. We travel this scenic corridor at the end of this chapter.

You can study the canyon in greater detail by hiking the gently inclined **Boulder Canyon Trail**. No, it doesn't go all the way to Nederland; it's just over two miles long, providing a nice workout. It's essentially an extension of Boulder Creek Path. A good starting point is **Red Rocks Settlers Park**; it's on the right, reached via Canyon Drive just before it starts uphill. Several exhibits in the park and along the trail discuss the establishment of Boulder. Other trails lead north from Settlers Park, taking hikers up to a red rock pinnacle area that affords nice views of the city. To start the Boulder Canyon hike, simply follow the trail uphill from Settlers Park. It tunnels under the highway and merges with the upper end of Boulder Creek Path.

6 *CHAUTAUQUA PARK* • *900 Baseline Road; (303) 442-3282. (www.chautauqua.bouldernet.com; e-mail: cha@usa.net) GETTING THERE: From the downtown area, drive south on Broadway and turn right (west) on Baseline Road. Follow it toward the foothills and turn left into the Chautauqua parking area.*

The national Chautauqua organization was formed more than a century ago to create cultural retreats in rural America. Most have long since disappeared, although the Boulder community survives, founded in 1898 and operated by the non-profit Colorado Chautauqua Association. No longer a mere summer retreat, it has become Boulder's community cultural center. The large complex includes a grassy public park, several rental cottages and a restaurant (see below). An imposing old wooden auditorium is the site of year-around concerts, live drama and cultural workshops. The 26-acre complex, which is at the base of the Flatirons, borders on Boulder Mountain Park. Visitors can get hiking maps and other park information from the Ranger Cottage, near the main parking lot. Hiking trails extend from here into the park. A good morning's workout is a three-mile hike toward Flagstaff Mountain for spectacular views back down to Boulder.

7 *BOULDER MOUNTAIN PARKS* • *Large wilderness area immediately west of Boulder. Modest daily parking fee. GETTING THERE: From the downtown area, drive south on Broadway, then turn right (west) on Baseline Road and follow it up into the foothills; it becomes Flagstaff Road as it passes Chautauqua Park.*

This huge natural area is Boulder's direct link to the Rocky Mountain Front Range. One can reach this great swatch forest, canyons, meadowlands and rocky outcroppings within minutes. The park contains many of the city's mountain landmarks—Boulder Canyon, Flagstaff Mountain with its grand city views, and those great sandstone slabs, the Flatirons.

For a quickie tour or an all-day outing, head up Flagstaff Road past Chautauqua Park. The road almost immediately begins a series of paper-clip turns, doubling back on itself as it climbs steeply up the Front Range. Frequent turnouts along the way invite you to pause for splendid views down to Boulder and up into the rocky heights. Trailheads extend from many of the turnouts, leading into the surrounding wilderness. About three miles from Chautauqua Park, a road to the right takes you to **Flagstaff Summit and amphitheater.** It has a seasonal ranger station, picnic areas and lofty views of the Continental Divide to the west and the City of Boulder below. The road ends about a quarter of a mile above the ranger station, at Artist Point, offering one of the park's best panoramas. Back on Flagstaff Road, watch on your right for **Lost Gulch Overlook**, a few miles above the Flagstaff Summit turnoff. (If you top a crest and leave the park, you just missed it.) Drive into a rough, eroded parking lot, then walk to the left where a platform provides the park's best view of the eternally snow-patched Great Divide. If you feel like rock-hopping, you can climb to a nearby outcropping for an even higher vantage point.

Just beyond the overlook, Flagstaff Road tops a crest around 7,000 feet at the park's upper boundary.

8 NATIONAL CENTER FOR ATMOSPHERIC RESEARCH
● *1850 Table Mesa Dr.; (303) 497-1174. (www.ncar.ucar.edu) Weekdays 8 to 5 and weekends 10 to 4; free. Cafeteria and science store. GETTING THERE: Drive a mile and a half south on Broadway, then turn right (west) onto Table Mesa Drive and follow it about two miles into the foothills.*

Although its studies are conducted worldwide, the National Center for Atmospheric Research was built in the foothills above Boulder. Why? Because the Rockies' downslope creates its own distinctive weather patterns as disturbances from the west spill over the Continental Divide. Completed in 1966, the dramatic complex—which suggests a highrise Pueblo dwelling—was designed by I.M. Pei, who went on to become of the world's leading architects.

NCAR isn't a museum, although corridors on the second and third floors are lined with fascinating hands-on science exhibits that concern worldwide weather patterns. Visitors can play with artificial lightning, create their own microbursts (simulated wind shears) and disrupt the twisting of a mockup tornado. A seven-minute video explains NCAR's role—to understand the behavior of the atmosphere as it relates to weather patterns. Its scientists seek to anticipate such potential disasters as flooding rains, tornadoes, winds sheers and other destructive forces of nature.

Behind the building, the short Walter Orr Roberts Weather Trail extends toward the sandstone foothills. Signs along the path discuss the Boulder area's terrain and its effect on weather patterns. It's a pleasant hike through a sloping meadow and woodland, with dramatic views up to the Front Range and down to the city.

9 *CELESTIAL SEASONINGS TOUR OF TEA • 4600 Sleepytime Dr.; (800) 351-8175 or (303) 581-1202. (www.celestialseasonings.com) Free tours hourly Monday-Saturday from 10 to 3 and Sunday 11 to 3. Tea Shop open weekdays 9 to 6, Saturday 9 to 5 and Sunday 11 to 4. Celestial Café open weekdays 7:30 to 9:30 for breakfast and 11 to 2:30 for lunch. Summer hours may be longer. GETTING THERE: Drive north from downtown on Foothills Parkway, which becomes Diagonal Way (Highway 119), go right at a stoplight at Jay Road for a mile, then turn left and go north on Spine Road. After passing through a residential area on the edge of an industrial park, turn left into the plant.*

What's a nice place like this doing in an industrial park? Manufacturing eight million bags of tea a day, that's what. There's an almost excessively pristine ladies' tea room ambiance at Celestial Seasonings, with its frilly décor and signs bearing inspirational messages. However, a 45-minute tour takes you past sophisticated equipment that looks capable of assembling a space station. Some of it is so specialized that photos are prohibited. Yet, all this machinery does is cut (teas are never ground like coffee), blend and package all sorts of teas—herbal and caffeinated.

The tour begins with a video, which is shown in a small art gallery exhibiting the original paintings of many of Celestial's cutesy, wholesome tea labels. Visitors are then walked through the large blending and bagging factory. Here, they can view great stacks of sacks containing tea ingredients, smell the plant's pleasant herbal dustiness and the heady aroma in the Mint Room, and watch those great big machines put the blended products into little tiny bags. The tour ends in a gift shop that is at once very large and very dainty. Before or after the tour, folks can sip some of the firm's teas. A nearby café with indoor and outdoor tables serves breakfast and lunch.

10 *LEANIN' TREE MUSEUM OF WESTERN ART • 6055 Longbow Dr.; (303) 530-1442. (www.leanintree.com) Weekdays 8 to 4:30 and weekends 10 to 4; free. GETTING THERE: It's best visited in conjunction with Celestial Seasonings. Continue past the plant for less than half a mile, then turn right onto Longbow Drive.*

You've seen those droll comic cowboys and inspirational Western and native people scenes on the Leanin' Tree line of greeting cards and giftwares. This is where they're produced. There are no tours, although the firm has opened a museum here to exhibit one of America's largest collections of Western art. Devotees of this art form can spend hours admiring more than 200 paintings and eighty bronze sculptures. Virtually all are by twentieth century "cowboy artists." Most are realistic paintings and finely detailed bronzes that typify this art form, although there are a few impressionistic paintings. Subjects range from romantic Western scenics that became popular in the late nineteenth century to paintings and bronzes of native folks and working cowboys. A few of the paintings are originals that were done for Leanin' Tree products. Many of these items are on sale at an adjacent gift shop.

THE TEN BEST RESTAURANTS

This small city has a big appetite, with more than 300 restaurants with a remarkable dining variety. The largest culinary concentration is along Pearl Street, both on and off the pedestrian mall. Many fine restaurants are found elsewhere as well, generally near the downtown area. And the really good news about Boulder dining is that all restaurants are smoke-free, by local statute. And that includes bar areas of restaurants.

PRICING: Dinner with entrée, soup or salad, not including drinks, appetizers or dessert: *$* = less than $10 per entrée; *$$* = $10 to $19; *$$$* = $20 to $29; *$$$$* = "Did you say you were buying?"

1 *DOLAN'S* • *2319 Arapahoe Ave.; (303) 444-8758. Contemporary American; full bar service. Lunch weekdays, dinner nightly and Sunday brunch. Major credit cards; $$ to $$$. GETTING THERE: It's just east of downtown at Arapahoe and Folsom.*

Locals and visitors-in-the-know like to congregate at one of Boulder's most popular restaurants, presided over by affable host Michael Dolan. The name may sound Irish, although the fare in this attractive, casual restaurant is contemporary American. The menu tilts toward seafood, featuring whatever Dolan can get flown in fresh. He has one of the best wine lists in town, and his chef likes to match wines with foods on the dinner special menu, which might feature grilled mahi mahi with polenta and fruit salsa with an Edna Valley Chardonnay, or seared *kajiki* with Carmenet Sauvignon Blanc. Among regular entrées are New Zealand rack of lamb with *cous-cous* and vegetables, beef tenderloin with buttermilk whipped potatoes; salmon-wrapped sea scallops over fresh vegetables, and macadamia crusted ahi with baby spinach and basmati rice.

2 *CHAUTAUQUA DINING HALL* • *900 Baseline Rd.; (303) 440-3776. Contemporary American; wine and beer. Breakfast, lunch and dinner daily. Major credit cards; $$ to $$$. GETTING THERE: From the downtown area, drive south on Broadway, then turn right (west) on Baseline Road and follow it to Chautauqua Park. The dining hall is on the park's southwestern edge.*

The once simple dining hall of Boulder's historic Chautauqua retreat has been turned into an appealingly bright and airy restaurant with cuisine to match. Diners have a nice choice. They can nosh indoors beside white and beige wood paneled walls graced with cheerful framed floral prints, or on the wrap-around porch with fuschia baskets hanging over the tables and views of the park and city below. Appropriate to this health-conscious community, the menu focuses on fresh, organic ingredients. You may encounter such savories as honey-cured pork tenderloin, pepper-crusted ahi tuna steak, trout with herb *cous cous* or grilled lamb chops.

3 *CHEZ THUY RESTAURANT* • *2655 28th St.; (303) 442-1700. Vietnamese; full bar service. Lunch Monday-Saturday and dinner nightly. Major credit cards; $ to $$. GETTING THERE: It's about a mile northeast of downtown. Take Pearl to 28th Street, turn left and go north two blocks; the restaurant is on the left, just past Mapleton Avenue.*

It's pronounced *Twee* and she's one of the greater Denver-Boulder area's best Vietnamese chefs. In addition to typical Asian stir-fry and rice dishes, she features several tasty entrées such as frog legs in garlic and ginger, shrimp in tamarin sauce, wrapped shrimp and honey chicken, and duck with sautéed vegetables and garlic sauce. The huge menu also offers a long list of noodle, hot pot and stir fry dishes, plus a dozen vegetarian dishes. Our favorite here is *cari*, a peppy Vietnamese curry stew with coconut milk, vegetables and a choice of fish, chicken, pork or beef. Thuy's is a cheery café, with purplish booths with brocaded flower backs, drop lamps and some nice Asian artifacts.

4 *DA GABI CUCINA* • *3970 W. Broadway; (303) 443-9004. Italian; wine and beer. Dinner nightly. Major credit cards; $$ to $$$. GETTING THERE: It's on the north side of town, in the east end of North Village Shopping Center. Follow Broadway about two miles west and turn right into the center just short of a traffic light at Quince Avenue.*

Unlike bright and cheery *trattorias*, Da Gabi is a rather handsome restaurant with dark woods, drop lamps and oversized art works on the walls, brightened by a couple of large flower arrangements. The fare is tasty and rather traditional, including cannelloni, fettuccine with Portobello mushrooms, and chicken breast with Marsala wine sauce, and *Salmone Portofino* with sautéed rock shrimp, asparagus and tomatoes. A specialty is *Gamberoni Pulcinella*—jumbo shrimp sautéed with garlic, white wine and roasted peppers. Da Gabi also features several designer pizzas and the usual range of pastas.

5 FLAGSTAFF HOUSE • *1138 Flagstaff Rd.; (303) 442-4640. Contemporary American; full bar service. Dinner nightly. Major credit cards; $$$ to $$$$. GETTING THERE: Drive south from downtown on Broadway, then turn right (west) on Baseline Road and follow it up into the foothills. It becomes Flagstaff Road as it passes Chautauqua Park and the restaurant is just beyond, on the right.*

Notched dramatically into a steep downslope between Boulder and its mountain park, Flagstaff House is a Colorado institution—and a pricey one. One of Colorado's few AAA Four Diamond restaurants, it provides stunning city views with its new American cuisine. The décor is elegantly simple, consisting mostly of glass walls to showcase the view. Crystalware and flower vases provide formal accents to this imposing setting. A patio cantilevered over the hillside is a grand place to sip a drink and wait for your table. The restaurant's carefully crafted and handsomely presented cuisine has earned high marks from the Zagat Survey and Colorado food critics. Some examples include venison with roasted breast of duck with shiitake mushrooms, Dover sole with roasted sweet peppers and *meunier* sauce, and a halibut and lobster combination with purple Thai rice and spinach-carrot ginger sauce.

6 FULL MOON GRILL • *2525 Arapahoe Ave.; (303) 938-8800. Northern Italian with nouveau accents; wine and beer. Dinner nightly. Major credit cards; $$$ to $$$$. GETTING THERE: It's less than a mile from downtown in the North Village Shopping Center off Arapahoe. The easiest way to reach it is to turn north from Arapahoe onto Folsom, then go right into the shopping center parking lot. Continue straight ahead through the lot for about a block.*

Full Moon Grill is one of those places that the faithful find even though it's buried in a large shopping center. Colorado food critics are unanimous in their praise for its creative cookery, which is northern Italian, tilting sharply toward American *nouveau*. Some recent examples—although the menu changes frequently—were pistachio crusted Alaskan halibut, New York steak with garlic mashed potatoes and red wine glaze, and pan-seared duck breast with polenta. That's Italian? No, but several pasta dishes are, and the pasta is made fresh daily in house. The Grill is tucked into an odd little hexagonal building that's mostly windows, making it bright and airy. Two small dining areas with tables and brocaded booths are divided by a pony wall, upon which two large ceramic Chinese pigs preside. A small dining patio is popular in warm weather.

7 *JAX FISH HOUSE* • *928 Pearl St.; (303) 444-1811. American, mostly seafood with Southwestern accents; full bar service. Dinner nightly. Major credit cards; $$ to $$$. GETTING THERE: It's downtown, between Ninth and Tenth streets.*

Jax is one of those happening places that patrons have taken by storm. Don't come here for a quiet evening—at least not on a weekend—because this narrow slot of a brick-walled restaurant and its center bar are jammed with mostly youthful patrons. It obviously draws faithful legions from the University of Colorado. Jax is two blocks west of the Pearl Street Mall, yet it has that lively hip mall attitude. An open kitchen at the far end of the slender restaurant issues *miso* salmon sashimi, chioppino, a spicy scallop and shrimp Diablo, chipotle-rubbed Santa Fe trout with sweet corn polenta, and a Mississippi catfish platter with crayfish *etouffée* and corn pudding. About the only non-fish item on the dinner menu is Kansas City strip steak.

8 *JOHN'S* • *2328 Pearl St.; (303) 444-5232. American with foreign accents; full bar service. Dinner Tuesday-Saturday. Major credit cards; $$ to $$$. GETTING THERE: It's about a mile east of downtown, on the right between 23rd Street and 24th Place.*

Tucked into a tiny pink cottage, John's has been a Boulder institution since 1975, although the menu has kept pace with the current eclectic culinary trends. Some examples are bouillabaisse with salmon, bass, mussels, shrimp and scallops; herb-crusted chicken *Agrigento* with currants, pinenuts and caramelized onions; and pork tenderloin medallions with roasted garlic. Walls of the tiny foyer are papered with more than a score of awards and plaudits that chef-owner John Bizzaro has earned through the years. The cozy interior keeps the quaint country cottage look with lace curtains, petite table lamps and exposed beam ceilings.

9 *SUNFLOWER NATURAL FINE DINING* • *1701 Pearl St.; (303) 440-0220. Holistic American with Asian accents; wine and beer. Lunch and dinner daily and Sunday brunch. Major credit cards; $$. GETTING THERE: It's downtown at the corner of Seventeenth Street.*

Sunflower and Boulder are a perfect match—both focused on keeping people fit. This cheerful café features only organic foods that are pesticide free; it uses no red meats or refined sugars. Not surprisingly, it has a large vegetarian selection. However, it also does tasty things with fish and fowl. The menu lists grilled ahi tuna with pineapple salsa, herb-stuffed chicken breast, and sesame crusted salmon with *miso* saké. Among house specials are a bamboo steamer of organic vegetables with *udon* noodles, and Masuman curry with vegetables over brown rice topped with tofu, chicken or shrimp. This isn't a dusty hippy joint whose waitresses have been pierced strange parts of their bodies. It's a bright and cheerful place with high ceilings, light woods and stylized Asian prints on the walls. Strings of sidewalk tables wrap around its corner location.

10 WALNUT BREWERY • 1123 Walnut St.; (303) 447-1345. American brewpub; full bar service. Lunch and dinner daily. Major credit cards; $$. GETTING THERE: It's downtown, near Eleventh Street.

In addition to being an appealing brewpub, this is one of Boulder's most attractive restaurants, housed in an old brick building with lofty ceilings held in place by bold steel girders. Hanging flower baskets bring a bit of cheer to an outdoor dining and drinking area. The great open interior space offers dining in comfortable booths and tables on two levels. Stainless steel brewing tanks are visible through large windows behind the bar, where specialty beers such as Big Horn Butter Ale, Buffalo Gold Ale, Indian Peaks Ale and St. James Irish Red are brewed. Sampler tastings are available for a fee. The kitchen issues hearty brewpub fare such as buffalo fajitas, fried chicken, barbecued ribs and fish and chips.

THE TEN BEST LODGINGS

We've broken our lodging selections into a pair of categories—hotels or inns, and B&B's. We start with the very best in each category, then follow with runners-up in alphabetical order.

PRICING: Dollar sign codes indicate price ranges for two people, based on summer rates: $ = a standard two-person room for $99 or less; $$ = $100 to $149; $$$ = $150 to $199; and $$$$ = $200 or more.

1 THE VERY BEST HOTEL OR INN: Hotel Boulderado • 2115 Thirteenth St., Boulder, CO 80302; (800) 433-4344 or (303) 442-4344. (www.boulderado.com; e-mail: info@boulderado.com) Major credit cards; $$$ to $$$$. GETTING THERE: This historic hotel is on the corner of Spruce Street downtown. If you're approaching on the Boulder Turnpike, blend onto 28th street, turn left onto Spruce Street and follow it about a mile downtown to Thirteenth.

This is Boulder's most handsome and most historic hotel, built in 1907 and very nicely restored. It's focal point is an atrium lobby with antique furnishings, a stained glass ceiling and cantilevered cherry wood staircase leading to a hanging balcony. The 160 guest rooms have a mix of modern and old style furnishings, with contemporary amenities such as two-line phones, TV/movies and voice mail. **Q's Restaurant** serves contemporary American fare, breakfast through dinner and the adjacent Corner Bar is a favorite locals' hangout.

1 *THE VERY BEST B&B: Earl House Historic Inn* • *2429 Broadway, Boulder, CO 80304; (303) 938-1400. Six rooms and two carriage house units; all with private baths; full breakfast. Major credit cards; $$ to $$$$. GETTING THERE: The inn is near downtown, between High Street and Portland Place. Approaching from the Boulder Turnpike, go left onto Baseline at the turnpike's end, then right on Broadway for about two miles. The inn is on the left.*

Boulder's best bed & breakfast inn is simply gorgeous. It's housed in a rough-cut stone 1882 Gothic Revival mansion with multi-colored Victorian trim, sitting behind carefully manicured formal gardens. The interior is beautifully decorated with Victorian antiques, inlaid wooden floors, carved wainscotting and floral wallpaper. An ornately furnished sitting room features a painted ceiling and a mural of a comely harp player. Rooms are individually furnished, with marble bathrooms, spa tubs, TV and phones. Adjacent carriage houses are individual homes with three bedrooms, two baths, full kitchens and washer/dryers, available for extended stays.

The next best hotels & inns

3 *BOULDER MARRIOTT* • *2660 Canyon Blvd., Boulder, CO 80302; (303) 440-8877. Major credit cards; $$$ to $$$$. GETTING THERE: It's just east of downtown in a shopping complex between Folsom and 28th streets. If you're approaching on the Boulder Turnpike, blend onto 28th Street, then turn left on Canyon Boulevard and left again.*

One of Boulder's larger full-service hotels, the 155-room Marriott has a Southwestern look, with salmon pink stucco and turquoise accents. The small, appealing lobby is decorated with contemporary native American paintings. Rooms have large desks, two phones with modems and other amenities. Facilities include **JW's Steakhouse** and lounge, several shops, a small indoor pool, business center, spa and fitness room. Two VIP floors feature continental breakfast, evening refreshments and a roof terrace.

4 *COLORADO CHAUTAUQUA ASSOCIATION* • *900 Baseline Rd., Boulder, CO 80302; (303) 442-3282, ext. 11. (www.chautauqua.boulder.net; e-mail: chau@usa.net) Major credit cards; $ to $$. GETTING THERE: It's in Chautauqua Park southwest of downtown. From the Boulder Turnpike, turn west onto Baseline Road and follow it to the park, which is on the left.*

While not fancy, these little green cottages and lodge rooms are charming and historic—part of the century-old Boulder Chautauqua complex. They have been renovated, although they don't have TV or telephones; units with kitchens have utensils. All lodgings are non-smoking. The **Chautauqua Dining Hall** (listed above) is nearby, and guests have access to tennis courts, children's playgrounds, Chautauqua Park and the adjacent hiking trails of Boulder Mountain Park. They also receive discounts on many Chautauqua cultural activities.

5 *MILLENNIUM AT BOULDER* ● *1345 28th Street, Boulder, CO 80302-6899; (800) 545-6285 or (303) 433-3850. (www.millenni- umhotels.com) Major credit cards; $$ to $$$. GETTING THERE: It's near the corner of 28th Street and Arapahoe Avenue. Approaching on the Boulder Turnpike, turn left into the hotel complex just before 28th.*

Boulder's largest resort hotel, the 269-room Millennium (formerly Regal Harvest House) occupies sixteen acres of landscaped grounds on the banks of Boulder Creek. Facilities include two swimming pools and spas, tennis courts, exercise room and basketball courts. Rooms and suites have the usual resort amenities and most have balconies. The hotel's attractive restaurant and adjacent deli serve American fare, with seating indoors and out.

6 *QUALITY INN & SUITES BOULDER CREEK* ● *2020 Ara- pahoe Ave., Boulder, CO 80302; (888) 449-7550 outside Colorado only, or (303) 449-7550. (www.qualityinnboulder.com; e-mail: info@quality- innboulder.com) Major credit cards; $ to $$. Prices include a hot buffet breakfast. GETTING THERE: The lodge is just southeast of downtown, be- tween 20th and 21st streets. From the Boulder Turnpike, blend onto 28th Street, turn left onto Arapahoe, pass 21st Street and turn left into the inn's parking lot.*

This recently remodeled and upgraded inn is centrally located, in a quiet neighborhood near Boulder Creek Path. It's within walking distance of the university campus, downtown and Pearl Street Mall. The nicely furnished rooms and suites have TV movies, two-line phones with voice mail, data ports, refrigerators and microwaves. Amenities include an indoor pool, sauna, fitness room, guest laundry and a business center with free 24-hour DSL internet access.

The next best bed & breakfast inns

7 *ALPS BOULDER CANYON INN* ● *38619 Boulder Canyon Dr. (P.O. Box 18298), Boulder, CO 80302; (800) 414-2577 or (303) 444-5445. (www.alpsinn.com; e-mail: info@alpsinn.com) Twelve rooms with private baths; full breakfast. Major credit cards; $$ to $$$$. GET-*

TING THERE: It's about three miles up Boulder Canyon, on the right. From Boulder Turnpike, blend onto 28th Street, turn left onto Canyon Boulevard and follow it through town and up into the canyon.

This handsomely rustic old lodge is a comfortable retreat high in Boulder Canyon, across the highway from Boulder Creek. It has the look of an old style hunting lodge with river stone and rough log accents, game trophies and sturdy wood furniture. Breakfast is served in a large lodge-style dining room. All guest rooms have fireplaces and some have clawfoot tubs or spa tubs for two. A TV lounge is an inviting place to relax, with overstuffed couches and chairs.

8 *BRIAR ROSE BED & BREAKFAST* • *2151 Arapahoe Ave., Boulder, CO 80302; (303) 442-3007. (www.briarrosebb.com) Nine rooms and one suite, all with private baths; full breakfast. Major credit cards; $$ to $$$. GETTING THERE: It's just east of downtown, near the corner of 22nd Street. From the Boulder Turnpike, blend onto 28th Street, turn left onto Arapahoe and the inn is on the right, near 22nd.*

An pleasant garden area shaded by mature trees provides an inviting entrance to Boulder's first bed & breakfast inn, opened in 1981. The handsome brick home is trimmed in the style of an English country cottage, with antique Victorian furnishings, original art and cut flowers. Rooms are individually decorated and two have wood-burning fireplace. An extended stay suite has kitchen facilities with a TV/VCR.

9 *THE BOULDER VICTORIA HISTORIC INN* • *1305 Pine St., Boulder, CO 80302; (303) 938-1300. Seven rooms with private baths; full breakfast. Major credit cards; $$ to $$$. GETTING THERE: It's near downtown at Thirteenth and Pine, within two blocks of Pearl Street Mall. From the Boulder Turnpike, blend onto 28th Street, go about two miles, turn left onto Pine and follow it about a mile toward downtown.*

Rivaling the Earl House as Boulder's most attractive inn, the Victoria occupies an 1870s era square-shouldered mansion with ornate Victorian gingerbread trim on the façade. The interior is beautifully done in Victorian antiques, although its bright and cheerful, with no dark woods or somber wallpaper. Each room has a "discreetly hidden" TV and phone inside an armoire. In addition to a full breakfast, guests are served afternoon tea, pastries, and evening port. The handsome old home is set off by small formal gardens.

10 *THE COBURN HOUSE* • *2040 Sixteenth St., Boulder, CO 80302; (800) 858-5811 or (303) 545-5200. (www.coburnhouse.com; e-mail: tara@coburnhouse.com) Twelve rooms with private baths; full breakfast. Major credit cards; $$$. GETTING THERE: It's near downtown at the southeast corner of Sixteenth and Spruce. Approaching on*

the Boulder Turnpike, blend onto 28th Street, go about two miles, turn
left onto Spruce and follow it about a mile toward downtown.

Although it fits well into the old brick of adjacent Boulder neighborhoods, this imposing structure is rather new. The look is "modern
West" with large public areas done in carved woods and polished
wood floors. Although amenities are contemporary, occasional game
trophies and saddles straddling polished rails add the Western
touches. The Great Room is particularly inviting, with a river stone
fireplace and plush leather sofas. A church once occupied this corner
and several of its original stained glass windows add multi-colored accents to the inn. The large guest rooms have fireplaces, two-people spa
tubs, private balconies, ceiling fans, TVs and desks.

ROCKY MOUNTAIN NATIONAL PARK

Boulder works well as a gateway to Rocky Mountain National Park,
since that splendid 415-square-mile preserve is only thirty-five miles
away. Estes Park is even closer, of course, serving as the park's eastern
gateway. However, it's much smaller and provides fewer facilities, although it does have several motels, small resorts and restaurants.

U.S. Highway 34 makes winds west and south through the park,
then it links up with U.S. 40, which will take you back to Interstate 70
and the next chapter. The total distance of this driving route is about
140 miles.

NOTE: This is a summer-only trip; the highway through the park is
closed from mid-October to June and sometimes later after a heavy
snowfall year. If you plan to do some hiking, most of the high country
trails aren't freed of snow until late June or possibly July. Before you
drive through the park, call the road condition number at (970) 586-
1333. For trail conditions and general park queries, contact: Superintendent, Rocky Mountain National Park, Estes Park, CO 80517-8397;
(970) 586-1206.

Rocky Mountain National Park has few developed facilities, which
is surprising since it was founded in 1912, at the start of an era when
monumental stone and log lodges were being built in America's parks.
However, only a few small facilities were constructed here; this is primarily a drive-through and hike-about preserve. If you don't plan to do
much hiking, you can make the trip from Boulder and wind up in
Idaho Springs at the beginning of the next chapter in one long day.
However, if you plan to hike—and you really should—you could spend
days there. There are no overnight facilities in the park except campgrounds, so book your lodgings in Estes Park or Boulder.

To begin your trek, we suggest heading up Boulder Canyon to Nederland and going north on the **Peak to Peak Highway**, instead of
taking U.S. 36 to Estes Park. Peak to Peak is a high ridge route that
starts on I-70 near Idaho Springs and provides nice vistas of the Conti-

A RUSTICALLY ELEGANT RETREAT

Gold Lake Mountain Resort & Spa and Alice's Restaurant • *3371 Gold Lake Rd., Ward, CO 80481; (800) 450-3544 or (303) 459-3544. (WEB SITE: www.goldlake.com; e-mail:goldlake-@goldlake.com) Eighteen cabin units with private baths; full breakfast. Major credit cards; $$$$. Alice's Restaurant serves lunch, dinner and Sunday Brunch; $$$ to $$$$. GETTING THERE: This lakeside retreat and restaurant are near the town of Ward in the mountains above Boulder. Go west up Boulder Canyon to Nederland then turn north (right) onto State Highway 72 to Ward. Specific directions will be given when you make reservations.*

Karel and Alice Starek have fashioned an intriguing environmentally sensitive non-smoking art primitive resort in a thin pine forest. At the end of a three-mile dirt road, it's as far from the madding crowds as one can get and still be in Colorado. The lodgings are rustically comfortable cabins with a mix of antique, contemporary and hand-hewn furnishings, eclectic works of art, odd collector pieces and bits of whimsy such as skin drums for night stands. All bathrooms are modern, although some are hand-fashioned with oversized rough-tile tubs and shower heads emerging from stone walls. Cabins have no phones or TV, although phone service can be arranged. Resort facilities include lakeside hot tubs, tipis for quiet contemplations, fly fishing, horseback riding, boating on Gold Lake and ice skating in winter. The resort is particularly noted for its spa treatments.

Alice's Restaurant, which draws diners from Boulder and even Denver, occupies the resort's rough-hewn dining hall with log truss ceilings and a large fieldstone fireplace. It features contemporary American cuisine with an emphasis on fresh organic vegetables and meats. Entrées can range from pan roasted pheasant in cabernet sauce to duck confit and amaranth pudding. You can order a "light dinner," a three-course dinner designed to consume at least and hour and a half, or a tasting dinner with matched wines that will consume an entire evening. Basket dinners are available for those who want to dine outdoors.

nental Divide as it travels north into the park. It's a combination of state routes 119, 72 and 7, although it's essentially the same highway. The Idaho Springs-to-Nederland section isn't awesome, so you won't miss much by starting from Boulder.

Enroute from Nederland, you'll catch brief swatches of the Great Divide and pass the old mining towns of Ward, Raymond and Allenspark. Cantilevered steeply down from the highway, **Ward** looks interesting from afar but is rather scruffy on close scrutiny. (Locals say they keep it that way to discourage tourist traffic.) It's also home to Gold Lake Mountain Resort & Spa (above), which definitely is *not* scruffy.

Raymond sits at the junction of highways 72 and 7, and doesn't offer much of interest. **Allenspark** is a bit more appealing, with a few late nineteenth century buildings. To cruise through town, follow a sign to the left from the highway. You'll eventually rejoin the main route and pass through the mountain village of **Meeker Park,** which is a small resort town.

ESTES PARK

Eighteen miles north of Meeker Park, a fork in the road invites you to go left into Rocky Mountain National Park, or take a right and spiral downhill to Estes Park. It's a pleasant scatter of a town in a tree-rimmed basin. Although basically a tourist town comprised of shops, motels, restaurants and service stations, it's a rather neat and attractive little village.

If you choose the Estes Park route, Highway 7 will blend into U.S. 36. If you want to check out the **Estes Park Area Historical Museum,** backtrack two blocks on Highway 36 and turn right. It exhibits the usual pioneer artifacts. Admission fee is modest and it's open Monday-Saturday 10 to 5 and Sunday 1 to 5; (970) 586-6256. At a traffic signal where highways 34 and 36 merge, a right turn will take you to the **Information Center,** where you can load up on material about the town. It's open Monday-Saturday 8 to 8 and Sunday 10 to 5 in summer, with shorter hours the rest of the year. If you want to know before you go, write: Estes Park Chamber of Commerce, 500 Big Thompson Ave., Estes Park, CO 8051; (970) 586-4431.

The creek-sized Big Thompson River splashes through town, and a tree-shaded paved walk follows its course for about a quarter of a mile into the shopping area. You can pick it up near the visitor center. A couple of cafés along the walk have riverside dining—**Poppy's Pizza and Grill** and **Mamma Rosa's** Italian restaurant. Both serve lunch and dinner.

Back in your car, follow Highway 36 through the neat, tree-lined downtown area and into the national park. You can pause at the **Bear Meadows Visitor Center,** which offers a 22-minute introductory film, a book shop, information desk and a few interpretive exhibits. It's open daily 8 to 5.

Pressing onward, you'll soon hit the entry gate to one of America's most interesting wilderness parks. You'll be able to travel through every climate zone in the Colorado Rockies, including a treeless wind-buffeted Arctic tundra zone as you go over one of the highest paved highway passes in the country.

A handy guidebook for your upcoming drive is the inexpensive *Rocky Mountain National Park Road Guide,* available at the Bear Meadows Visitor and Moraine Park Museum (below). It describes practically every stream, glacier, peak and other geological feature you'll see on the road ahead.

THE TEN BEST THINGS TO DO AND SEE IN ROCKY MOUNTAIN NATIONAL PARK

Serious hikers spend days and even weeks in this splendid high mountain wilderness. However, if you're pressed for time, you can do everything we suggest here in a single day, and still arrive in the next chapter well before sundown. They're listed in their order of arrival as you drive. Shortly after entering the park, take a left onto Bear Lake Road for your first stop, which comes up quickly on your left:

1 MORAINE PARK MUSEUM • Bear Lake Road; open daily 9 to 4:30.

Located in an historic log structure built in 1923 as a social center, this fine little museum tells the geological history of the Rocky Mountains through displays, graphics and interactive exhibits. You can make a mountain, become a glacier and create an earthquake fault. Before or after visiting the museum, follow a short nature trail what winds into the thin ponderosa forest above.

2 EMERALD LAKE TRAIL • At the end of Bear Lake Road.

About nine miles beyond Moraine Park Museum, Bear Lake Road ends at a trailhead for several paths into the Rockies. Ninety percent of the people who pause here—and this is a crowded, popular stop—take the half-mile stroll around pretty little **Bear Lake**, jump back in their cars and continue on their way. For a much more interesting outing, join the ten-percenters who follow the **Emerald Lake Trail** to a series of three lakes, formed along a creek flowing from Tyndall Glacier. Ancient moraines created this trio of alpine ponds along the creek's route. You can pick up an area hiking map at an information booth. The round trip hike is about four miles; initially moderate and then with a bit of rock-hopping for the final lake.

An easy half mile stroll through a second growth Ponderosa forest will take you to Nymph Lake, no prettier than Bear Lake but much less populated. From here, the trail tilts upward somewhat steeply and soon you'll have a nice aerial0 view of the lake you just left. Just over half a mile from Nymph, you'll encounter long, slender Dream Lake, which is the widening of a creek partially dammed by an ancient moraine. You'll see a fantastic glacial cirque in the mountains to your right. From here, the trail becomes more difficult although the views improve with every step. A final rock scramble across this glacial creek takes you to Emerald Lake, an absolute jewel cupped in a basin rimmed by on three sides by dramatic, near vertical mountain walls. You're enjoying one of the most impressive views in Rocky Mountain National Park.

Retrace your route on Bear Lake Road and head west through the park on U.S. 36. It travels through a pretty tree-fringed meadowland, with the great broad shoulders of the snow-patched Rockies filling the horizon. The route soon blends into U.S. 34, which becomes Trail Ridge Road, one of the highest and most spectacular driving routes in America. It snakes into a high country of Ponderosa pine forests. Watch on your left for the park's first major vista point:

3 **MANY PARKS CURVE** ● *Just beyond the turnoff to Hidden Valley.*

From this boardwalk vista point, you can look back down into the valley that you just left, and across to a sawtooth horizon of snow-patched peaks. You're at an elevation of 9,620 feet.

From here, the road's upward climb is gradual with rather gentle curves, which is surprising since it's approaching one of the highest points of any paved highway in the country. This should be good news if you're driving a big RV or trailer rig. However, you're definitely gaining altitude, for the evergreens have thinned quickly, surrendering to a rocky, windswept, low-lying tundra.

4 **FOREST CANYON OVERLOOK** ● *About eight miles from Many Parks Curve, on the left.*

Fetch your jackets when you step out to enjoy this imposing vista point. You're now above 10,000 feet, in a treeless tundra where vegetation—although relatively thick—hugs the ground to hold its moisture and withstand the almost constant wind. Ironically, the view from the overlook is down into sheltered Forest Canyon, covered with a thick thatch of pine and fir. It's one of the most remote sections of the park; not even wilderness trails penetrate that great green void.

5 **TUNDRA COMMUNITIES TRAILHEAD** ● *A couple of miles beyond Forest Canyon, on the right.*

This is one of the most interesting stops on the route. You'll get a top-of-the-world feeling here, since you're more than 11,000 feet high. You appear to be on a level with the surrounding peaks, although many of them range up to 14,000 feet. The Tundra Communities Trail—about two-thirds of a mile—invites you to take a stroll over the low ground cover. It's on an asphalt path so you won't damage this delicate ecosystem. Although the hike is short and only gently inclined, it'll seem longer because of the elevation. A side trail leads to several mushroom rocks that were oddly shaped by wind-blasted erosion. The main trail ends at a rocky outcropping, where you can scramble up for a better look at this incredible top-of-the-world place. Or you might choose to use the rocks as shelter from the cold, driving wind.

6 *LAVA CLIFFS TURNOUT* • *Just beyond Tundra Communities Trailhead.*

At Lava Cliffs turnout, elevation 12,085 feet, you'll see some sheer, 400-foot walls of "welded tufa" from a volcanic eruption twenty-eight million years ago. About a mile beyond that, you'll pass—watch carefully for the sign—the highest point on the road, at 12,183 feet. Talk about being on top of the world! However, this isn't the Continental Divide. Because of the contour of the high wilderness, this watershed still drains into the Missouri-Mississippi river system.

7 *ALPINE VISITOR CENTER AND FALL RIVER PASS* • *Just beyond the road's high point. Open daily 10:30 to 4:30.*

Feeling lightheaded? Fall River Pass and the Alpine Visitor Center and Store are at 11,976 feet. The sturdy chink-long visitor center has interesting exhibits about life on the tundra, and the few hardy creatures who survive here. The adjacent store, which dates from 1935, has a surprisingly large stock of souvenirs, T-shirts and other clothing, plus a snack bar with tables that provide views of the tundra and its cradling mountains. You'll never experience a more dramatic vista with a hot dog and Coke.

From here, a short hike over the tundra on the Alpine Ridge Trail will take you up to 12,005 feet to a crest with a predictably awesome panorama.

8 *MEDICINE BOW CURVE* • *Just beyond Fall River Pass.*

And suddenly, you head back down into the real world. A vista point here provides a final look at tundra and mountain, and then the highway begins dropping sharply downhill; you'll be back into thick forest within minutes. And you will soon encounter what should be higher up:

9 *THE CONTINENTAL DIVIDE* • *At Milner Pass, about five miles below Medicine Bow Curve.*

The Continental Divide—also called the Great Divide—is only 10,759 feet at this point; it's nearly 1,500 feet lower than the road's highest reach. Actually, none of the water draining from this point flows directly into the Atlantic or Pacific. Eastside rainfall winds up in the Mississippi drainage basin and the Gulf of Mexico, while westbound water ends up in the Colorado River, which flows into the Sea of Cortez. However, in a very dry year, virtually no Colorado River water reaches its proper destination because of excessive upstream diversion. Chances are if you took a whizz in the westside woods, you'd would wind up watering watermelons in California's Imperial Valley.

The rest of the southbound run through Rocky Mountain National Park isn't very interesting. The highway travels throw a vee-shaped, heavily wooded valley with only occasional views of the higher peaks. You'll depart the park at the **Kawuneeche Visitor Center**, which provides the same services as the Bear Meadows gateway.

Just after you depart the park, watch on your left for a turnout to a grand old national park style lodge. In fact, you may want to end this day's Rocky Mountain outing there, although you should call in advance for reservations:

10 *GRAND LAKE LODGE ● P.O. Box 569 (15500 Highway 34), Grand Lake, CO 80447; (970) 627-3967. (www.grand-lakelodge.com) Open June to mid-September. Cabins and lodge rooms $ to $$$; major credit cards. Reservations required for restaurant; call (970) 627-3185.*

Completed in 1920 and now a national historic landmark, this grand old lodge sits on the edge of mountain-rimmed Grand Lake. It's built in the style of those great 1930s national park lodges, with heavy log beams and comfortable, rough hewn furniture. A handsome fireplace is a centerpiece of the spacious lobby. Three old fashioned porch swings on front veranda offer what lodge owners call "Colorado's favorite front porch view." Two more swings are suspended from ceiling beams before the fireplace. The **Lodge Restaurant** serves breakfast, lunch and dinner and an adjacent lounge has full bar service. Both provide fine lake and mountain views.

...and into the next chapter

From here, U.S. 34 follows the shorelines of Shadow Mountain Lake and Lake Grandby, traveling through a lowland area of woods, pasturelands and a string of resort communities. The town of **Grandby** has a few old wooden false front and brick buildings. Beyond, condo-busy and vaguely chalet-style **Winter Park** is noted mostly as a ski resort.

Pressing southward from Winter Park, you'll cross the Continental Divide a second time this day, spiraling up and over Berthoud Pass. Although you crest 11,314 feet, you won't quite reach a tundra zone. Twisting down the other side, you'll hit Interstate 70, where a quick nine miles east to Idaho Springs will take you into the next chapter.

Summertime, and the livin' is easy.
— From *Porgy and Bess* by George and Ira Gershwin, © 1934

Chapter thirteen

ROCKIES WEST

SUMMERTIME IN SKI COUNTRY

Most people think of the Rockies west of Denver as a winter playground. Indeed, some of the world's most famous ski resorts are near the Interstate 70 corridor—Keystone, Breckenridge, Vail and Beaver Creek.

However, it's summer now and the livin' is easy in Colorado's central Rockies. The region offers an outdoor abundance of hiking, mountain biking, fishing, river running, chairlift and gondola rides, jogging along wooded creekside trails and more. The communities and resorts have active summer programs, the hotels and inns are open, the rates are down and the best restaurants are cooking up summer savories. Major hotel and resort rates drop by as much as fifty percent in summer, since this is still primarily a winter sports area.

What follows is a sampler of the best that this region has to offer, focused in two areas—Clear Creek and Gilpin counties on the eastern slope of the Rockies, noted for their historic mining towns; and Summit and Eagle counties on the far side of the Great Divide, where most of Colorado's ski resorts are located.

"MUD SEASON"

If you're planning a vacation in this area, don't come before Memorial Day weekend. After ski season has ended, many resorts, restaurants and attractions temporarily close their doors during what locals call "mud season." This is the spring thaw period from April to May, the slowest time of the year. Many hotels reduce their activities and some close completely, as do many restaurants. Because snow—and mud—may still be on the higher slopes, the area's scenic summer gondola rides generally don't begin operating until Memorial Day weekend. If you're a hiker, you'll discover that the high country trails suffer the same snow and mud problems.

THE TEN MOST INTERESTING COMMUNITIES & RESORTS

This isn't a region of large museums, parks and zoos—the sorts of things that would be defined as attractions back down there in Denver. The "attractions" of this area are primarily the communities themselves. Some are historic mining towns, others are mountain villages that have become winter and summer activity centers, while others are ski resorts that have evolved into communities.

This section is fashioned into a logical driving route from Denver, or from the tail-end of the Rocky Mountain National Park tour in the previous chapter. The route will take you through the historic mining towns of Clear Creek County, with a side trip to a couple of gaming centers, and up Clear Creek Canyon on I-70 through the Eisenhower Tunnel to the ski areas of Summit and Eagle counties. From there, it heads south to Leadville and then southeast toward Colorado Springs and this book's final chapter. We begin with an old mining town that has retained much of its yesterday look:

1 IDAHO SPRINGS • *About twenty-five miles west of Denver; I-70 exits 240 or 241-A. FOR MORE INFORMATION: Clear Creek County Tourism Board, P.O. Box 100, Idaho Springs, CO 80452; (800) 88-BLAST or (303) 567-4660. Also Idaho Springs Visitor Center and Heritage Museum, 2200 Miner St., Idaho Springs, CO 80452; (800) 685-7785 or (303) 567-4382.*

This old charmer of a town was born in 1859 when George Jackson found two things of interest—gold bearing rock in Clear Creek and some natural hot springs nearby. Thousands naturally flocked to the area when word spread and the gold camp initially was called Jacksons Diggins. The name later was changed to Idaho Springs after a popular mineral water resort in that state. It enjoyed brief success as a hot spring spa, and mining carried it well into the twentieth century until increasing costs made it unprofitable.

If you take I-70 exit 240, you'll be in the heart of old town, which has been declared a national historic district. If you use the lower approach, exit 241, you'll be in the newer, more strung out section of town. A short drive uphill on Miner Street will deliver you to the historic district.

First, pause at the **Idaho Springs Visitor Information Center & Museum** at 2200 Miner Street. If you want to spend more time in this region, the helpful staff can point you in several directions, including some interesting scenic drives. The small museum recalls the town's mining days, with old photos, mining equipment and a gem and mineral display. The museum and chamber are open 8 to 6 daily; hours may be shorter in the off-season.

When you reach Idaho Springs' historic district, find a place to park and stroll its streets, which are lined with old two-story brick and masonry buildings. Most house small shops, curio stores and cafés. One, the **Buffalo Restaurant**, occupies a saloon dating back to 1885; (303) 567-2729. Another essential stop, not historic but tasty, is **Beau Jo's Pizza** at 1517 Miner Street, a local favorite; (303) 567-4376.

If you'd like to sample the region's mining history, visit the **Argo Gold Mine and Museum** at 2350 Riverside Dr.; (303) 567-2421. It's a former ore processing mill open for self-guided tours. The **Phoenix Mine** is a former hard rock gold mine also open for tours; (303) 567-0422. To reach it, take the I-70 frontage road a mile west from Idaho Springs, then go south on Trail Creek Road just under a mile.

2 BLACKHAWK • *Exit 244 from I-70 (four miles east of Idaho Springs), then ten miles north on State Route 119. FOR MORE INFORMATION: Gilpin County Chamber of Commerce, (303) 582-5077.*

If you want a little Nevada-style gambling, head up a narrow creek canyon to Blackhawk. If you want to sample the history of one of Colorado's oldest mining towns, forget it. While preserving many of their fine old buildings, the people of Blackhawk have sacrificed their heritage to the golden lure of gambling. Other guidebooks comment that Blackhawk and neighbor Central City have "preserved" their heritage through an infusion of gambling money. What we see is towns with lost heritages.

Certainly, Blackhawk is worth a look. While gaming may have blurred its identity, its proceeds have spruced up the town's small historic section, particularly along Gregory Street, uphill from the highway. Its history began in the spring of 1859 when prospector John H. Gregory found gold in North Clear Creek. A profusion of mining camps quickly sprang up as thousands came to sluice the creek—now called Gregory Gulch—. When the easy pickin's were gone, hard rock mining kept the area going until the 1880s. Then as the veins became more elusive, most of the towns disappeared. Only Blackhawk and Central City survived into the twentieth century and they seemed unlikely to make it to the Millennium. Then Coloradans approved limited stakes gambling in 1989, and the two slowly dying towns came back to life.

Walking the streets of Blackhawk, you'll note that many of its old brick and masonry buildings have been preserved. However, most have been merely hollowed out for the installation of casinos. It's difficult to find any historic plaques or exhibits that discuss their glory days. Further, the recent creation of several newer casinos along the highway is pulling business away from the smaller "uptown" places along Gregory Street. Many have closed.

The larger casinos, financed mostly by Nevada money, are marching downhill along Main Street until they're stopped—ironically—by the county's sewer plant at the lower end. Despite their advertising hoopla, these are not "Las Vegas style" casinos. They're much smaller, with none of the big showrooms, top stars, theme architecture and glitter of the Las Vegas Strip resorts. Further, this once attractive ravine has been gutted, widened and gunnited to make more room for casinos and parking lots. This is progress?

3 **CENTRAL CITY** • *Just uphill from Blackhawk on Gregory Street. FOR MORE INFORMATION: Central City Marketing, (303) 582-5251; or Gilpin County Chamber of Commerce, (303) 582-5077.*

Central City was—and still is—the largest town in the Gregory Gulch mining district. Because it's a bit off Highway 119, it suffered an even worse decline than Blackhawk after the mines closed. Many citizens were relieved when legalized gambling came. Ironically, because of competition from Blackhawk, poor old Central City has gone from gold mining boom to bust to gambling boom and now back to bust. Most of its gaming parlors and many of its restaurants have closed. The only surviving casino of any size is Harvey's, built by Nevada money.

While this can't be good news for its citizens, Central City is more appealing than Blackhawk for visitors—at least for those not interested in gambling. You can still catch that sense of yesterday, walking up steeply tilted Eureka Street, past old memory-filled buildings. Among the more interesting ones—all along upper Eureka—are the red brick twin-towered Gilpin County Courthouse, the 1872 St. James United Methodist Church, the rough-cut stone Eureka Opera House, and the weathered brick Williams Stables building. The handsome Teller House casino and museum, occupying an 1872 building, was closed when we last visited. Just below, at Eureka and Main, is one of the town's few still-active gaming parlors. **Doc Holiday's** definitely is worth a peek for its crystal chandeliers, old wall sconces and pressed tin ceilings.

The small **Gilpin County Historical Society Museum** will give you some sense of the area's history, with a large if rather cluttered collection of yesterday memorabilia. It occupies an 1869 school house building at 228 E. High St.; (303) 582-5283. Hours are 11 to 4 daily from Memorial Day through Labor Day weekend; call for off-season hours.

4 GEORGETOWN • *Twelve miles north of Idaho Springs; take I-70 exit 228. FOR MORE INFORMATION: Georgetown Visitor Information Center, (800) 472-8230 or (303) 569-2405.*

Like Idaho Springs, Georgetown began in 1859 as a mining center, and it has an even more appealing historic district. Its downtown area is a virtual architectural museum of nineteenth century brick, masonry and wooden false front buildings and ornate Victorian homes. Unlike most early mining towns, it escaped disastrous fires, so many of its old wood frame buildings still stand. More than 200 historic structures occupy the downtown area, which is cheerfully dressed in hanging flower baskets and planters. Many structures contain shops, boutiques and restaurants, along with a couple of interesting museums.

Hotel de Paris Museum is an impressive restoration of an 1875 lodging. Rooms are furnished to the period and many of the objects are original. It's at the corner of Sixth and Taos streets, open daily 11 to 4:30 in summer, with shorter hours the rest of the year; (303) 569-2840. The **Georgetown Energy Museum,** just up from the hotel at Sixth and Griffith, is in a small hydroelectric plant that has been active since 1906. It features photos and exhibits tracing the development of hydro power in the area, plus early electric appliances such as a 1900 stove and 1919 washing machine. Through an adjacent window, you can see two generators still in operation. The museum is open Monday-Saturday 10 to 4 and Sunday noon to 4; by appointment only the rest of the year; (303) 569-3557.

The town is best known for the **Georgetown Loop Railroad** that takes tourists on an impressive six-mile spiral up Clear Creek Canyon to the town of Silver Plume and back. The hour and a half ride behind an old narrow gauge oil-burning steam train is operated by the Colorado Historical Society and tickets are moderately priced. Trains run late May through September. You also can catch the train on the other end by taking Silver Plume exit 226 and following signs to the depot. For a small additional fee you can tour the Lebanon Gold Mine at a midpoint in the ride. For information and schedules, call (800) 691-4FUN or (303) 569-2403. (*www.georgetownloop.com*)

Silver Plume is just two freeway miles from Georgetown. However, it's downtown area isn't very well preserved. It would be unkind but accurate to call it scruffy. If you didn't take the Georgetown Loop, the restored Silver Plume railroad station is worth a look, and there are several pieces of old rolling stock on display nearby. From Silver Plume, I-70 continues a deceptively gradual climb toward the Eisenhower Tunnel, one of the world's longest and highest road tunnels at 11,013 feet. If you're willing to tackle a dizzying spiral, take the alternate U.S. 6 route over Loveland Pass—the original highway route—where you can straddle the Continental Divide and enjoy grand views west to the mountains and east to the Great Plains.

Across the Great Divide

By either route you'll arrive in Summit County and Eagle County's Vail Valley, which are Ski Country USA. Only California's Sierra Nevada has a greater number of ski resorts. And, as we noted before, all of the resorts here have active summer programs, and they're gateways to a grand mountain wilderness. The Rockies don't end at the Continental Divide. They extend nearly a hundred miles west to Glenwood Springs.

5 KEYSTONE • *Seven miles southeast of I-70 on Highway 6, via exit 205. FOR MORE INFORMATION: Keystone Resort, P.O. Box 38, Keystone, CO 80435; (800) 222-0188 or (970) 496-2316. (www.keystoneresort.com) Also Summit County Chamber of Commerce, P.O. Box 214, Frisco, CO 80443; (970) 668-5800 or 668-0376. NOTE: If you take Highway 6 over Loveland Pass, you'll pass through Keystone before returning to I-70.*

Keystone isn't a town; it's a large planned resort complex that's getting larger. The eastern-most of Colorado's major ski resorts, it's noted for upscale accommodations and excellent restaurants, and it offers an active summer program. It has two major resorts, Keystone Lodge and the Inn at Keystone, plus several smaller ones, with ranks of condominiums around and between them.

To reach Keystone, take exit 205 through **Dillon**. This small town is worthy of a brief side trip. Shortly after leaving I-70, turn right at a stoplight onto Lake Dillon Drive for a brief cruise through this well-tended alpine style village. After a few blocks, you'll hit a T-bone intersection opposite Dillon Reservoir, with an attractive shoreside park and picnic area. Retrace your route back up Lake Dillon Drive, turn right on Buffalo Street and then left on La Bonte and go a block to the **Summit Historical Museum** on your left. Occupying an old bell tower church at 403 La Bonte, it offers the usual exhibits and pioneer relics concerning the development of Summit County. It was being restored when we passed by, so call the Summit County Historical Society for hours; (970) 453-9022.

After about five miles, you'll enter the planned Keystone development. Its focal point is Keystone Lodge (see below, page 214), a luxury resort built around a small lake. To reach it, continue past ranks of condos and the Inn at Keystone; you'll see the lodge on your right.

Keystone Lodge occupies a pretty basin surrounded by low wooded hills, with snow-streaked peaks in the background. Much of this scene is reflected in a small lake diverted from a lively little stream that dances through the property. You can rent paddleboats and mini-kayaks, or just take a leisurely stroll around the lake, admiring this elegant resort. Several other resorts, an eighteen-hole golf course and some of Colorado ski country's better restaurants are located within the Keystone community. One of its restaurants, Alpenglow Stube, is listed below on page 209.

Beyond the lodge, you'll note some construction activity, since the resort's parent company is in the midst of a $1 billion expansion program to transform Keystone into a more broad based year-around resort community. Current summer activities include an eighteen-hole golf course and putting green, horseback riding, hiking, gondola rides, cycling and tennis.

From Keystone, drive northwest on Highway 6 for a couple of miles, then turn west (left) at a stoplight onto Swan Mountain Road and follow it along the eastern shore of Dillon Reservoir. As you top a rise, watch on your right for the **Sapphire Point Overlook,** where a short path will take you to a vista point with views of the lake and craggy mountains beyond. Overly friendly chipmunks and ground squirrels will plead for peanuts or sunflower seeds, insisting that they haven't eaten for days. Don't believe them. Beyond Sapphire Point, you'll spiral lazily downhill, then hit a traffic light on State Route 9. Turn left for the next stop, six miles away:

6 BRECKENRIDGE • *About fourteen miles southeast of I-70 on Highway 9. FOR MORE INFORMATION: Breckenridge Resort Chamber of Commerce, 309 N. Main St. (P.O. Box 1909), Breckenridge, CO 80424; (970) 453-6018 or (970) 453-5000. Also Breckenridge Central Reservations, (888) 533-9880. (WEB: www.gobreck.com; e-mail:cenres@gobreck.com)*

Unlike many Colorado ski areas, Breckenridge is a town with a real history. In the fateful year of 1859 when gold was discovered on the eastern slope of the Rockies, more glitter was found in what is now Summit County. The ensuing gold rush brought the usual swarms of fortune hunters, fallen angels and overnight mining camps. Only Breckenridge, Dillon and Frisco survive; of the three, Breckenridge is the most attractive. It's also the oldest Colorado town west of the Rockies. Its small downtown area retains much of its late nineteenth century Victorian look. It has been designated as a national historic district. More than 250 of its buildings have been placed on the National Register of Historic Places.

Skiing didn't arrive in the form of a multi-million dollar resort. It evolved slowly in the mountains just across the Blue River from downtown. The Breckenridge Ski Area is one of the oldest west of the Rockies, opening in 1962. It has become one of the region's largest, spread over three mountains above the community. It rivals Vail in skier attendance and in fact topped the larger resort during a recent dry season because of its extensive snow-making capability.

As you approach the town, Highway 9 becomes Main Street. The **Breckenridge Resort Chamber** and **Summit County Histori-cal Society** are on your right at 309 N. Main; open daily 9 to 5. It offers the usual tourist information and a few historical exhibits. Continue past the chamber and you'll soon be in the historic district.

Although condos are crowding Breckenridge's edges, the heart of downtown still retains its yesterday look. Most if its old wood frame and brick buildings are now occupied by boutiques, outdoor outfitters and restaurants. At midtown, a one-block section of Washington Avenue has been converted into a small park that reaches to the Blue River. A walkway extends through the downtown area and merges onto the Blue River Bikeway that travels for several miles north alongside Highway 9.

Breckenridge has several appealing restaurants, including Café Alpine, which made our Ten Best list below, on page 210.

To Frisco and Vail

As you return to I-70 on State Route 9, you'll pass through the charmingly funky old town of **Frisco,** one of the survivors of the 1859 gold rush. Pause at the **Frisco Historic Park** on Main Street, a collection of seven restored buildings brought to this area. The Frisco Schoolhouse is the only one on its original site and it serves as the park's museum headquarters. The park is open Tuesday-Sunday 11 to 4 in summer; closed Sunday the rest of the year; (970) 668-3428.

Heading west on I-70, you'll spiral up and over 10,662-foot Vail Pass and then sweep down into one of the prettiest—and certainly most affluent—valleys in the American West. Vail Valley is cradled between sawtooth peaks to the west and east and it is home to some of the world's most famous ski and summer resorts.

7 VAIL ● *Just south of I-70 in the heart of the Vail Valley. FOR MORE INFORMATION: Vail Valley Tourism & Convention Bureau, 100 E. Madrone Dr., Suite 34, Vail, CO 81657; (800) 525-3875 or (970) 476-1000. (www.-visitvailvalley.com)*

Vail Village is the center of this prosperous valley. To reach it, take exit 176, loop around a traffic circle, then go briefly east to the **Vail Visitor Center.** It's open daily 9 to 5. You can leave your car at the adjacent parking lot here and walk to the village, or take a free shuttle to the town's further reaches.

This is a tidy and attractive little community with several swatches of green parklands and trees tucked among its condos, resorts and shopping areas. It's actually a string of small villages stretching for nearly seven miles along Gore Creek and the Eagle River. They are, reading from east to west, East Vail, Vail Village, LionsHead Village, Cascade Village and West Vail. They're pleasant places to explore by foot or bike. Vehicles are barred from some Vail streets and those free shuttle buses encourage folks to abandon their cars. (This is America's largest free public transit system.) An attractive biking/walking trail alongside cascading Gore Creek links the village to LionsHead and Cascade, providing further incentive to use feet and pedals.

The Vail complex is North America's largest winter resort and it also has an extensive summer program. Virtually all hotels, restaurants and recreational facilities operate then. However, some close during the spring mud season.

Vail is younger than most of its winter and summer visitors. The area remained virtually undeveloped until the 1960s. Aspen, farther west, was well established before the first ski facilities were built here in 1966. Vail hit its stride after major expansion in 1988, followed by is hosting of the World Alpine Ski Championships in 1989. It has passed long-established Aspen as Colorado's largest ski area. Seven of its lifts rise directly from the village, within walking distance of many of its resorts and condos.

Exploring Vail

This resort complex extends through its namesake valley for more than six miles along I-70. Frontage Road—and that's its proper name—parallels the freeway, linking the valley's towns. The heart of the community—Vail Village to Cascade Village—is best explored on foot. If you grow foot-weary, you can hop that free shuttle to return to your starting point. From the parking lot at the Vail Visitor Center, you can take a stairway directly into the village. Pick up a *Vail Walking Map* and wander at will past its many shops, restaurants and resorts. Definitely worth a look is **Village Inn Plaza** at Vail Road and East Meadow Drive. Busy with art galleries, it's a virtual outdoor museum of bronzes, with more than a score of statues with Western, wildlife, kids at play and other themes.

After exploring Vail Village, follow Meadow Drive west, perhaps pausing to admire the elegant Bavarian style **Sonnenalp Resort** (see page 214 below). Continue along the drive for about two blocks past the fire department, then fork left just beyond the Vail Valley Medical Center and pick up the **Gore Creek Recreation Path** in a small park. It follows this tumbling, cascading creek for about two miles through LionsHead and Cascade villages and beyond to Stephens Park.

LionsHead is a mini Vail Village with several shops, restaurants and lodgings just up from the creek. You can catch a scenic gondola ride on the **Eagle Bahn** which begins operating on or shortly after Memorial Day weekend, or play a round of miniature golf at a creek-view course next to the ski lift. Strolling onward, you'll reach **Cascade Village,** primarily a hotel and condo area. The path bumps into a street and appears to end at the west side of Cascade Village. However, you can shift slightly uphill, pick it up again and follow it another mile and a half to Stephens Park. It remains a sheltered creekside trail for about half a mile, then it loses its charm and runs alongside Frontage Road the rest of the way. Once you arrive at **Stephens Park,** you'll find a nice tree-lined swatch of green on both sides of Gore Creek, with restrooms, picnic tables and a large kiddie playground.

8 *AVON CALLING?* • *Just west of Vail off I-70. GETTING THERE: Take I-70 exit 167 and go briefly south. For the Chamber of Commerce visitor center, go east at a third roundabout onto East Beaver Creek Boulevard. After a block, turn right onto Beaver Creek Place, then turn left into the large City Market parking lot. The visitor center occupies the west end of that building. It's open daily 8:30 to 6 in summer and 9 to 5 the rest of the winter. FOR MORE INFORMATION: The Chamber of Commerce, 260 Beaver Creek Place (P.O. Box 1437), Avon, CO 81620; (970) 949-5189. (www.vailvalleychamber.com)*

The gateway to Beaver Creek Resort, Avon is a mini-boomtown of condos and shopping complexes, plus housing for folks who work in Vail or Beaver Creek and can't afford to live there. For visitors, Avon's lodgings generally are less expensive than those in the two resort areas. And the small town offers such realities as Wal-Mart and a large supermarket. It's a good base of operations for those of us who smuggle picnic coolers into hotel rooms to cut down on food costs.

Once a rather ordinary bedroom community, Avon is now a rather prim, well-planned village. Its main street, Avon Road, wraps through a series of landscaped roundabouts several are graced with large Western style bronze sculptures. The Eagle River cascades through the heart of town, providing a nice centerpiece. Avon is growing like a spring weed. When we last passed through, several hotels, condos and shopping complexes were under construction.

The town's recreational focal point is **Nottingham Park** at Avon's west end, wrapped around a reservoir of the same name. To reach it, go right onto Benchmark Road (at the fourth roundabout from the freeway) and drive less than half a mile past the Avon Municipal Complex. An walking/cycling trail, just under a mile long, circles the reservoir. The park has a kids' playground, volleyball and soccer facilities and picnic areas, plus paddleboat and bike rentals. You can get light snacks in an old restored cabin near the lake.

9 *BEAVER CREEK RESORT* • *Just south of Avon on Village Road. GETTING THERE: From downtown Avon, cross Highway 6 on Avon Road and you'll enter the Beaver Creek gate. A car pass will be issued and you can ask for directions. For the main village area, go about two and a half miles uphill and turn left into a parking structure, just after you've passed under a pedestrian overcrossing. If you've reserved condo lodgings at Beaver Creek, you may be asked to check in at the Beaver Creek Reception Center near the entrance gate. FOR MORE INFORMATION: Vail-Beaver Creek Resort Properties, P.O. Box 36, Avon, CO*

81620; (800) 525-2257 for lodging reservations or (970) 845-9090 for general information. Also contact Vail Resorts, Inc., P.O. Box 7, Vail, CO 81658. (www.beavercreeksummer.com)

Colorado's most upscale resort, Beaver Creek is many things in one tightly bundled architectural package. Tucked carefully into a narrow wooded valley instead of being scattered all over it, it's a rather vertical two-to six-story Bavarian-style village. It features a shopping complex that rivals Rodeo Drive, several fine restaurants, hotels and condos, a serious ski area and a major summer resort.

Conceived by the creators of Vail, Beaver Creek was opened in 1980 as a carefully planned package—the ultimate winter-summer mountain playpen. Virtually all parking is underground and the village is small enough to be easily walkable. Three tiers of outdoor escalators carry shoppers and browsers from one level to the next and ultimately to a winter-summer ski lift that carries them high into the mountains. For destinations outside the immediate village area, Beaver Creek has free dial-a-ride service for guests.

This complex of multi-storied condos and hotels hugs the edge of Beaver Creek while allowing that pretty little stream to cascade freely. Pathways invite folks to stroll along its banks. The village is immaculately maintained; not a plant stem is out of place. Dogs aren't allowed, to prevent doggie accidents and to protect wildlife. Shopping is mostly higher end, and the village has more art galleries per square block than Santa Fe. The best selection of galleries is beneath **Market Square**.

The entire development, with a year-around population of 2,500 lucky souls, is one large gated community, with that gate just outside Avon. However, friendly gatekeepers are there to give directions, not restrict entry. Anyone who wants to explore Beaver Creek is free to do so. The resort even has a concierge staff to answer visitors' questions. The information office is near the top of the second escalator by Coyote Café; (970) 845-9090.

Although Beaver Creek is an upscale shopping and dining complex, it's also a major outdoor center. The main gateway to the conifer and aspen forests of adjacent White River National Forest is the **Centennial Express,** which carries summer visitors up to Spruce Saddle Lodge, 10,200 feet above sea level and more than 2,000 feet above the village. This isn't a gondola, but an open-air chair lift, which is part of the fun. Summer ride tickets are a fraction of the cost of ski passes. The Express runs weekends only from late May through mid-June, then daily through Labor Day, and weekends only until the end of September. Hours are 9:30 to 4:30, with the last lift down the mountain at 5; (970) 845-9090.

The views of the sawtoothed Gore Range to the east and the surrounding tree-thatched mountains are dazzling from up there, and the Express puts visitors in touch with an extensive webwork of hiking and mountain biking trails. Visitors can rent mountain bikes at the base and drape them on special hooks on the backs of the lifts, or rent them at the top, ride the mountain trails and then spiral back down to the village.

For those who prefer hiking, miles of trails beckon. Pick up a copy of the *Beaver Creek Summer Biking & Hiking Map*, available at both ends of the chair lift, at the lift ticket office and in brochure racks all over town. Most of the trails follow access roads and ski runs. While they aren't very esthetic, the views from them are great. If hiking or biking works up an appetite, you can get lunch at a barbecue or snack bar, then carry your prize to a picnic table for dining with a view. Beaver Creek also has a guided hiking program; call (970) 845-5373.

Back down in the village, you can follow cascading Beaver Creek for about half a mile to pretty little **Creekside Park,** with a playground and picnic areas. If you like romantic midnight strolls, the path is lighted after dark. The creekside path ends at Offerson Road, where you can cross Village Road and pick up the **Beaver Creek Recreational Path.** This walking/cycling path leads down the hill to Avon.

If you prefer your activities sitting down, **Vilar Center for the Arts** in the lower level of Market Square has a summer-long season of pops, country, jazz, rock and classic music, plus dance recitals, a children's theater, stand-up comics and other performers. A special feature is the summer long *Bravo! Vail Valley Music Festival*, featuring assorted concerts in Beaver Creek and Vail, from symphony orchestras to soloists. For information and schedules, contact: Vilar Center for the Arts, P.O. Box 3822, Avon, CO 81620; (888) 920-ARTS or (970) 845-TIXS.

Heading for legendary Leadville

From Beaver Creek, you can either return to I-70 through Avon's many roundabouts, or turn east just outside the Beaver Creek Gate and follow U.S. Highway 6. After about five miles, the highway blends onto U.S. 24 and heads south toward Leadville. (If you use the freeway, take exit 171.) The route, designated the "Top of the Rockies Scenic Byway," travels through the pretty green Eagle River Valley, rimmed by wooded slopes. It's particularly attractive in the fall.

Heading southward, you'll shortly encounter **Minturn,** an old railroad town with a few brick and wooden false front stores along the highway. They house a handful of shops, antique stores and inexpensive restaurants. The Western style **Minturn Saloon** is a favorite locals' hangout. You can pick up a walking map at some shops, although there isn't much else to see here, unless you enjoy browsing around funky old towns. Minturn was founded in 1887 as a railroad division point and the walking map brochure calls it a "diamond in the rough," although there's more rough than diamond.

Highway 24 continues south through some rather spectacular mountain scenery, highlighted by 11,308-foot Shrine Pass. The route follows the Eagle River, and then crosses it on a bridge several hundred feet high. As you drive through a broad meadow, watch on your left for a group of historical signs concerning **Camp Hale,** a special facility built in 1943 to train ski troopers for mountain combat. Nothing of the camp remains except for a few foundations and road patterns. Just beyond, you'll cross the Continental Divide at 10,424-foot Tennessee Pass, and then spiral down into one of America's most famous mining boomtowns:

10 *LEADVILLE • Thirty-two miles south of I-70 exit 171 on U.S. Highway 24. FOR MORE INFORMATION: Greater Leadville Area Chamber of Commerce, P.O. Box 861, Leadville, CO 80461; (888) LEADVIL or (719) 486-3900. (www.leadvilleusa.com; e-mail: leadville@leadvilleusa.com)*

Colorado's most famous boomtown and America's highest incorporated city at 10,152 feet, Leadville never was a major lead producer. It got its name from silver-bearing carbonate of lead, which kept clogging the sluices of the area's early goldseekers. Gold was discovered here in 1860, triggering one of Colorado's largest rushes. Later, miners realized that the lead-bearing black sand also was rich in silver. By 1878, Leadville was booming with 30,000 residents.

The town's most famous personages were not "Leadville Johnny" and Molly Brown, despite what was portrayed in that silly "Unsinkable" movie. Its museums and historic sites focus mostly on Horace Austin Warner Tabor and his pretty young wife Elizabeth McCourt Doe. Tabor was a general store owner who grubstaked a couple of prospectors with $50 for a one-third share of their silver mine. When they struck paydirt, all three became rich. With this and other mining investments, he became one of Leadville's richest citizens. He divorced his frumpy wife Augusta and married pretty little "Baby Doe" McCourt. Tabor eventually became governor of Colorado and then a U.S. Senator. When America went off the silver standard in favor of gold in the 1890s, the Tabors and many others went bust almost overnight, along with the city of Leadville. Tabor died of a ruptured appendix in 1899 and Baby Doe eventually moved into a toolhouse in one of their mines called the Matchless. She lived there in poverty for thirty-six years until she froze to death during the harsh winter of 1935.

Although Leadville was seriously wounded by the collapse of the silver market, it didn't quite die. Determined men went back to the town's beginning—seeking more gold. They eventually found it far underground, aided by a system of shoring up the deep shafts that was designed by—guess who?—J.J. Brown. More of a mining engineer than a miner, the so-called "Leadville Johnny" was rewarded with company stock and this led to his fortune. (See Chapter Two, page 36.)

The town experienced a resurgence at the turn of the last century—even as Baby Doe was wasting away in her mining shack. The discovery of molybdenum—a steel hardening agent—and the development of the huge Climax Molybdenum Mine in 1918 kept Leadville going for several decades more. At its peak, the mine near Fremont Pass was producing eighty percent of the world's supply. When that finally shut down in the 1970s, Leadville discovered another lode—tourist money.

Doing Leadville

The downtown core of Leadville has been declared a national historic district. In addition to this five-block area busy with old brick and masonry buildings, Leadville offers four museums, an opera house tour and a scenic train ride. Highway 24 enters town on Poplar Street, turns right onto Ninth Street and left onto Harrison Avenue, which is the main drag. After completing the turn, watch on your right for the **Chamber of Commerce Visitor Center** at 109 Harrison. It's open daily 9 to 5, with shorter hours in the off-season.

Three of town's museums are near here—the **Leadville Heritage Museum** at Ninth and Harrison, the **Healy House and Dexter Cabin** just above at Tenth and Harrison, and the **National Mining Hall of Fame Museum** just to the west on Ninth between Harrison and Pine. If you drive two blocks down Harrison and turn left (east) onto Seventh Street, you'll reach the **Leadville, Colorado & Southern Railroad** excursion train. Just beyond, Seventh Street enters the tailing dumps of the main mining district. On the left is the entrance to the **Matchless Mine and Baby Doe Tabor Cabin.** Finally, if you return to Harrison and go south for a few blocks, you can tour the **Tabor Opera House,** across from the **Silver Dollar Saloon.** This 1879 bar is worth a peek and maybe a beer. It's a classic Western saloon turned into a virtual museum clutter of pioneer and mining artifacts, old prints and other doodads.

Leadville's attractions

PRICING: Dollar sign codes indicate the cost of adult admission: **$** = under $5; **$$** = $5 to $9; **$$$** = $10 to $14 ; **$$$$** = $15 to $19; **$$$$$** = $20 or more.

Healy House and Dexter Cabin Museum ● *912 Harrison Ave.; (719) 486-0487. Daily 10 to 4:30 Memorial Day through Labor Day, then weekends only through September; closed the rest of the year; $.* □ The "cabin," which houses the ticket office and gift shop, isn't a miner's shack. Although built of rough logs, it was elegantly furnished by business tycoon and mine owner James V. Dexter as a bachelor pad where he and his buddies gathered to play poker and sip whiskey. The adjacent three-story Healy House was built by Leadville developers August and Emma Meyer in 1879, then it later became a boarding house. It contains elegant Victorian furnishings of the first owners and the more elementary late nineteenth century furniture of its boarding house era.

Leadville, Colorado & Southern Railroad ● *326 E. Seventh St,; (719) 486-3936. Rides daily at 1 p.m. from late May through mid-June, then 10 and 2 through Labor Day weekend, and again at 1 p.m. only* *through September; closed the rest of the year. MC/VISA; $$$$$* □ Railroad buffs will enjoy this ride high into the mountains above a valley of the Arkansas River. It's not an awesome trip and it's a bit pricey, but the scenery's nice. This isn't an historic train; the comfortable open coaches are pulled by a modern diesel electric. For the best views, choose the open car and sit on the left side. The turnaround point is just short of Climax, the now-defunct molybdenum mine near 11,320-foot Fremont Pass.

Leadville Heritage Museum • *Ninth and Harrison; (719) 486-1878. Daily 10 to 6 May through October; by appointment only the rest of the year; $.* □ Occupying the 1902 Carnegie Library, this museum does a fine job of relating the story of Leadville through mini-dioramas and historic photos. It also has a room grouping of late nineteenth century furnishings, an exhibit on Camp Hale and the usual pioneer and mining artifacts. The most interesting exhibit is a detailed styrofoam and wood replica of the Ice Palace, a fantasy structure built during the winter of 1895-96.

Matchless Mine and Baby Doe Tabor Cabin • *East Seventh Street; (719) 486-1899. Daily 10 to 4:45 in summer and 10 to 4 the rest of the year; $.* □ This "museum" is a reconstruction of the rough toolshed and lift house that Baby Doe Tabor converted into a crude cabin after her husband died. Visitors are first ushered into the cabin, furnished with a crude bed, stove, table and chairs and papered with old newspapers. They hear the story of Horace and Baby Doe, then they're taken for a look at the adjacent Matchless mine shaft and a blacksmith shop.

The National Mining Hall of Fame & Museum • *120 W. Ninth St.; (719) 486-1229. Daily 9 to 5 from May through October then weekdays only 10 to 2 the rest of the year; $.* □ This large museum traces the history of mining not only in Leadville but around the world. Professionally done exhibits include a striking display of huge and multi-colored crystals, two mock-up mine shafts and a cute model railroad setup intertwined into a nineteenth century mining operation. Several display cases focus on gold discoveries and gold rushes in several states, with ore samples and historic photos.

Tabor Opera House • *308 Harrison Ave.; (719) 471-0984. Sunday-Friday 9 to 5:30 from Memorial Day through Labor Day; closed the rest of the year.* □ Tours take visitors through this lavish opera house built by H.A.W. Tabor in 1879. Much of the interior is still intact, including the original cashier's cage, the stage and its "oleo" backdrop, fancy Victorian style boxes, the backstage area and the now-dusty dressing rooms. Tabor lost his opera house in the silver panic of 1893, although it continued under new owners for several decades, hosting John Philip Sousa's Marine Band, boxer Jack Dempsey, Harry Houdini, Lillian Russell and Anna Held. A local group called the Crystal Comedy Company presents family shows there during the summer.

Biking and hiking

If you have your bikes aboard, you can ride the dirt and gravel roads of nearby tailing dumps, and follow the 10.5-mile Mineral Belt Bike Trail that loops the town. You also can explore the mining area on foot or by car, although you'll encounter occasional barriers as you drive, since some of the old access roads are intended for cyclists and walkers only. Another nice ride—or stroll—is around Turquoise Lake, reached by heading west on Highway 24 onto Mountain View Drive. Pick it up on the north side of town, just beyond a Safeway.

Dining in the Rockies West:
THE MOST INTERESTING RESTAURANTS

Since this chapter covers a wide region, we've chosen an area-wide sampler of restaurants. If we focused on the absolute best, our geographic reach would be rather narrow, since they tend to cluster around Vail and Beaver Creek. Our favorite restaurant tops the list, and the rest are listed in the order of their encounter on our Rockies West driving tour.

PRICING: Dinner with entrée, soup or salad, not including drinks, appetizers or dessert: *$* = less than $10 per entrée; *$$* = $10 to $19; *$$$* = $20 to $29; *$$$$* = "Did you say you were buying?"

1 ALPENGLOW STUBE ● *Keystone Resort at 154 Soda Ridge Road, reached by two gondola rides; (970) 496-4386. Contemporary American; full bar service. Dinner Thursday-Sunday and Sunday brunch in summer; lunch and dinner Monday-Saturday and Sunday brunch during ski season. Major credit cards; $$$$. GETTING THERE: It's part of the Keystone Resort complex, which is seven miles south of I-70 on U.S. Highway 6. Reservations are required, so ask specific directions when you make them.*

This handsome Bavarian style restaurant requires some effort to reach, and once accomplished, it offers one of Colorado's most fascinating dining experiences. Sitting at 11,444 feet in the log and stone Outpost Lodge atop North Peak Mountain, it's America's highest gourmet restaurant. It has earned an AAA Four Diamond Award and was called the country's "finest on-mountain dining experience" by *Ski Magazine*. Six-course dinners are served *prix fixe* and—like the altitude—are quite high. The open kitchen produces savory entrées of game, seafood, veal and full flavored vegetarian dishes. Among recent menu items were roasted rack of wild boar, marinated game birds, rack of lamb with minted blackberry chutney, and a mixed grill of caribou and salmon.

Idaho Springs

2 **BUFFALO RESTAURANT & BAR** • *1617 Miner St., Idaho Springs; (303) 567-2729. (www.buffalorestaurant.) American; full bar service. Breakfast through dinner daily. Major credit cards; $ to $$. GETTING THERE: Take Idaho Springs exit 240 from I-70, drive briefly north to Miner Street, then go right for about three blocks.*

The Buffalo is a great old Western saloon turned tourist attraction restaurant, with high pressed tin ceilings, wooden floors, maple furniture and antique signs on raw brick walls. The facility spills into four buildings in historic downtown Idaho Springs. The main part is an 1881 structure originally occupied by a mercantile, and it's been a saloon since 1906. Note particularly the handsome backbar. A restaurant specialty is buffalo meat, issued in burgers, barbecue strips, steaks, hot dogs and even bratwurst. Buffalo meat is much leaner and therefore more mild tasting than beef, so don't order it well done or it'll be dry and chewy. The menu also features barbecued chicken and pork, assorted steaks and other basic American fare. No matter what you order, ask that it be accompanied by the restaurant's excellent thick-cut seasoned fries.

Keystone and Breckenridge

3 **KEYSTONE RANCH** • *In the Keystone Resort complex, (800) 253-7758 or (970) 468-1334. (www.keystoneresort.com) Colorado nouveau; full bar service. Dinner nightly with two seatings. Major credit cards; $$$$. GETTING THERE: Take I-70 exit 205 and drive southeast through Dillon for about seven miles; the resort is on the right.*

Rustic Western elegance best describes this fine restaurant, which occupies a grand old ranch house in the Keystone Resort complex. It's also expensive, with lavish six-course *prix fixe* dinners starting around $70. Those courses may feature wild game, Rocky mountain trout, Colorado steak, lamb or fowl. They're embellished with savory soups, salads and starters that employ fresh local ingredients such as wild mushrooms, quince relish, celery roots and rhubarb sauce. After dinner, diners adjourn to overstuffed leather furniture beside a crackling fireplace in the original living room to enjoy in-house created desserts and sip after dinner drinks. Keystone is one of the most elegant dining experiences in the Rockies. The restaurant sits at the edge of the Keystone Golf Course, where elk often are frequent visitors.

4 **CAFÉ ALPINE** • *106 E. Adams Ave., Breckenridge; (970) 453-8218. Eclectic; full bar service. Breakfast, lunch and dinner daily. Major credit cards; $$ to $$$. GETTING THERE: Take exit 201 from I-70 and* *follow State Route 9 fourteen miles southeast to Breckenridge. It becomes Main Street and the restaurant is at the corner of Main and Adams.*

This upbeat chalet style restaurant, one of the most popular in Summit County, serves an interesting mix, ranging from innovative breakfasts and monumental lunch salads to international *nouveau* fare for dinner. A popular hangout is the Tapas Bar where tasty appetizers are matched to the Alpine's lengthy wine-by-the-glass list. Although *tapas* are traditionally Spanish, the Alpine version takes on international airs, ranging from sashimi tuna to marinated quail breast. Evening fare on the changing menu may include Thai prawns, Szechuan spiced lamb chops, cornbread crusted orange roughy and Moroccan grilled chicken breast with *cous-cous* and lemon cilantro oil. The Alpine's extensive wine cellar has won a *Wine Spectator* "Award of Excellence."

Vail and Cascade Village

5 BIGHORN BISTRO • *4695 Meadow Dr., East Vail; (970) 479-7864. Contemporary Asian-American; full bar service. Lunch and dinner daily. MC/VISA; $$. GETTING THERE: The Bistro is in the Vail Racquet Club complex, although it's open to the public. Take I-70 exit 180 and follow Bighorn Road east alongside the freeway for over a mile, go right and then left onto Streamside Circle and continue eastward. After a brief distance, fork right onto Meadow Drive and the racquet club comes up shortly, on your left.*

Although a bit out of the way, this locals' favorite serves some of the least expensive fare in the Vail Valley, and it's excellent. As you enter the restaurant, sniff the potted plants sitting on a railing; they're various herbs that are used fresh in the kitchen. The menu dances from modest hamburgers and rice flour battered fish & chips to creative entrées such as cornmeal crusted chipotle and sage trout, "Drunken pork chops" with tamarind plum sauce and cashew fried rice, and black Angus pepper steak. Desserts are tasty as well, and the list includes warm sour apple pie, key lime cheesecake and ginger creme brulé. In a state where restaurants almost universally overcharge for wine, the Bistro's prices are modest, and the list is quite good. The restaurant's décor is casual, with an A-frame ski chalet look and light knotty pine walls.

6 CHAP'S GRILL & CHOPHOUSE • *At Vail Cascade Resort, 1300 Westhaven Dr., Vail; (970) 476-7111. (www.vailcascade.com) American; full bar service. Breakfast, lunch and dinner. Major credit cards; $$ to $$$. GETTING THERE: The resort is in the Cascade Village section of Vail. Take I-70 exit 173 or 176 (depending on your direction of approach), take Frontage Road to Cascade Village and follow signs to the resort. Chap's is just off the lobby.*

Although the menu is contemporary at this handsome restaurant, the focus is more on hearty grilled entrées than on *nouveau* raspberry purée and air-dried tomatoes. The open kitchen issues a variety of beef, pork, lamb, chicken, seafood and wild game dishes. For a sampler, try the Colorado Trio of lamb, elk and venison. Chap's also offers fresh pasta dishes. Meats come with a choice of interesting dipping sauces; our favorite is Napa Valley merlot demi-glace. An extensive California and European wine list provides suitable matches to Chap's grilled entrées. The "mountain eclectic" décor is as robust as the fare, with distressed wood table tops, wrought iron accents, and multicolored fabrics. Perhaps its most appealing "decoration" is its window walls with a view of Gore Creek and the mountains. When weather permits, diners can adjourn to an outdoor deck.

7 *LUDWIG'S* • *At the Sonnenalp Resort of Vail, 20 Vail Rd.; (970) 476-5656. Continental-American; full bar service. Dinner nightly. Major credit cards; $$$. GETTING THERE: The Sonnenalp is in downtown Vail Village at the corner of Vail Road and Meadow Drive. Take I-70 exit 176 and go two blocks into the village.*

The old world ambiance of the area's finest resort (see below, page 214) is reflected in the understated elegance of its primary restaurant. Candle-lit tables with white and blue nappery and white stucco walls graced with artwork provide a pleasing setting for its continental cuisine with American *nouveau* accents. During summer, diners can adjourn to a patio rimmed by sheltering trees. Dinner entrées—always beautifully presented—may include beef tenderloin with black truffles, grilled salmon on a bed of julienne vegetables, maple duck breast with spicy Mediterranean vegetables and topped by a potato basket, lamb loin with braised pearl onions and thyme juice, and a trilogy of sea bass, red snapper and scallops in balsamic vinegar essence. Ludwig's has earned *The Wine Spectator's* "Distinguished Restaurants of North America" award.

8 *WILDFLOWER* • *The Lodge at Vail, 174 E. Gore Creek Dr., Vail; (970) 476-5011. Contemporary American; full bar service. Lunch and dinner daily. Major credit cards; $$$ to $$$$. GETTING THERE: The restaurant is upstairs off the lobby of The Lodge at Vail, in central Vail Village at the corner of Gore Creek Drive and Willow Bridge Road.*

Dressed like a spring garden, Wildflower is the prettiest restaurant in the Colorado Rockies. Light woods, pastel colors and mint green and white nappery are accented by gorgeous floral arrangements and small "jug vase" bouquets on each table. A courtyard sheltered from traffic is particularly inviting on warm evenings. Of course, we've come to smell the flowers, not to dine on them. The creative kitchen has earned raves from local residents and food critics; the Zagat Survey rated it among the top three Vail area restaurants. Typical entrées are herb-crusted swordfish with baby spinach, seared halibut with ginger balsamic and Asian vegetables, grilled honey marinated ostrich with jack cheese grits, and steak with bacon-cheddar potato purée.

Beaver Creek

9 **GROUSE MOUNTAIN GRILL** • *Beaver Creek Resort at 141 Scott Hill Rd.; (970) 949-0600. (http://vail.net/dining/gmg) Contemporary American; full bar service. Breakfast and dinner daily. Major credit cards; $$$ to $$$$. GETTING THERE: It's just above Beaver Creek Village in the Pines Lodge. Take I-70 exit 167 and drive south through Avon into the Beaver Creek resort complex. Just short of the village, turn right up Scott Hill Road and follow it about four blocks to the lodge.*

This handsome restaurant's three-course *prix fixe* dinners are surprisingly affordable, even by Beaver Creek standards, and they're excellent. Diners have wide choices of starters, entrées and side dishes. Main offerings when we dined included New York steak with stuffed roasted onions, pretzel-crusted pork chops with orange and hot mustard sauce, pepper grilled tuna, and pine nut studded breast of chicken with caramelized onions and roasted garlic. This culinary happiness happens in a pleasant, open dining room with large windows onto Beaver Creek Resort and its surrounding mountains. Knotty pine panels and framed art works provide nice accents to its white stucco walls. A huge wrought iron chandelier and a New Mexico *kiva* style fireplace are interesting focal points.

10 **TOSCANINI** • *Market Square in Beaver Creek Village; (970) 845-5590. Italian; full bar service. Dinner nightly. Major credit cards; $$ to $$$. GETTING THERE: Take I-70 exit 167 and drive south through Avon into the Beaver Creek resort complex. Just beyond the first pedestrian overcrossing, turn left into an underground parking garage. Toscanini is located on the mall, adjacent to the Black Family Ice Arena.*

Pick a warm summer night to enjoy Italian food at Toscanini's outdoor dining patio and watch skaters play on the adjacent ice arena. Or dine inside and admire its light Italian-modern décor with mirrored walls and open kitchen. Of course Toscanini features several fresh pasta dishes; angel hair with olive oil-poached tomatoes is a favorite. Other entrées include herb rotisserie chicken, veal short ribs with wild mushroom risotto cakes, Italian sausage with morrel mushrooms and penne pasta, fresh fish of the day, and several designer pizzas. Dessert specialties include tirimasu and lemon pistachio torte. The restaurant has a very good wine list with several interesting Italian and California selections.

THE TEN BEST LODGINGS

Like the restaurant selections, our lodging choices are spread out somewhat, to catch the best hotels or resorts in each of the areas we visited. We begin with the absolute best—the Sonnenalp in Vail, then follow with the rest in the order that they appear in our driving tour.

PRICING: Dollar sign codes indicate price ranges for two people, based on summer rates: **$** = a standard two-person room for $99 or less; **$$** = $100 to $149; **$$$** = $150 to $199; and **$$$$** = $200 or more.

1 *SONNENALP RESORT OF VAIL* • *20 Vail Rd., Vail, CO 81657; (800) 654-8312 or (970) 476-5656. Major credit cards;* **$$** *to* **$$$$**. *GETTING THERE: The Sonnenalp is in downtown Vail at the corner of Vail Road and Meadow Drive. Take I-70 exit 176 and go two blocks into Vail Village.*

Sonnenalp owner-manager Johannes Fässler, whose grandparents opened their first resort in Bavaria in 1919, has created a haven of simple luxury amidst the slick condos and major hotels of Colorado's ski country. It has won awards from *Condé Naste Traveler* and *Travel & Leisure* as one of the world's better resorts. It has eighty-eight suites, plus two smaller rooms that are quite modestly priced for a resort of this caliber. The suites have gas log fireplaces, mini-bars, TV/VCRs, Bavarian décor with white stucco walls and dark wood beam ceilings, and oversized bathrooms with heated marble floors. The hotel's lobby blends into the Kings Club, a comfortable lounge with a fireplace, intimate seating areas and nightly live piano music. Adjacent is a cozy library with a fireplace and shelves busy with books. Other resort amenities include a spa, and golfing at nearby Singletree Resort. Summer activities—for adults and kids—include wilderness hikes, bike rides and photography workshops. **Ludwig's** restaurant (reviewed above) serves guest breakfast plus dinner, while the upbeat **Bully Ranch** is a Western style café serving lunch and dinner.

Keystone & Breckenridge

2 *KEYSTONE LODGE* • *At Keystone Resort complex, 22010 Hwy. 6 (P.O. Box 38), Keystone, CO 80435; (800) 253-7758 or (970) 468-1334. (www.keystoneresort.com) Major credit cards;* **$$** *to* **$$$$**. *GETTING THERE: Take I-70 exit 205 and drive southeast through Dillon for about seven miles; the resort is on the right.*

Although Keystone Lodge is one of the area's most elegant resorts, midweek summer rates are rather affordable. Large, comfortable rooms have all the usual amenities and most have balconies or patios.

The resort is built around a small lake and rental boats and mini-kayaks are available. Other Keystone facilities include an eighteen-hole golf course, tennis, walking paths, cycling, gondola rides, putting green, pool, spa, sauna and a kids' playground. Several **restaurants** are in the lodge or elsewhere in the Keystone resort complex, including **Alpenglow Stube** and **Keystone Ranch,** listed above.

3 **BEAVER RUN RESORT** • *620 Village Rd. (P.O. Box 2115), Breckenridge, CO 80424; (800) 525-2253 or (970) 453-6000. (www.beaverrunresort.com; e-mail: thebeaver@colorado.net). Major credit cards; $$ to $$$$. GETTING THERE: The resort is half a mile south of Breckenridge on State Highway 9 at Village Road and Park Avenue.*

This modern 519-unit resort at the base of a ski mountain has a full range of accommodations, from hotel rooms to studios and condos with one to four bedrooms. They're attractively furnished and most have VCRs, dataports, refrigerators, fireplaces and spa tubs. The large family-oriented resort's amenities include shops, two indoor-outdoor pools, eight hot tubs, a tennis court, exercise room, miniature golf, videogames and horseback riding. The resort is near the Blue River and its recreation trail, and it offers ski-in, ski-out facilities in winter. Three restaurants—**Spencer's Steak & Spirits, Tiff's Night Club** and the affordable **GB Watson's Deli** that's popular with families.

Vail

4 **HOTEL-GASTHOF GRAMSHAMMER** • *231 E. Gore Creek Drive, Vail, CO 81657; (800) 610-PEPI or (970) 476-5626. (WEBSITE: www.pepis.com; e-mail: info@pepis.com) Major credit cards; $$ to $$$$. GETTING THERE: It's in the western part of Vail Village, near the corner of Bridge Street. Take I-70 exit 176.*

Step into this ornate mustard yellow and dark wood trimmed hotel and you've stepped back into old Austria. It is in fact Austrian-owned—the creation of Pepi and Sheika Gramshammer, who opened it in 1963 as one of Vail's first resort hotels. The thirty-five rooms and five apartments have modern amenities, with European artifacts and ornate hand-carved woods to retain that old country feel. The hotel's large European style shopping complex features giftwares, art and sports wear. **Pepi's Restaurant** serves Austrian-Bavarian and other European cuisine while the **Antlers Room** focuses on wild game and veal. Pepi's Porch and lounge is a popular people-watching place.

5 **VAIL CASCADE RESORT** • *1300 Westhaven Dr., Vail, CO 81657; (800) 420-2424 or (970) 476-7111. (www.vailcascade.com; e-mail:vailcasc@vail.net) Major credit cards; $$$$. GETTING THERE: The resort is in the Cascade Village section of Vail. Take I-70 exit 173 or*

176 (depending on your direction of approach), take Frontage Road to Cascade Village and follow signs to the resort.

Vail Cascade is a full service facility with 291 large guest rooms, twenty-eight suites and seventy-two condominiums. It's arrayed along-side Gore Creek and many of its units have creek and mountain views. Most have balconies or patios. Nicely decorated rooms have ceiling fans, refrigerators, desks and other amenities. Some larger rooms and suites have couches, multiple phones, gas fireplaces and spa tubs. Facilities include two swimming pools (one beside the creek); a full-service health spa; tennis, racquetball and squash courts; and several shops. Vail Cascade is particularly popular with skiers because one of the lifts operates right from the property. Summer visitors like the fact that it's on the biking/walking path to LionsHead and Vail Village. Dining areas include **Chap's Grill and Chophouse**, reviewed above.

6 *VAIL MARRIOTT MOUNTAIN RESORT* • *715 W. Lions-Head Circle, LionsHead Village, Vail, CO 81657; (800) 648-0720 or (970) 476-4444. Major credit cards; $$ to $$$$. GETTING THERE: Take exit 173 or 176 and follow Frontage Road to LionsHead Village, turn south and follow signs.*

The 349-unit Marriott has a pleasing "mountain modern" look and offers extensive resort facilities such as indoor and outdoor pools, a European style spa, tennis courts, health club and jogging trail. One of it's most inviting spots is the Avalanche Pub just off the lobby, with a fireplace and large color action photos of Colorado outdoors. The Marriott's 311 rooms and thirty-eight condominiums have TV movies, refrigerators and voice mail. Many have balconies, ceiling fans and a few have fireplaces. Condo units have full kitchens with one to three bedrooms. The **Mountain Grill** serves American fare, breakfast through dinner, and the **Avalanche Pub** has light snacks. The hotel is a short walk from LionsHead Mall and the Gore Creek path to Vail Village.

Beaver Creek

7 *BEAVER CREEK LODGE* • *26 Avondale Lane (P.O. Box 2578), Avon (Beaver Creek), CO 81620; (800) 525-7280 or (970) 845-9800. (www.beavercreeklodge.net; e-mail: suitesatbc@vail.net) Major credit cards; $$ to $$$. GETTING THERE: It's in the heart of Beaver Creek Village. Take I-70 exit 167 south through Avon to Beaver Creek Village and turn left onto Avondale Lane.*

This small 73-suite resort is built around an impressive five-story atrium lobby topped by a skylight, from which dangle two massive hammered copper Western-theme light fixtures. It has two cozy fireplace lounges; one off the lobby and another on the mezzanine. Most units are two-room suites with fireplaces, mini kitchens, TV/VCRs and dataport phones with voice mail. Guests also can rent privately-owned condos with two to four bedrooms, full kitchens, laundry units and spa tubs. The lodge's amenities include an indoor-outdoor pool, hot tub and a small health club. The **Beaver Creek Chophouse** serves contemporary American fare; breakfast through dinner, with full bar service. A coffee shop has light fare and the Chophouse bar features live entertainment.

8 *THE CHARTER AT BEAVER CREEK* • *120 Offerson Rd. (P.O. Box 5310), Avon (Beaver Creek), CO 81620; (800) 525-6660 or (970) 949-6660. (www.vail.net/charter; e-mail: charter@vail.net) GETTING THERE: Take I-70 exit 167 south through Avon to Beaver Creek Village, turn left on Offerson Road below the village and drive up about two blocks; the hotel complex is on the right.*

One of Beaver Creek's first hotels remains its most opulent. Built in 1980 and since remodeled, it features attractive public areas with thick carpeting, floral accents and European decorator touches. A large view lounge with a circular bar just off the lobby provides nice Beaver Creek vistas. The Charter offers 135 units, including lodge rooms and one- to five-bedroom condominiums. All are nicely decorated, with matched floral prints, stylish furnishings and art works. The condo units have full kitchens, washer-dryer units, fireplaces and balconies or patios. Other amenities include indoor and outdoor pools and hot tubs, sports shop, game room, exercise room, sauna and steam room. A short path leads from the resort complex to Beaver Creek Village. Dining options are **TraMonti Restaurant**, serving Italian fare; and **Pacific Ranch**, with an interesting Asian décor, serving American and Asian entrées. Both have outdoor dining areas.

9 *HYATT REGENCY BEAVER CREEK* • *136 E. Thomas Place (P.O. Box 1595), Avon (Beaver Creek), CO 81620; (800) 55-HYATT or (970) 949-1234. (www.hyatt.com) Major credit cards; $$$ to $$$$. GETTING THERE: Take I-70 exit 167 south through Avon to Beaver Creek Village, turn left on Offerson Road below the village, then right into Thomas Place.*

Beaver Creek's largest resort, the 276-unit Hyatt has a "rustic mountain modern" décor. It's located on the village mall with quick access to shops and the Centennial Express winter-summer ski lift. Public areas have distinctive antler chandeliers, large fireplaces and carved woods. Amenities include a spa and health club, pool, hot tub and kids' play area. The attractively decorated rooms and suites have TV with rental VCRs available, ceiling fans and the usual resort amenities. Restaurants are the **Patina**, serving continental and American fare; the informal **Double Diamond Deli**; and the **Crooked Hearth**, serving American fare.

Leadville

10 *COLUMBINE INN & SUITES* • 2019 N. Popular St., Leadville, CO 80461; (800) 954-1110 or (719) 486-5650. (www.columbineinn.com) Major credit cards; $ to $$. Prices include a large continental breakfast. GETTING THERE: Approaching from the north, the inn is on the right side of Highway 24, about a mile from Leadville's historic district.

In a weathered old mining town that's short on good lodgings, the Columbine is an exception. The cheerful lobby lounge has a European country inn feel with hardwood floors, throw rugs, a riverstone fireplace and a comfortable couch and chairs. Outside, hanging flower baskets brighten the entryway. The forty-one rooms and suites are spotless and nicely done with light wood custom furniture and old fashioned prints. All have TV with HBO and suites have spa tubs. Most offer views of the snowcapped peaks on Leadville's skyline. The inn also has a spa and meeting room. The entire complex is non-smoking.

Leadville to Colorado Springs

The easiest route to the Colorado Springs-Manitou Springs area and the next chapter is south and then east on U.S. 24. It's an exceptionally pretty drive, following the Arkansas River for much of its course, with some of Colorado's highest peaks on the western horizon.

Fifteen miles south of Leadville, you'll hit the turnoff to **Twin Lakes,** established in 1879 as a provisioning center for nearby silver mines. En route, you'll see a visitor center for the **Mount Elbert Power Plant** and **Frying Pan Arkansas River Recreation Area,** open Monday-Thursday 10 to 6 and Friday-Sunday 9 to 6. Many of Twin Lakes' old log buildings are still intact and the two-block downtown area has been declared a national historic district. The town and its namesake Twin Lakes sit dramatically in a glacial scoop below several of Colorado's "Fourteeners," including the state's highest peak, 14,433-foot Mount Elbert.

The most interesting element here is **Twin Lakes Nordic Inn,** which has been serving travelers since the town's founding. Its a charming old European style inn with rough bark log walls, painted flower boxes and knotty pine interior. It offers rustic lodge rooms and cabins at rather modest rates. A restaurant serves breakfast through dinner, with a mix of German and American fare. The owners of the inn boast quite proudly that this was once a brothel, as well as a stage stop. *For information: Twin Lakes Nordic Inn, 6435 Highway 82, Twin Lakes, CO 81251; (800) 626-7812 or (719) 486-1830. (www.twinlakesnordicinn.com; e-mail: nordicinn@chaffe.net)*

Back on Highway 34, you'll soon enter a rugged canyon carved by the Arkansas River as it works its way resolutely toward the Mississippi and ultimately the Gulf of Mexico. This is a major whitewater rafting area, and one of the more popular outfits running this stretch is **River Runners**, offering half-day, all-day and multiple day trips; (888) 350-7782. (*www.riverrunnersltd.com; e-mail: raft@amigo.net*)

You'll soon encounter **Buena Vista,** a small town with an old fashioned business district and an interestingly cluttered historic museum. It's also a good place to gas up for the long drive east to Colorado Springs. To cruise Buena Vista's downtown, turn right onto Main Street at its only traffic signal. A couple of blocks beyond, you'll see the former county courthouse at Main and Court streets, now housing the **Buena Vista Heritage Museum**, open daily from 9 to 5, June through Labor Day weekend. It's one of those wonderfully cluttered small town museums with almost no interpretation but lots of interesting stuff, like antique pianos, a Victrola, hunting trophies, flapper era clothing, blacksmith tools and a large model railroad layout.

A bit below Buena Vista, Highway 24 swings northeast to cross the Rockies Front Range en route to Colorado Springs. Just after you make the turn, watch on your left for a scenic overlook. Here, several interpretive signs discuss the Arkansas River Valley's geology and history, and point out half a dozen "Fourteeners" on the dramatic Great Divide across the valley. From here, U.S. 24 gallops through high meadowlands flanked by wooded hills in remote ranching country. This is a solitary land where both your cell phone and buffalo roam.

After topping a couple of gently inclined 9,000-foot passes, the highway drops down toward woodsy **Woodland Park** headed for what may be—after this pleasant high lonesome country—an excess of civilization.

We will never have a true civilization until we have learned to recognize the rights of others.
    — Will Rogers quote at the Colorado Springs Shrine of the Sun

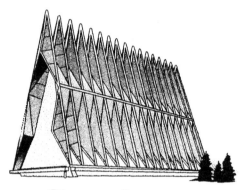

Chapter fourteen

ROCKIES SOUTH
THE BEST OF MANITOU SPRINGS
AND COLORADO SPRINGS

T he Colorado Springs-Manitou Springs area has been for decades the state's favorite family playground. In fact, both communities were founded as vacation resorts and both were named for mineral springs in the area.

General William J. Palmer of the Denver & Rio Grande Railroad platted Colorado Springs in 1871, not far from the already existing mining and ranching provisioning center of Colorado City, which dates back to 1859. Six years later, London physician William Bell founded Manitou Springs at the base of Pikes Peak. However, the man who *really* established this area as a tourist lure was mining millionaire and philanthropist Spencer Penrose, whose fortunes built the Broadmoor resort, Pikes Peak Cog Railway, Pikes Peak Highway and Will Rogers Shrine of the Sun. He also gave his private animal collection to the people of Colorado Springs as the basis for Cheyenne Mountain Zoo.

In the years that followed, Manitou Springs has maintained its mountain resort look, since it's tucked into a wooded ravine. On the other hand, Colorado Springs—sitting on the edge of the prairie—had lots of room to spread and it did. It has become a major commercial center and the second largest city in Colorado, with a population approaching 300,000. The creation of the United States Air Force Academy just to the north has done much to boost the city's growth.

Both are attractive communities—one small and quaint and the other large and bustling. And in our minds, both have a common fault. Since they began more than a century ago as vacation spas, early entrepreneurs turned many of its natural wonders into tourist attractions. Lures such Seven Falls and Cave of the Winds are commercial operations instead of state or federal preserves. Garden of the Gods, an area of sculpted red sandstone originally was privately owned, although it has been a Colorado City Park for many years. Privately owned Manitou Cliff Dwellings is a fabrication, created more than a century ago in a way that wouldn't be tolerated today. The builders took stones from real ruins at present-day Mesa Verde National Park and reassembled them here.

The Pikes Peak Cog Railway is a commercial operation as well, although we can't fault that, since it's a spectacular ride up one of the world's most isolated mountains. And of course the U.S. Air Force Academy and its famous Cadet Chapel is an outstanding local attraction. Another major lure is the Broadmoor, one of the world's most famous hotels.

All of these lures have made Colorado Springs and Manitou Springs immensely popular. And as the crowds have come, more gimmicks have followed, such as Santa's Workshop, Hall of Presidents Wax Museum, Flying W Ranch chuckwagon dinners and the Ghost Town and Wild West Museum. Other museums—most quite interesting—have been drawn to the area as well. They focus on professional rodeo cowboys, figure skating, the mining industry, the Pikes Peak auto hill climb, aviation, numismatics carriages and "giant and exotic insects."

Obviously, the area has some grand and some corny tourist attractions. It's understandable that the area suggests Orlando and Walt Disney World—with a dramatic mountain backdrop. Expect the region to be crowded in summer and avoid driving from one attraction to the next on I-25 during commute hour, since Colorado Springs is large enough to have some traffic headaches.

Information sources

Both communities have active tourist bureaus, and a third organization represents the area's many commercial attractions. You may want to send for information before you arrive.

Colorado Springs Convention & Visitors Bureau, 104 S. Cascade Ave., Suite 104, Colorado Springs, CO 80903; (800) DO VISIT or (719) 635-7506. (*www.coloradosprings-travel.com*)

Manitou Springs Chamber of Commerce, 354 Manitou Ave., Manitou Springs, CO 80829; (800) 642-2567 or (719) 685-5089. (*www.manitousprings.org*)

Pikes Peak Country Attractions Association, 354 Manitou Ave., Manitou Springs, CO 80829; (800) 525-2250. (*www.pikes-peak.com*)

If you're coming into the area on U.S. 24 from the previous chapter, you'll first encounter Manitou Springs. Take Highway 24 business east, which puts you in the heart of town on Manitou Avenue. Continue downhill through the historic district and you'll see the Manitou Springs Chamber of Commerce on your left, at the corner of Mayfair. It's open weekdays 8 to 7 and weekends 8:30 to 5, with shorter hours the rest of the year.

If you're southbound from Denver on I-25, Colorado Springs will be the first stop. Take exit 143 (Uintah Street) and follow signs to the Colorado Springs Convention and Visitors Bureau at Cascade and Colorado Avenue. It's in Sun Plaza opposite a large Wells Fargo Bank building, open daily 8:30 to 5. Incidentally, if you're coming from Denver, you might want to hop off I-25 at exit 156-B (Northgate Boulevard) and tour the U.S. Air Force Academy, since it's north of Colorado Springs.

The first thing you should do on arrival—assuming you have lodging arrangements—is make reservation for the Pikes Peak Cog Railway by calling (719) 685-5401. It books up several days in advance in summer. If you haven't made lodging reservations, you'll find the usual motels and hotels clustered around I-25 exits and a couple downtown. Manitou Avenue is lined with small motels—some neat and some scruffy. Despite the area's tourist lures, many of these motels are relatively inexpensive.

Doing downtown Colorado Springs—briefly

Most of the area's attractions are in Manitou Springs or on the outskirts of Colorado Springs. However, the downtown section of Colorado Springs is worth a brief look. We've devised a simple paperclip shaped tour that hits the highlights.

Begin by taking I-25 exit 143 and going briefly east on Uintah Street, then south on Cascade Avenue. A divided boulevard with a landscaped median strip, Cascade takes you through the pretty campus of **Colorado College.** Just beyond, note the elegantly restored and rather gaily painted twin Victorians at Cascade and St. Vrain Street, which comprise the **Hearthstone Inn,** listed among our Ten Best restaurants and lodgings below. You'll then enter the compact downtown area. Another of our selected lodgings, the pink multi-story **Antler Adam's Mark Hotel** sits behind a plaza called Palmer Center.

Just beyond, at the corner of Cascade and Colorado is the **Colorado Springs Convention and Visitors Bureau.** Continuing south, you'll pass the attractive **Colorado Center for the Performing Arts.** Turn left just below here onto Vermijo Street, go two blocks east then turn left again onto Nevada Avenue, passing the **Smokebrush Center for the Arts/Colorado Actors' Theatre.**

This route takes you out of the downtown area and through a mixed neighborhood of fine old late nineteenth century homes that's being invaded by spreading commercialism. (It seems odd to find a Blockbusters Video among stately Victorian homes.) Within a few blocks, you'll again pass through that pretty **Colorado College** campus.

At the southern edge of the campus, go left on Cache la Poudre and left again onto Tejon Street. Note the **Grace Episcopal Church** at the corner of Tejon and Monument, with its classic squared Gothic bell tower. Just beyond, you'll pass through an interesting area of small shops, boutiques and a few sidewalk cafés. They occupy some of Colorado Springs century-old low rise brick and masonry buildings that have escaped downtown renovation (also called demolition). After several blocks, you'll be back in the newer downtown area with its few modest highrises.

You can end your brief driving tour with a stop a the **Colorado Springs Pioneers Museum** at 215 Tejon. It's housed in a wonderful 1899 cut stone clock tower building that once served as the El Paso County Courthouse. It's open Tuesday-Saturday 10 to 5 the year around and Sunday 1 to 5 from May to October; closed Monday; (719) 385-5990. It's worth a look both for its fine exhibits and its gorgeous marble interior.

THE TEN BEST ATTRACTIONS

With our Ten Best format, we can't possibly cover all of the area's attractions, nor would we want to. The *Colorado Springs and Pikes Peak Region Official Visitor Guide,* available free at visitor centers, lists forty-four of them! What appears below is our favorites. Some are commercial and some are not, and some aren't even "attractions" in the touristic sense of the word. After our top pick, the U.S. Air Force Academy, we list the next nine in a logical visitation order, starting with the popular Pikes Peak Cog Railway.

The convergence point of Manitou Springs and Colorado Springs is I-25 and Highway 24, so our directions begin from there.

PRICING: Dollar sign codes indicate the cost of adult admission to various attractions and activities: *$* = under $5; *$$* = $5 to $9; *$$$* = $10 to $14 ; *$$$$* = $15 to $19; *$$$$$* = $20 or more.

1 UNITED STATES AIR FORCE ACADEMY ● *I-25 exit 156-B. For information: Public Affairs, U.S. Air Force Academy, CO 80840-9400; (719) 333-2025. (www.usafa.af.mil) Grounds open to the public 6 a.m. to 10 p.m. Cadet Chapel hours 9 to 5 weekdays and 1 to 5 weekends; Visitor Center open daily 9 to 6.*

Set against a dramatic backdrop of Rocky Mountain foothills, the large U.S. Air Force Academy looks more like a university campus than a military facility. It's both. Much of it is open to the public and a driving map with seven point-of-interest stops is available at area visitor bureaus. Or ask at the gate when you enter. Whether you're approaching from the north or the south, enter through the north gate, since that's the beginning of the driving route. If you don't have a route map, follow Northgate Drive which becomes Academy Drive, and watch for "Falcon Tour" signs. The first stop is hard to miss—a **B-52 Stratofortress** on your left. Take a left turn onto Stadium Boulevard, then go left again into a parking area for a closeup look at this monster of the skies. Return to Northgate Boulevard and watch on your left for the huge **Cadet Field House,** open to the public from 9 to 5. At this point, Northgate has become Academy Drive.

The next stop combines the **Visitor Center** and one of the most striking churches ever constructed—the dramatic multi-finned **Cadet Chapel.** It's the most recognized and most photographed building on the academy campus and probably in Colorado. Drive past the chapel, curving around to the left on Academy Drive and enter the Visitor Center parking lot. The center focuses on the cadets' scholastic and military training and their daily lives on campus. A 14-minute film about the academy, *In Pursuit of Excellence,* is shown every half hour. The center also has a large gift shop, in case you'd like a U.S. Air Force Academy refrigerator magnet for AFA Falcons football jersey.

From the visitor center, a short nature trail leads to the chapel. (If you're running late, go there first since it closes at 5, while the visitor center remains open until 6.) This is actually three separate chapels, with the large Protestant section occupying the main floor with its dramatically soaring winged roof. The smaller Catholic and Jewish chapels are a floor below. The building is composed of seventeen aluminum tetrahedron triangles that mesh and converge, meeting 150 feet in the air to form one giant triangle. They're separated by thin strips of multicolored glass, creating a very dramatic interior space.

Just north of the chapel, on the courtyard near Harmon Hall, is an interesting display of bronzed fighter planes and bombers from World War II.

Beyond the visitor center are three more "Falcon Tour" stops—an overlook of the main cadet area and officers club complex; Falcon Stadium where the Air Force Academy football team plays; and the landing field, where you may see cadet training flights, and possibly parachuting and glider flights. Exit the south gate for the return to Colorado Springs.

Adjacent to the Academy's north gate entrance is the **Western Museum of Mining and Industry** on Gleneagle Drive (an eastern extension of Northgate Boulevard). It's open Monday-Saturday 9 to 4 and Sunday noon to 4; (719) 488-0880; *$$.* It has exhibits on area and Western states mining, with several huge pieces of mining equipment on the grounds outside. They're worth a look even if the museum is closed.

2 *PIKES PEAK & THE COG RAILWAY* • *Ruxton Avenue in Manitou Springs; (719) 685-5401. (www.cograilway.com; e-mail: cogtrain@iex.net) Daily late April through early November; departure times vary. Major credit cards; $$$$$. GETTING THERE: Follow Highway 24 west from Colorado Springs, take the Manitou Avenue exit and follow it uphill through the Manitou Springs historic district. Fork left onto Ruxton Avenue and follow it to the depot.*

Western America's most famous little engines that could have been hauling tourists to the rocky top of Pikes Peak since 1891. These aren't conventional choo-choos. They're diesel cog-wheel trains that use a notched center track to crawl up slopes that tilts as much as twenty-six degrees. The ride is immensely popular in summer so make reservations as early as possible. We recommend catching the early-morning train—8 o'clock in summer—since it's sometimes less crowded and the odds of sunshine are much better. (Although the eastern slope of the Rockies gets plenty of summer sunshine, afternoon clouds and showers aren't uncommon.) Also, take a warm coat, since the temperature is forty to sixty degrees colder on top. It's not uncommon to encounter a snowstorm up there in August!

The tilted little train climbs from 6,571 feet at Manitou Station to the Pikes Peak summit at 14,110 feet in about an hour and twenty minutes. It passes from a pretty evergreen creek valley into a rocky tundra, where the odds are likely that you'll see some bighorn sheep and chubby little marmots. The top of Pikes Peak—more of a ridge than a peak—isn't a pretty place; it's essentially a rockpile. However, the views from here are predictably awesome, especially to the west where you can see a great span of the Continental Divide. The view to the east once was nice until habitation placed an almost permanent haze over Colorado Springs and other Front Range cities. On rare clear days, you can see all the way to Denver.

Passengers have thirty to forty minutes on top and they spend most of that time in the Summit House, since it's *cold* outside, baby! Naturally, the Summit House is a large souvenir and snack shop. The crunchy homemade doughnuts, often still warm from the oven, are particularly tasty.

Incidentally, you can drive to the top of Pikes Peak on a nineteen-mile toll road leading from Cascade northwest of Manitou Springs. However, it's gravel much of the way and very hard on brakes and windshields. The scenery's great, although there are 156 turns so keep your eyes on the road, please. You also can hike to the top on a thirteen-mile trail that begins at the cog railway station, and they're a campground midway. Hikers can by partial tickets, hiking one way and riding the other. During busy periods however, round trip tickets take precedence.

3 MANITOU SPRINGS HISTORIC DISTRICT ● *Manitou Avenue between El Paso Boulevard and Ruxton Avenue.*

Manitou Springs has retained much of its early twentieth century tourist town look, although modern shops and restaurants now occupy the old low-rise brick and masonry buildings. A walk along Manitou Avenue, with spur trips on Cañon and Ruxton avenues, will reveal both yesterday and today in this old town. Along the way, you'll encounter several public fountains where you can taste the sweet-salty mineral water that attracted yesterday tourists. It's definitely an acquired taste.

Beginning at on the south side of Manitou Avenue across from Memorial Park, you'll encounter an assortment of shops and boutiques as you stroll upward. If you're in need of lunch, the family-style **Old European Restaurant** in the restored Barker House Victorian at 819 Manitou serves inexpensive American and European fare; (719) 685-4945. A block above at 907 Manitou, **Townhouse Lounge** serves burgers and other light fare, with an outdoor patio; (719) 685-1085. At the corner of Manitou and Ruxton, you'll see a small monument and a stylized "Indian maiden" fountain where you can sample the mineral water. Just uphill on Ruxton, **Marysha's Pastries** serves very tasty American and European style pastries, plus light lunch; (719) 685-1710.

Most of the shops stop beyond Marysha's, although you can reach the **Pikes Peak Cog Railway** complex by continuing up Ruxton. Before you get that far, you can go right for a visit to **Miramont Castle,** a 28-room mansion offering self-guided tours for a modest fee; (719) 685-1011. Return to Manitou Avenue and cross to the north side, where you'll encounter pretty little **Soda Springs Park** along Fountain Creek. A block downhill is another tasting fountain at **Cheyenne Springs.** The adjacent century-old Manitou Spa is shut but an old fashioned fun zone and arcade are still operating. Just below here, at the 1870 St. Paul's Episcopal Church, follow Cañon Avenue a block back uphill and you'll encounter several art galleries and shops, plus one of our recommended restaurants, **Adam's Mountain Café.** Continuing farther on Cañon, you'll encounter the **Cliff House** inn and restaurant, listed below.

Reverse your route and continue downhill on Manitou Avenue. The **Dulcimer Shop** at 740 Manitou sells old style musical instruments, neat T-shirts and cool sounds on CDs and tapes. Just below, the **Keg Lounge** at 730 Manitou is an anomaly—an old fashioned bar that serves health-conscious food, such as vegetable and berry salads and chicken croissant sandwiches. Just beyond is the closest thing you'll find to a head shop in the conservative Colorado Springs-Manitou Springs area, **The Hemp Store.** It sells—not *cannabis*—but tie-dyed T-shirts, scented candles and anti-establishment bumper stickers.

4 *COLORADO CITY HISTORIC DISTRICT* • *Colorado Avenue between 24th and 27th streets. GETTING THERE: Go west from Colorado Springs on Colorado Avenue or southeast from Manitou Springs on Manitou Avenue, which becomes Colorado Avenue.*

"Pikes Peak or bust" came the cry in 1859 when gold and silver were discovered in the nearby foothills. A hasty mining camp appropriately called El Dorado was established, later renamed Colorado City. The first permanent town in the Pikes Peak region, it had its fifteen minutes of fame when it became the territorial capital. The assembly met here in 1861, then moved on to Denver.

The gold strike proved to be rather small, although the town survived as a supply center. By 1887, it boasted a railway repair center, a glass works founded by a group that included Adolph Busch of Anheuser-Busch fame, and a good number of saloons and brothels. However, the town was caught between the thriving new resort centers of Manitou Springs and Colorado Springs, and it was annexed to the latter in 1917.

The old town's brick and masonry buildings have been renovated and preserved as a national historic site, with about 200 shops, galleries, boutiques and cafés. It has been dressed up with brick sidewalks, shade trees, and hanging flower baskets on its old fashioned lamp posts. The historic district extends only four blocks, so an exploration consists simply of walking up one side of Colorado Avenue and then down the other. A good starting point—noted for its breakfast— is 1930s style **Bon Ton's Café** on the south side of the street at 26th, with a patio out front; (719) 634-1007. Stroll east and try not to notice the ugly Sno-White Linen and Uniform Rental between 25th and 26th; it was built before restoration had begun.

A lattice shade ramada at the corner of 26th has a map showing the historic district and its stores. **Henri's Mexican Restaurant** just beyond at 2427 Colorado Avenue is the oldest Hispanic diner in the Colorado Springs area, dating from 1949; (719) 634-9031. For bakery goods and designer coffees, pause at **La Baguette** at 2417 Colorado; (719) 577-4818. Next-door **Beau Jo's** at 2417 claims to serve the best pizza in Colorado, and it was quite good; (719) 442-0270.

Cross to the north side of Colorado Avenue at 24th, where you'll find tree-shaded **Bancroft Park** and a chink log cabin, the only structure to survived the city's brief days as territorial capital. Also worth a look here is a classic Carnegie Library still in operation, opposite the backside of the park at 2418 Pikes Peak Avenue. At the corner of 24th and Pikes Peak, the **Old Colorado City History Center** occupies an 1891 clapboard and shingled Baptist church. This neatly arrayed, uncluttered museum is open daily except Monday, 10 to 5 in summer and 11; (719) 636-1225. (*www.history.oldcol.com*)

Two blocks beyond, check out the large old fashioned **Meadow Muffins** bar at the corner of 26th, a virtual museum of Western and pioneer regalia. Two buckboard wagons and scores of other odds and ends hang from the ceiling, and check out the very voluptuous nude portrait to the left of the entrance. This is a lunch and dinner restaurant as well as an old timey saloon; (719) 633-0583. Just beyond, another shop with a museum personality is the **Thunder Mountain Trading Company** at 2508 Colorado Avenue; (719) 632-7331. It sells Western and native art and artifacts and old Western movie memorabilia. What's not for sale are the several game trophy heads that line the upper walls.

A good way to end your stroll is to order an overpriced but delicious ice cream cone at **Colorado Creamery** at 2602 Colorado Avenue, corner of 26th; (719) 634-1411. It's set back off the street away from traffic, with several outdoor tables. Next door, **Colorado Microbrew**, carries more than 100 Colorado specialty beers.

While you're in the neighborhood, drive briefly east on Colorado Avenue, then take 21st Street up to Highway 24, where you'll encounter the **Art Pottery Factory and Showroom**; (719) 633-7729. It's open Monday-Saturday 8:30 to 5 and Sunday 1 to 5. The original pottery studio was founded in 1902 by Artus Van Briggle, whose works are now in some of the world's major museums. The Van Briggle pottery specialty is a soft sheen "secret glaze," and some of the pieces are surprisingly affordable. A self-guided tour will take you past a working potter, the huge kilns and the etching department where skilled artists add designs to the pieces. The tour ends in a sales room, of course. The Van Briggle operation moved to this site in 1953. The structure was built in 1899 as a railroad roundhouse.

5 CAVE OF THE WINDS • *Cave of the Winds Road off U.S. 24; (719) 685-5444. Tours daily 9 to 9 in summer and 10 to 5 the rest of the year. Laser Canyon Show at 9 p.m.; Friday and Saturday in May, then nightly from Memorial Day through Labor Day. MC/VISA; cave tour $$$$; laser show $$. GETTING THERE: From Colorado Springs, follow U.S. 24 west to the traffic light at Cave of the Winds Road. From Manitou Springs, go west through town on Manitou Avenue, then fork right at the "Highway 24 east" sign and drive across the highway at the traffic light.*

The setting for Cave of the Winds is as impressive as the cave itself. The entrance building/gift shop is cantilevered over the edge of sheer-walled Williams Canyon and a deck offers nice views of Manitou Springs and the mountains. The cave system is extensive and while it doesn't offer a fabulous collection of formations, it as a goodly number. Forty-minute guided tours take visitors past assorted stalactites, stalagmites, columns and other formations such as cave popcorn, soda straws and flowstone. It's fifty-four degrees in the caverns, so take a light wrap. Tours begin in Canopy Hall, the largest natural room, and follow both natural and manmade paths through the catacombs. The most striking feature is the Oriental Garden, where stalagmites have formed into chubby shapes that suggest Asian temples.

HIKING OPTION: An abandoned dirt road that originally led to the cave complex offers access to Williams Canyon, where you can follow a riparian trail along its small trickling creek. To hike the canyon, you must sign a permission waiver at the Cave of the Winds ticket office; there's no charge. It's a pleasant walk alongside the creek's slickrock bed, with beige limestone walls rising several hundred feet above. Some of its sylvan pools are so pretty that you expect to encounter a sexy little nymph admiring her reflection. The trail ends after about a mile, although you can continue farther in you're in a rock-hopping mood. Few people know about this trail and the cave folks don't advertise it, so you'll likely have the canyon to yourself.

6 *MANITOU CLIFF DWELLINGS* • *Cliff Dwellings Road off Highway 24, just west of Colorado Springs; (800) 354-9971 or (719) 685-5242. Daily 9 to 8 in summer; closes at 5 or 6 the rest of the year. Major credit cards; $$. GETTING THERE: It's less than a mile below Cave of the Winds, on the north side of the highway.*

Two things bother us about the Manitou Cliff Dwelling Museum. The "dwellings" were taken from Mesa Verde and then reconstructed here about a hundred years ago by tourist promoters. And the gift shop is three times larger than the museum. The promotional material never quite admits that the cliff dwellings are reconstructions, cannibalized from a real archeological site. (The fabricators blew their cover by failing to put smoke stains on the ceilings.)

Of course the raiding of the ruins was done in a less environmentally sensitive era. On the positive side, folks can scramble over, under, around and through this mortar-reinforced replica—something that would be frowned on in a national park or monument. The "ruin" is quite extensive, so there are plenty of rooms and kivas through which to crawl.

The adjacent pueblo, which promoters freely admit is not authentic, is the same age as the cliff dwelling. Its museum contains some nice examples of early Southwestern pottery and other artifacts, and its exhibits do a good job of telling the story of these ancient people. However, it's practically dwarfed by a huge gift shop complex, which even has sales rooms gouged out of the cliff face. As one explores the pueblo, it's easier to find rubber tomahawks and kokopeli refrigerator magnets than museum displays.

As an added dimension to this tourist site, native dances are presented several times daily and the dancers proudly insist that they *are* authentic.

7 GARDEN OF THE GODS • *Visitor center at 1805 N. 30th St.; (719) 634-6666. (www.gardenofgods.com) Park open daily 5 a.m. to 11 p.m. Visitor Center open daily 8 to 8 in summer; shorter hours the rest of the year. Park admission is free; small charge for movies and bus tours. GETTING THERE: Coming from Manitou Cliff Dwellings, continue west about a mile, then turn north onto Garden of the Gods Road.*

No one created the Garden of the Gods except God, or faulted up-lifting followed by erosion, if you prefer the scientific explanation. Op-erated by the Colorado Springs Parks and Recreation Department, this fine 1,300-acre park at the base of Pike's Peak contains some excellent examples of uptilted and eroded red sandstone formations. One could spend the better part of a day here, following the park's many trails and exploring these wind-shaped spires, ridges and castles. The park also preserves a slice of an interesting ecosystem of ancient junipers and desert flora where the plains meet the Rockies.

If you enter the park from Highway 24, you'll first encounter the in-teresting old **Garden of the Gods Trading Post**, built in 1900 as yet another tourist attraction. Colorado Springs took over the park in 1909 and leases the trading post to a concessionaire. It's now essen-tially a gift shop, although a few displays trace the park and post's his-tories. From there, follow roads randomly through the park, stopping now and again to admire some godlike shape reaching skyward, or to hike a nature trail. Signs will direct you to the handsome **Garden of the Gods Visitor Center**, where you can catch a park tour bus, watch a film about the park's geological history and—you guessed it—visit a large gift shop. (C'mon, someone has to pay the bills!) The cen-ter also has a snack bar, with tables on an outdoor deck that offer nice park views.

Nearby and within the park complex is the **Rock Ledge Ranch Historic Site**, a living history center set in a restored 1880s home-stead. You can watch blacksmiths at work, sip sarsaparillas and "shop" for old timey items in a general store. There's a modest fee for entry to the ranch complex. It's open daily 10 to 5 in summer; (719) 578-6777.

THE NEXT STOPS

The final three attractions are rather close together on the slopes of Cheyenne Mountain. We suggest seeing them in the order listed, based on their locations and closing hours.

Getting to this area is rather complicated, so we're going to suggest the simplest instead of the most direct approach. Drive south on I-25 to exit 138 (Circle Drive) and follow Lake Avenue west toward the mountains for about three miles. It runs right into the grounds of the **Broadmoor**, which you may want to visit; see the listing below. Then skirt around the edge of the Broadmoor golf course by going west on Lake Circle, and south on El Pomar Road, following Cheyenne Mountain Zoo signs. It blends into Penrose Boulevard which in turn blends into Cheyenne Mountain Zoo Road. All the while, you'll be driving through Colorado Springs' swankest residential area.

Once you hit the zoo, you can either park and walk in, or continue through the parking area to a toll gate and drive through the zoo—yes, right through it—to the Will Rogers Shrine of the Sun. It sits high on the flanks of Cheyenne Mountain. One admission price covers both attractions.

8 *CHEYENNE MOUNTAIN ZOO • 4250 Cheyenne Mountain Zoo Rd.; (719) 633-9925. (www.cmzoo.org) Daily 9 to 6 in summer and 9 to 5 the rest of the year. MC/VISA; $$.*

While not large, Cheyenne Mountain Zoo has two distinctions. It's America's only zoo built onto a mountain slope and it's one of the world's highest zoos, at 8,000 feet altitude. The mountainside location limits space somewhat, and many of the occupants are in small enclosures instead of open areas. However, it's a very well kept zoo with a good selection of critters—more than 500 animals representing 146 species. This also is a zoo with a view. When you tire of trading stares with the giraffes, you can enjoy nice vistas of Colorado Springs far below. Since the giraffes' enclosure is on a downslope, you're nearly eye-to-eye with them. With its mountainside site, this is a hiking zoo, although can rest your feet by catching a zoo train.

The two most interesting exhibits are the **Asian Highlands** and **Wolf Woods**. These larger compounds are tilted steeply uphill, enclosing a slice of the attractive wooded terrain of Cheyenne Mountain. Rare Siberian tigers and Amur leopards can be seen lurking in the Asian Highlands and you're likely to spot one or more wolves skulking in their namesake woods.

The Cheyenne Mountain Zoo and Will Rogers Shrine of the Sun are the work of the same man—Colorado mining millionaire and philanthropist Spencer Penrose. The zoo grew from his private animal collection, which he deeded to a public trust in 1938. He was a close friend of Will Rogers, and when the great humorist and philosopher died in a plane crash in 1935, Penrose was moved to build an imposing shrine to his memory.

9 *WILL ROGERS SHRINE OF THE SUN • At the end of Russell Tutt Scenic Highway above Cheyenne Mountain Zoo; (719) 634-5975. Daily 9 to 6 in summer, 9 to 5 through October, then 9 to 4 the rest of the year; free.*

I was just over a year old when Will Rogers and his pilot Wiley Post died in an Alaska plane crash. However, my grandfather Walter C. Dallas knew Will slightly and bore an amazing resemblance to him. And they had things in common; both had tried their hand at cowboying and writing and they both did a lot of traveling. Of course Will was eminently more successful. Grandad Dallas—whose greatest skill apparently was fathering children—was a fan of the great humorist and he taught me to respect Will's simple wit and wisdom.

For any fan of America's greatest cowboy philosopher, a visit to the Will Rogers Shrine of the Sun will be a moving experience. It's a tall castle-like structure with a view tower reached by several levels of stairways. At each level, old photos and newspaper clippings present a retrospective of the humorist's life. Every fifteen minutes, the tower carillon tolls mournfully and its sound can be heard throughout Colorado Springs.

For those who aren't will Rogers fans, the shrine offers a fantastic viewpoint. Here more than anywhere else, you can appreciate the dramatic convergence of the Rocky Mountains and the Great Plains. You're standing high on the slopes of Cheyenne Mountain, looking down upon a vast flatness that extends to Chicago and beyond. It's even more impressive from here than from Pikes Peak, since you're much closer to Colorado Springs and the prairie and you can see much more detail.

10 SEVEN FALLS • *At the end of Cheyenne Canyon Road South; (719) 632-0765. (www.sevenfalls.com) Daily 8 to 11:15 mid-May through Labor Day, 9 to 4:15 the rest of the year. Major credit cards; $$. GETTING THERE: Take Cheyenne Mountain Zoo Road back to Penrose Boulevard and follow signs to Seven Falls. A couple of left forks and left turns will put you on Cheyenne Canyon Road South, which leads uphill to this attraction.*

Seven Falls is a 181-foot cascade that bounces seven times down a dramatic rocky gorge. It's an impressive sight and would be even more so if its private developers hadn't built an ugly set of 224 stainless steel steps up the side of the canyon. These lead to the top of the falls, and then into the forest on a half-mile trail to the gravesite of novelist Helen Hunt Jackson, best known for her book, *Ramona.* She's no longer there; her body was moved to a Colorado Springs cemetery after the site was desecrated.

This is a steep hike and I'm glad I wasn't one of the pallbearers at her funeral. A sign suggesting that she wrote *Ramona* while sitting on this very spot is inaccurate. The book is a love story inspired by her visit to a Spanish ranch near San Diego, and she wrote most of it in New York. But never mind that. This is a nice hike through the woods, and it ends at an impressive Colorado Springs overlook, just beyond the grave. Midway to the gravesite, a second trail leads to a small cataract called Midnight Falls. Again, it's a nice woodsy hike.

If you need more exercise, take a second ladder—185 steps—up to Eagles nest, where you can see the entire series of cataracts. You also can ride an elevator up here, or take it back down after hiking up. Its rather interesting, since the shaft was blasted through solid rock. You may want to visit the falls after dark, when multicolored spotlights turn them into liquid rainbows.

THE TEN BEST RESTAURANTS

PRICING: Dinner with entrée, soup or salad, not including drinks, appetizers or dessert: **$** = less than $10 per entrée; **$$** = $10 to $19; **$$$** = $20 to $29; **$$$$** = "Did you say you were buying?"

1 THE PENROSE ROOM • *The Broadmoor, One Lake Ave., Colorado Springs; (719) 634-7711. (www.broadmoor.com) Contemporary continental; full bar service. Dinner nightly. Coat required for gentlemen; ties preferred. Major credit cards; $$$$. GETTING THERE: Drive south on I-25 to exit 138 (Circle Drive) and follow Lake Avenue west toward the mountains for about three miles. It runs right into the Broadmoor grounds.*

If you seek a special occasion restaurant in Colorado Springs there are two good selections—both at the Broadmoor. Charles Court is sumptuously elegant and serves contemporary American fare. However, we favor the rooftop Edwardian style Penrose Room, with its excellent and creative continental cuisine and its dazzling view of the Broadmoor's lake, Cheyenne Mountain and the rest of the Rockies. Sample menu items are grilled lamb with cumin herbs, filet of prime rib, filet of Dover sole, and chicken breast with potato basket of turnip confit. Wild game appetizers and an assortment of caviars are specialties. The wine list is outstanding; the hotel is said to have more than 100,000 bottles in its extensive cellars.

2 ANTLERS GRILLE • *Antlers Adam's Mark Hotel, 4 S. Cascade Ave., Colorado Springs; (719) 473-5600. (www.antlers.com) Contemporary American; full bar service. Breakfast through dinner. Major credit cards; $$ to $$$. GETTING THERE: It's in the heart of downtown Colorado Springs, between Colorado and Pikes Peak avenues. Take I-25 exit 142 and go east on Bijou, then south briefly on Cascade.*

Just off the lobby of Adam's Mark, the grill has a handsome men's club look, with dark woods and brass chandeliers, yet it's also light and airy. Seating is at comfy curved banquettes or tables. Menu offerings include pan-seared scallops, grilled pork tenderloin with sautéed spinach, herb crusted salmon with batter corncakes, grilled beef tenderloin with mashed sweet potatoes and chipotle Bearnaise, Southwest chicken breast with black bean and charred corn salsa, and yellowfin tuna with mashed sweet potatoes.

3 ADAM'S MOUNTAIN CAFÉ • *110 Cañon Ave., Manitou Springs; (719) 685-1430. Eclectic menu; wine and beer. Lunch and dinner Tuesday-Thursday, breakfast through dinner Friday-Saturday and Sunday brunch; closed Monday. MC/VISA; $ to $$. GETTING THERE: Follow Manitou Avenue uphill into the historic district, then fork to the right on Cañon Avenue; the restaurant is on the right.*

This charming little café in Manitou's historic district serves health-focused fare in a kind of European tearoom environment. Ceiling fans, rough beams, tulip wall sconces, wallpaper and old fashioned prints create a pleasant setting for its mixed menu. Among its offerings are *wasabe* grilled tuna with a blood orange and ginger glaze, lime chicken with polenta and roasted green chiles in red chile sauce, a Thai vegetarian dish with peanut sauce and *soba* noodles, rosemary lemon chicken with grilled spinach, and several pastas.

4 BRIARHURST MANOR • *404 Manitou Ave., Manitou Springs; (719) 685-1864. (www.briarhurst.com) American; wine and beer. Dinner Monday-Saturday. Major credit cards; $$ to $$$$. GETTING THERE: The manor is just beyond the Manitou Springs Chamber of Commerce, in the Blue Sky B&B complex near the corner of Mayfair Avenue.*

Dining at Briarhurst is like dining in an Old English castle or hunting lodge, with its rough-cut stone walls, game trophies and brass chandeliers. Tables are set with cute little mauve colored lamps over pink and burgundy nappery. Set back off Manitou Avenue between a creek and a red rock bluff, this pink sandstone manor house was built in 1876 by Manitou's founder, Dr. William Bell. Several rooms have been styled into attractive dining areas and on warm nights, diners can adjourn to a terrace. The kitchen departs from American *nouveau*—a refreshing departure these days—to offer more traditional American and continental fare such as chicken breast with herbs, trout in a light egg batter with capers and lemon, lamb chops with mint sauce, and filet mignon with sauce Bérnaise or Cabernet Sauvignon wine sauce. Candlelight buffet dinners are served Wednesday nights.

5 CLIFF HOUSE RESTAURANT • *306 Cañon Ave., Manitou Springs; (719) 685-3000. (www.thecliffhouse.com) American nouveau; full bar service. Breakfast, lunch and dinner daily. Major credit cards; $$$ to $$$$. GETTING THERE: Follow Manitou Avenue uphill into the historic district, then fork to the right on Cañon Avenue and follow it two blocks to the corner of Park Avenue.*

The dining room of this newly reopened 1873 inn has been restored to its earlier finery with lace café curtains, tulip chandeliers and white nappery. The menu is considerably more contemporary, serving savories such as lamb with leek and smoked tomato compote, pork tenderloin with red cabbage and apples, fish of the day with orange onion confit and *beurre blanc*, and crabcakes with arugula and aged balsamic vinegar. A lighter menu is served on the hotel's handsome front porch, which offers views of the town and mountains.

6 CRAFTWOOD INN • *404 El Paso Blvd., Manitou Springs; (719) 685-9000. (www.craftwood.com) "Colorado cuisine"; full bar service. Dinner nightly. Major credit cards; $$ to $$$. GETTING THERE: From Manitou Springs, go southeast on Manitou Avenue, fork left onto El Paseo Boulevard near the city hall and park, and follow it for about half a mile. From Colorado Springs, head west out Colorado Avenue, blend onto Manitou Avenue, turn right onto Mayfair at the visitor center, drive up to El Paseo and turn left; it appears quickly on your right.*

Housed in a red sandstone English Tudor style mansion, the Craftwood Inn offers splendid views of Manitou Springs and its mountains, particularly from its outdoor deck. It was built as a private home and coppersmith shop in 1912 and became a restaurant in 1940. Now carefully restored, it has several European style dining rooms, plus that sunny outdoor deck and a separate cocktail lounge. Its "Colorado cuisine" is best defined as contemporary American with an accent on wild game, and without raspberry purée or air dried tomatoes. Hearty entrées include filet of salmon, grilled loin of wild boar, mixed "wild grill," caribou steak, braised herbal chicken and a tasty vegetarian platter. Prices are quite modest for such an elegant place with fine views.

7 FLYING W CHUCKWAGON SUPPER • *3330 Chuckwagon Rd., Colorado Springs; (719) 598-4000. (www.flyingw.com) Western style supper. Nightly at 7:15 from mid-May through September; reservations required. Winter Steakhouse open the rest of the year with two sittings, at 5 and 8. MC/VISA; $$$. Prices include Western show and admission to a reconstructed Western village.*

Of course it's corny. And is it really one of the area's ten best dining experiences? Well, it's probably the area's most *fun* dining experience. Visitors chow down in a chuckwagon corral on barbecued steak or chicken, plus salad, a baked potato and "famous Flying W beans." How can baked beans be famous? Ask yourself in the morning. There's spice cake for dessert, the sort of thing a real cowboy would never eat in public. However, it's quite tasty. Supper is followed by a one-hour show of cowboy music and cowboy humor. (The difference between cowboy music and country music is that one is about cows and the other is mostly about pickups and bad women.) Visitors can browse through fourteen restored buildings in an adjacent "ghost town." Some are museums and some are gift shops; most are both. In winter and during bad summer weather, the cowboy feed adjourns to a heated shelter. Flying W didn't make the Zagat Survey and it's missing from other Colorado dining guides. Do the owners care? They've been baking famous beans and packing in the tourist since 1953.

8 **HEARTHSTONE INN** • *514 N. Cascade Ave., Colorado Springs; (719) 473-4413. (www.hearthstoneinn.com; e-mail: hearthstone@worldnet.att.net) French; wine and beer. Breakfast and lunch Monday-Saturday and Sunday brunch; dinner Thursday-Saturday (may be extended to Tuesday-Saturday). Major credit cards; $$ to $$$. GETTING THERE: The restaurant is part of the Hearthstone Inn B&B, is near downtown at the corner of St. Vrain. Take I-25 exit 143, go briefly east on Uintah to Cascade and drive south; or exit 142 and go east on Bijou, then north on Cascade.*

The Hearthstone restaurant reflects the Victorian elegance of the adjacent inn, with print wallpaper, wainscotting, carved high back chairs and brass lighting fixtures. Seating is divided into two dining areas; the smaller one has an inviting fireplace. The fare is classic French without trendy *nouveau* accents. Some examples are scallops *a la Normande* with mushrooms and shallots in white wine, sea bass *Grenabloise* with lemon and capers, steak Diane with garlic and sherry demi-glace, and chicken *Marsala*. For diners who just aren't into French cuisine, the menu also features New York steak and several pasta dishes.

9 **LA PETIT MAISON** • *1015 W. Colorado Ave., Colorado Springs; (719) 632-4887. French and American nouveau; wine and beer. Dinner Tuesday-Saturday. Major credit cards; $$ to $$$. GETTING THERE: The restaurant is located between Tenth and Eleventh streets. From downtown Colorado Springs, follow Colorado Avenue West. From Manitou Springs, take Manitou Avenue southeast; it becomes Colorado Avenue.*

This charming little restaurant occupies a blue and creme clapboard cottage in an older neighborhood that's transitioning from residential to commercial. The house is indeed petit and the interior is even cozier, divided into a pair of intimate dining rooms. The menu wanders pleasantly from "new American" to French continental, featuring entrées such as roast chicken breast stuffed with goat cheese and spinach, pork *tournedos* wrapped in applewood bacon with peppercorn Marsala sauce, roasted duck with plum sauce, and cumin-dusted shrimp with fennel and pickled watermelon salad. The paté appetizers are excellent. While dinners are modestly priced for a restaurant of this quality, an even less expensive menu is available for early diners, from 5 to 6:30. La Petit has a good selection of wines by the glass and by the bottle.

10 MONA LISA FONDUE • *733 Manitou Ave., Manitou Springs; (719) 685-0277. European fondue; wine and beer. Dinner Tuesday-Sunday. Major credit cards; $$ to $$$. GETTING THERE: Follow Manitou Avenue uphill into the historic district. Mona Lisa is in the 1886 Park Place Hotel building.*

This second-story restaurant with a candle-lit Olde European look offers fondue fare with some interesting twists. It's a "do it yourself" operation; diners are furnished with utensils for melting their choice of three different cheese fondues and grilling their chosen entrées. Chunks of bread, sliced apples and chunks of carrots, broccoli and cauliflower are provided for the cheese fondues, along with a choice of seasoned salmon, shrimp, steak, chicken or mixed grill, with five different dipping sauces. These are more American *nouveau* than traditional European, ranging from honey mustard to cranberry horseradish. The cheese fondues are contemporary as well; choices include "new world" and "South of the Border" in addition to traditional Swiss. All of this savory dipping finally ends with a variety of chocolate and other dessert fondues.

THE TEN BEST LODGINGS

Our favorite Colorado Springs-Manitou Springs lodgings come in two categories—hotels and resorts, and bed & breakfast inns. As usual, we begin with the very best in each category, then follow with runners-up in alphabetical order.

PRICING: Dollar sign codes indicate price ranges for two people, based on summer rates: $ = a standard two-person room for $99 or less; $$ = $100 to $149; $$$ = $150 to $199; and $$$$ = $200 or more.

1 THE VERY BEST RESORT HOTEL: The Broadmoor • *P.O. Box 1439 (One Lake Ave.), Colorado Springs, CO 80901-1439; (800) 634-7711 or (719) 634-7711. (www.broadmoor.com) Major credit cards; $$$$. GETTING THERE: Drive south on I-25 to exit 138 (Circle Drive) and follow Lake Avenue west toward the mountains for about three miles. It runs right into the Broadmoor grounds.*

Built by Spencer Penrose and opened in 1918, the Broadmoor is the grand hostelry of the Rockies. It's the only AAA Five Diamond and Mobil Five-Star hotel in the Intermountain West. Everything about this great pink Italianate structure and its park-like grounds are gorgeous and impeccably done. This is more of an upscale pleasure city than a resort, with thirty buildings on 3,500 acres. Amenities include a large lake circled by a jogging track, fifty-four holes of golf, twelve tennis courts, three swimming pools and a lap pool, a spa and fitness center, a movie theater, stables and several upscale shops. If you can't afford the rates (we can't), stop by for a visit and act as if you belong; the staff is quite polite. The 700 rooms and suites are handsomely done in period furnishings, with honor bars, phones and voice mail, safes and every conceivable amenity. Ten **restaurants** and cafés serve a broad range of fare, from the casual Tavern with a European bistro look and the Lake Terrace Dining Room to the elegant Penrose Room (reviewed above) and Charles Court.

The **Carriage House Museum** is just across from the Broadmoor entrance, open 10 to noon and 1 to 5 Tuesday-Saturday. It displays some nicely restored old carriages and surreys.

1 THE VERY BEST B&B: Old Town GuestHouse ● *115 S. 26th St., Colorado Springs, CO 80904; (888) 375-4210 or (719) 632-9194. (bbonline.com/co/oldtown/; e-mail: oldtown@databahn.net) Eight units with private baths; full breakfast. Major credit cards; $$ to $$$$. GETTING THERE: The inn is at the corner of 26th and Cucharras in the Old Town section of Colorado City. Take Colorado Avenue west from Colorado Springs or Manitou Avenue from southeast Manitou Springs, then and go south for one block to 26th.*

Handsomely crafted of brick to match the old style look of Colorado City's historic district, this inn is quite new and opulent. It's one of only two B&B's in the state to earn an AAA Four Diamond award. The look is more of deliberate elegance than country inn cozy, with modern amenities, art works and wrought iron chandeliers. A comfortable library has a fireplace and shelves lined with books and video films. The cheerful breakfast room is decorated with dried flower and twig wreaths.

Each of the rooms and suites is individually furnished, with themes ranging from Victorian and Asian to Western and mountain lodge. All have amenities that would rival those of a full service hotel, such as TV/VCRs (tucked into armoires), CD players, refrigerators, phones with voice mail and computer ports, and desks. Most have balconies or porches with views of Pike's Peak, Garden of the Gods or the Old Town district; some have spa tubs and fireplaces. A full breakfast is served in the dining room or on a patio.

The next best hotels and resorts

3 ANTLERS ADAM'S MARK HOTEL ● *4 S. Cascade Ave., Colorado Springs, CO 80903; (800) 444-ADAM or (719) 473-5600. (www.antlers.com) Major credit cards; $$ to $$$$. GETTING THERE: It's in the heart of downtown Colorado Springs, between Colorado and Pikes Peak avenues. Take I-25 exit 142 and go east on Bijou, then south briefly on Cascade.*

One of the area's most attractive lodgings and the only major downtown hotel, the Antlers is within easy reach of area attractions. The handsome carpeted and marble lobby has a comfy seating area with a two-way fireplace. **Antlers Grill** (reviewed above) and a lobby bar are adjacent. A second restaurant and bar, **Judge Baldwin's Brewing Company**, is part of the hotel's adjacent shopping complex. Amenities include a health club, indoor pool and spa. The 292 rooms and suites have desks, phones with dataports and voice mail, and TV movies. Many rooms have views of Pikes Peak.

4 *THE CLIFF HOUSE* ● *306 Cañon Ave., Manitou Springs, CO 80829; (888) 212-7000 or (719) 685-3000. (www.thecliffhouse.com; e-mail: information@thecliffhouse.com) Major credit cards; $$ to $$$$. GETTING THERE: Take Manitou Avenue uphill into the historic district, then fork to the right on Cañon Avenue and follow it two blocks to the corner of Park Avenue.*

This handsome turreted and bay windowed 1873 resort hotel recently was renovated and reopened. It features fifty-seven rooms and suites with late eighteenth century décor. Many offer views over the town to Pikes Peak, and all have modern amenities. The hotel's porch is particularly appealing, with white wicker couches and chairs where guests can relax and admire the view. Light fare is served on the porch for breakfast, lunch and dinner. A sitting room is equally inviting, with plush period furniture and a grand piano. Historic displays of the hotel's earlier days line a corridor off the lobby. The Cliff House began as a stage stop on the old road between Colorado Springs and Leadville. The **Cliff House restaurant** is reviewed above.

5 *COURTYARD BY MARRIOTT* ● *2570 Tenderfoot Hill St., Colorado Springs, CO 80906; (800) 321-2211 or (719) 576-1100. Major credit cards; $$ to $$$. GETTING THERE: Drive south on I-25 to exit 138 (Circle Drive) and follow Lake Avenue west toward the mountains for about a mile, then turn left onto Tenderfoot Hill Street and right into the hotel complex.*

Opened in 2000, this new hotel is located near the Broadmoor and Cheyenne Mountain attractions. Although not large, it's appealing and cozy, with a small lobby, fireplace lounge and breakfast café. Amenities include an indoor pool, spa and hot tub and a small garden area with a gazebo. The attractive rooms have dual phones with dataports and large screen TVs. Within a short walk are **Bennigan's Grille**, an Irish style pub and restaurant; and **Macaroni Grill**, serving Italian fare. Both are open for lunch and dinner daily. Although they aren't part of the hotel, both provide room delivery service, and menus are available at the hotel desk.

6 *DOUBLETREE HOTEL COLORADO SPRINGS WORLD ARENA* ● *1775 E. Cheyenne Mountain Blvd., Colorado Springs, CO 80906; (800) 222-TREE or (719) 576-8900. (www.doubletreehotels.com) Major credit cards; $$ to $$$. GETTING THERE: It's on the southwest corner of I-25 interchange 138. Drive south on I-25, take exit 138 right onto Lake Avenue, then go left twice to reach the hotel grounds.*

A spacious lobby with the skylighted Coffee Garden and Atrium café are focal points of this large, low rise hotel complex. Two bars are just off the lobby—the Quiet Bar, and Maxi's Lounge that features live entertainment. Its 299 rooms and suites have phones with dataports and voice mail. Refrigerators are available for a fee. The hotel is built around a central courtyard and its amenities include a pool, spa, sauna, fitness center and gift shop. It's conveniently located, just off the freeway and near Cheyenne Mountain attractions.

The next best bed & breakfast inns

7 *HEARTHSTONE INN* ● *506 N. Cascade Ave., Colorado Springs, CO 80903; (800) 521-1885 or (719) 473-4413. (www.hearthstoneinn.com; e-mail: hearthstone@worldnet.att.net) Twenty-five rooms and suites with some private and some shared baths; full breakfast. Major credit cards; $ to $$$$. GETTING THERE: The inn is near downtown at the corner of St. Vrain. Take I-25 exit 143, go briefly east on Uintah to Cascade and drive south; or exit 142 and go east on Bijou, then north on Cascade.*

Two fine Victorian mansions in Colorado Springs' best-kept old neighborhood have merged to become an elegant inn and restaurant. The noble structures are cheerfully multi-colored on the outside and quite stylish within, with beveled glass doors, Victorian and American antiques, brass light fixtures, tile fireplaces and museum quality artwork. Some of the lavishly decorated rooms have brass beds, window seats, wall sconces and lots of floral prints. The comfortable main floor parlor has built-in bookshelves, a fireplace and upright piano. Wide corridors feature art works, antique furnishings and little tucked-away sitting areas.

8 *HOLDEN HOUSE 1902 BED & BREAKFAST INN* ● *1102 W. Pikes Peak Ave., Colorado Springs, CO 80904; (719) 471-3980. (www.bbonline.com/co/holden/; e-mail: holdenhouse@worldnet.att.net) Five suites with private baths; full breakfast. Major credit cards; $$. GETTING THERE: It's at the corner of Eleventh Street and Pikes Peak Avenue, which is parallel to Colorado Avenue. From Colorado Springs,* go west on Colorado Avenue and then north (right) one block to Pikes Peak Avenue. From Manitou Springs, go southeast on Manitou Avenue, which blends onto Colorado Avenue. Pass through the Colorado City historic district, then go left on Eleventh Street.

Holden House is two Victorian homes and a carriage house that have been fashioned into a fine B&B complex. Two spacious suites are in the main house and carriage house, and a fifth is in the next-door rose Victorian. They're all elaborately decorated with Victorian and early American motifs—busy floral patterns, antique furnishings, four-poster beds, marble bathrooms and family heirlooms. The stairwell of the main house is lined with several generations of family photos, giving the inn a nice homey touch. All units have fireplaces, sitting rooms and elaborate bathrooms with oversized "tubs for two."

9 RED STONE CASTLE • *601 South Side, Manitou Springs, CO 80829; (719) 685-5070. Two suites with private baths; full breakfast. Major credit cards; $$ to $$$. GETTING THERE: The "castle" is reached via Pawnee Avenue from Manitou Avenue, below the historic district. Admission is by reservation only, so ask for specific directions.*

Castle indeed! This stone mansion at the end of a short, twisting red dirt road is perched high on a hillside with commanding views of Manitou Springs. It's part of a rambling twenty-acre estate with terraced lawns, woods and lots of privacy. Built in the 1890s, this red sandstone mansion features Victorian décor with gilt-edge mirrors, print wallpaper, brass light fixtures and comfy turn-of-the-last-century furniture. Guests can absorb vistas of the surrounding countryside from wicker chairs on a circular porch and wrought iron chairs a lawn below. The two suites, located in "castle" turrets, are furnished with antiques and family heirlooms.

10 TWO SISTERS INN • *10 Otoe Place, Manitou Springs, CO 80829; (800) SIS-INN or (719) 685-9684. (www.twosisinn.com) Four rooms and a cottage; some private and some share baths; MC/VISA, DISC; $ to $$. GETTING THERE: Follow Manitou Avenue west toward the historic district and turn left (south) on Otoe Place; the inn is on your right.*

This American style inn, pink with green trim, is a short walk from old Manitou Springs. It's dressed in lace curtains, early American furnishings, plate rails and a welcoming cuckoo clock. A cozy library offers lots of reading material. White wicker chairs on the front porch provide views of the town and its surrounding hills. The four rooms feature American antiques and fresh flowers. Two that share a bathroom are quite affordable. The "honeymoon cottage" out back has a kitchenette and private bath.

INDEX: Primary listings indicated by *bold face italics*

Remarkably useful DISCOVERGUIDES
By Don & Betty Martin

Critics praise the "jaunty prose" and "beautiful editing" of travel, wine and relocation guides by authors Don and Betty Martin. They are recent winners of a gold medal for best guidebook of the year in the annual Lowell Thomas Travel Writing Competition. Their DISCOVERGUIDES are available at bookstores throughout the United States and Canada, or you can order them on line at **www.amazon.com, bn.com** or **borders.com.**

ARIZONA DISCOVERY GUIDE

This guide covers attractions, scenic drives, hikes and walks, dining, lodgings and campgrounds in the Grand Canyon State. A "Snowbird" section helps retirees plan their Arizona winters. *— 408 pages; $15.95*

ARIZONA IN YOUR FUTURE

It's a complete relocation guide for job-seekers, retirees and "Snowbirds" planning a move to Arizona. It provides essential data on dozens of cities, from recreation to medical facilities. *— 272 pages; $15.95*

THE BEST OF DENVER AND THE ROCKIES

Discover the very finest of the Mile High City, from its Ten Best attractions, museums and parks to its leading restaurants and lodgings, and then explore attractions of the nearby Rockies. *— 256 pages; $16.95*

THE BEST OF THE WINE COUNTRY

Where to taste wine in California? More than 350 wineries are featured, along with nearby restaurants, lodging and attractions. Special sections offer tips on storing and serving wine. *— 352 pages; $16.95*

CALIFORNIA-NEVADA ROADS LESS TRAVELED

This is a "Discovery guide to places less crowded." It directs travelers to interesting yet uncrowded attractions, hideaway resorts, scenic campgrounds, interesting cafes and other discoveries. *— 336 pages; $15.95*

LAS VEGAS: THE BEST OF GLITTER CITY

This impertinent insiders' guide explores the world's greatest party town, with expanded Ten Best lists of casino resorts, restaurants, attractions, buffets, shows, pubs, clubs and more! *— 296 pages; $15.95*

THE BEST OF PHOENIX & TUCSON

Head for the Sunbelt to explore Arizona's two largest cities. Discover their Ten Best attractions, desert parks, walking and biking trails, restaurants, resorts, dude ranches and much more! *— 256 pages; $16.95*

MORE BOOKS AND ORDERING INFORMATION ON NEXT PAGE

NEVADA IN YOUR FUTURE

It's a complete relocation guide to the Silver State, with useful information for job-seekers, businesses, retirees and winter "Snowbirds." A special section discusses incorporating in Nevada. — *292 pages; $16.95*

NEW MEXICO DISCOVERY GUIDE

This useful guide takes travelers from Santa Fe and Taos to busy Albuquerque, Carlsbad Caverns and beyond. — *384 pages; $16.95*

OREGON DISCOVERY GUIDE

From wilderness coasts to the Cascades to urban Portland, this book guides motorists and RVers throughout the state. —*448 pages; $17.95*

SAN DIEGO: THE BEST OF SUNSHINE CITY

Winner of a Lowell Thomas gold medal for best travel guide, this lively and whimsical book picks the finest of sunny San Diego, featuring its Ten Best attractions, restaurants and much more. —*248 pages; $15.95*

SEATTLE: THE BEST OF EMERALD CITY

This upbeat and opinionated book steers visitors to the very best of Emerald City and the rest of Western Washington. —*236 pages; $15.95*

THE ULTIMATE WINE BOOK

This great little book covers the subject in three major areas—Wine and Heath, Wine Appreciation and Wine with Food. And it does so with good humor, poking harmless fun at wine critics —*194 pages; $10.95*

UTAH DISCOVERY GUIDE

It's a remarkably useful driving guide covering every corner of the Beehive State, from its splendid canyonlands to Salt Lake City to the "Jurassic Parkway" of dinosaur country. —*360 pages; $13.95*

WASHINGTON DISCOVERY GUIDE

This handy book steers motorists and RVers from the Olympic Peninsula to Seattle to the Cascades and beyond. —*464 pages; $17.95*

DISCOVERGUIDES ARE AVAILABLE
AT BOOKSTORES EVERYWHERE

If your store doesn't have a title in stock, tell the clerk it can be ordered from any major distributor, such as Publishers Groups West, Ingram or Baker & Taylor. And you can buy our books on-line from *www.amazon.com, bn.com* and *borders.com*.

TRADE BOOK BUYERS
DISCOVERGUIDES are available through
PUBLISHERS GROUP WEST — (800) 788-3123